Narratives of a Vulnerable God

Also by William C. Placher
and published by Westminster John Knox Press

Unapologetic Theology:
  A Christian Voice in a Pluralistic Conversation

Readings in the History of Christian Theology,
  Volume 1: From Its Beginnings to the Eve of the Reformation

Readings in the History of Christian Theology,
  Volume 2: From the Reformation to the Present

A History of Christian Theology: An Introduction

With David Willis-Watkins

Belonging to God:
  A Commentary on "A Brief Statement of Faith"

William C. Placher

Narratives of a Vulnerable God

Christ, Theology, and Scripture

Westminster John Knox Press
Louisville, Kentucky

Scripture quotations from the New Revised Standard Version of the Bible are copyright © 1989 by the Division of Christian Education of the National Council of the Churches of Christ in the U.S.A. and are used by permission.

Book and cover design by Drew Stevens
Cover illustration: Pieta, 1946. *Bernard Buffet. Courtesy of Superstock.*

First edition

Published by Westminster John Knox Press
Louisville, Kentucky

This book is printed on acid-free paper that meets the American National Standards Institute Z39.48 standard. ∞

PRINTED IN THE UNITED STATES OF AMERICA

00 01 02 03 04 — 10 9 8 7 6 5 4

Library of Congress Cataloging-in-Publication Data

Placher, William C. (William Carl), date.
   Narratives of a vulnerable God: Christ, theology, and scripture /
William C. Placher. — 1st ed.
         p.   cm.
   Includes bibliographical references and index.
   ISBN 0-664-25534-5 (alk. paper)
   1. God—Love.   2. Narration in the Bible.   3. Church.   I. Title.
BT140.P53 1994
231'.6—dc20   93-47618

To my students at Wabash over the years

Contents

Acknowledgments

The invitation from Princeton Theological Seminary to deliver the Stone Lectures for 1993 provided the impetus that led to this book, and I am grateful to President Thomas Gillespie and the faculty of the seminary for that invitation and to the seminary community for a generous reception and for thoughtful responses and questions. Earlier versions of chapters 1, 3, 4, 5, and 6 constituted the Stone Lectures. Different versions of chapter 1 have also appeared in *The Future of Reformed Theology*, edited by Michael Welker and David Willis-Watkins (Grand Rapids: Wm. B. Eerdmans Publishing Co., 1993), and in the July 1993 issue of the *Princeton Seminary Bulletin*. Chapter 4 appeared in an earlier form in the April 1994 issue of *Modern Theology*; chapter 6, in the Winter 1993 issue of *Pro Ecclesia*. Chapter 7 has had the most complicated history of all. It began as a Lafollette lecture at Wabash (published by the college in a collection of Lafollette lectures, *The Community of the Humanities*, edited by Raymond B. Williams, in 1992). After one revision it became one of my Niebuhr lectures at Elmhurst College, was revised again for the Spring 1992 issue of *Theology Today*, and is now here revised yet again. I am grateful to all the relevant editors and publishers for permission to republish these essays.

Ever since the publication of *Unapologetic Theology*, I have been telling people that I was at work on a book on Christology. This isn't it. I will need to traverse other ground before I can attempt what I have in mind for that project. This is a programmatic sketch of some of my christological ideas and some of their broader implications, the sort of enterprise for which a series of lectures provided the ideal opportunity. Although this work may clearly have some of the disadvantages that a work has when it covers much ground quickly, I hope it has some of the concomitant virtues too—that it indicates where things are going and why they might matter in a way that can get lost in a more detailed study of one particular topic.

Much of the book was written during a pleasant summer in Chicago, and I want to thank the staff of Windermere House for their helpfulness; President David Ramage of McCormick Seminary for getting me into Regenstein library; and David Tracy, Brian Gerrish, Dawn DeVries, Scott Seay, and Stephen Pavy for making me feel welcome in Hyde Park. Like many who have worked around the University of Chicago, I am particularly indebted to that marvelous institution, the Seminary Co-op Bookstore.

Raymond Williams generously read various parts of the manuscript at several stages; Christopher Runge provided all sorts of help—finding references, teaching me more of the mysteries of my computer, and even deciphering my handwriting—during the summer when he was our departmental student intern. A number of hearers and readers have made helpful comments along the way. Keith Geiselman and some other Princeton Seminary students properly challenged me on something I initially said about power. I am particularly grateful to the Yale-Washington Theology Group, not only for their reading and discussion of this manuscript but for a continuing intellectual community without which I am not sure I could have been a theologian.

I have dedicated the book to my students at Wabash. Their interest and friendship has been one of the joys of my life for nearly twenty years now. One of those students, Steve Webb, has become my friend and colleague, and an ongoing conversation with him has been one of the two principal influences on this book—the other being an ongoing conversation with the memory of Hans Frei.

W. C. P.

A Note on Language

At some future time, Christians may find a language for their talk about God that captures the truths of the Christian tradition, that speaks helpfully to contemporary concerns about the relations of female and male, and that moves and inspires us all. In past generations, the most powerful and appropriate new language has often entered Christian discourse by way of ordinary Christian congregations, and the work of liturgists and hymn writers, with theologians trailing in their wakes. But just now the signals from these and other sources are mixed, and anyone who writes theology must inevitably settle for a series of more or less awkward compromises; this book is no exception. Here are some rough-and-ready rules that I have followed:

1. I have used standard translations of sources, only rarely commenting on the linguistic biases of texts or translators. The biblical quotations are cited from the New Revised Standard Version. This version at least has tried not to introduce into the English translation male language when it was not present in the Greek or the Hebrew.

2. I have tried to avoid the use of either male or female pronouns with respect to God.

3. I have not hesitated to use male pronouns in reference to Jesus. Jesus of Nazareth was a male human being; denying his maleness risks denying his sex and thereby denying his full humanity. Chapter 5 discusses this issue at greater length.

4. My own hope is, in general, for the enrichment rather than the diminution of theological vocabulary. With respect to the Trinity, I am therefore inclined to use the language of Father, Son, and Holy Spirit while also introducing other terms, but, like many other writers, I am still trying to find appropriate balances in such matters. Chapter 3 of this book presents some rather technical historical arguments about the Trinity, and most of the sources cited use "Father" and "Son." It seemed confusing and awkward, when commenting on a passage that was just quoted, to switch away from the language it used, so I have there stuck with the traditional language with a consistency that will annoy some readers. If I had been writing in a less historical mode, I would have used more varied terms—but even then, I should clearly acknowledge, I would not have given up "Father" and "Son" altogether.

All these policies constitute a kind of experiment, pursued without any sense that they constitute "*the* right answer" and only with the hope that progress and consensus emerge only through a variety of such experiments. In one of his essays Paul Ricoeur dreams of a "prophetic preacher" who "would be able to make a radical return to the origins of Jewish and Christian faith and, at the same time, make of this return an event which speaks to our own time." But then he admits, "The philosopher, however, is not this prophetic preacher."[1] Neither, with rare exceptions, is the theologian. If one finds oneself with a theologian's vocation in a time when neither the preaching of prophets nor the practice of Christian communities has generated an altogether satisfactory language of Christian discourse, one has to struggle along as best one can.

NOTE

1. Paul Ricoeur, "Religion, Atheism, and Faith," in *The Conflict of Interpretations: Essays on Hermeneutics*, trans. Charles Freilich (Evanston, Ill.: Northwestern University Press, 1974), 447–48.

Introduction

Most people, in cultures where Christianity has been a dominant religious influence, assume that they know roughly what the word "God" means. Whether or not they believe in God, whether or not they find God an attractive notion, they do have an idea of God, an idea that tends to center on power. God is all-powerful, omnipotent. God is in charge of everything. God is like a king, and one who rules very much without parliament as an absolute monarch. God is like a father, and a patriarchal, domineering father at that. God is "the Lord." Even the classic conundrums posed about God—If God is all-powerful, why is there evil? If God is all-powerful, how can human beings have any freedom?—take God's power for granted as central to the setting of the problem.

The Christian gospel, however, starts its understanding of God from a very different place. To read the biblical narratives is to encounter a God who is, first of all, love (1 John 4:8). Love involves a willingness to put oneself at risk, and God is in fact vulnerable in love, vulnerable even to great suffering. God's self-revelation is Jesus Christ, and, as readers encounter him in the biblical stories, he wanders with nowhere to lay his head, washes the feet of his disciples like a servant, and suffers and dies on a cross—condemned by the authorities of his time, undergoing great pain, "despised and rejected by others; a man of suffering and acquainted with infirmity" (Isa. 53:3). Just this Jesus is the human face of God, not merely a messenger or a prophet but God's own self come as self-revelation to humankind. If God becomes human in just this way, moreover, then that tells us something about how we might seek our own fullest humanity—not in quests of power and wealth and fame but in service, solidarity with the despised and rejected, and the willingness to be vulnerable in love.

One might therefore expect that Christians who care most about the outcasts and the suffering people of the world, who are most suspicious of raw power, would be most drawn to a theology that begins with Jesus Christ as encountered in these biblical stories. Yet many such contemporary Christians see an emphasis on Christology or the Bible as part of the problem rather than part of the solution. Their attitudes are understandable. The Bible indeed also contains stories and sayings that seem to be authorizations of bigotry and celebrations of brutality. Perhaps even worse are some of the ways scripture and christological and other doctrines have been misused throughout Christian history.[1] Many who today are anxiously fighting rear-guard actions to preserve power and privilege and delay justice and equality adopt the slogans of "biblical Christianity" or claim to speak in the name of Jesus.

Little wonder that many women, to say nothing of gays and lesbians, hear appeals to the Bible or to christological doctrines as the instruments of their oppression. Nor do such concerns focus exclusively on issues about gender. Some argue, for instance, that much of the world's recent history has involved the oppression of the rest of the world by people from Europe and North America and that, since most Europeans and North Americans during much of that time were at least nominally Christian, theology that emphasizes a Christian starting point (Jesus Christ, the Bible, the Trinity) simply continues such patterns of oppression. "Christian absolutism," John Hick remarks, "in collaboration with acquisitive and violent human nature, has done much to poison the relationships between the Christian minority and the non-Christian majority of the world's population by sanctifying exploitation and oppression on a gigantic scale."[2] The Trinity and the incarnation must therefore be treated as an "intellectual construction" to be "left behind when the disciple of Jesus discards the cultural packaging in which Western Christianity has wrapped the Gospel."[3]

The list of examples could easily continue, and the attitude grows widespread in certain academic circles that, if you care deeply about injustice and oppression, it is all right to be somehow religious, but problematic to be too deeply and explicitly Christian—

all right to believe in God, but problematic to ground one's belief too much in the Bible. But that gets things exactly backward: it is vague religiousness, a culturally derived general belief in God, that so often thinks about God as power, and faith in Jesus Christ as known in the biblical stories that points instead to the divine but oh so human one on the cross, vulnerable in love for the outsiders of the world.

Too often it seems that one set of angry voices asks, "Do you care about justice and equality, or are you one of those people still obsessed with Christology and biblical authority?" while other voices demand, "Do you really care about Jesus and the Bible, or are you one of those folk always talking about peace and justice?" It becomes difficult to say, "I really care about Jesus and the Bible, and *therefore* I want to talk about justice, and peace, and vulnerable love."

Hasty generalizations are dangerous, and some qualifications need attention right at the start. Some committed feminists, some deeply engaged in interreligious dialogue, some fighting hard for social justice understand full well that the biblical Jesus is their ally. In addition, the gospel of Jesus Christ does not provide the only way of challenging a picture of God as first of all about power— other religious traditions, for instance, make similar points in their own different ways, as does the metaphysics of process thought. Moreover, those who are suspicious of many elements in the Christian tradition are not just imagining the problems that concern them. Throughout much of Christian history the symbols and stories of Jesus have been misused to become the emblems of power. Explorers and conquerors about to plunder new territories did often pause to plant a flag that bore a cross. Women, gay men, and lesbians have often found that theologies that began with the Bible were used as the instruments of their oppression.

But still, in a world all too full of the idols of power, when the stories of how love led very God of very God to end up hanging on a cross are taken as somehow the allies of oppression, something has surely gone desperately wrong.

This book will seek to recover more authentic interpretations of those stories, to ask, in the first place, what sort of God one would believe in if one took the biblical narratives, especially the Gospel stories about Jesus, as the best clue to who God is. Chapter 1 lays out the beginning of an answer: God is the one who loves in freedom, and in that free love God is vulnerable, willing to risk suffering. One problem posed by such an account is that the Christian

xv

tradition has usually thought of God as eternal and often thought of the eternal as timeless and unchanging and therefore impervious to being affected by the changing world. Chapter 2 will give a different interpretation of eternity: as the fullness of life experienced in all its richness, and therefore not at all closed off from the changing vulnerabilities of love. Thinking about divine vulnerability and divine eternity in the context of the Christian tradition will already have led to some questions about the doctrine of the Trinity, and chapter 3 will turn to the Trinity as the working out of the identity of the God self-revealed in the biblical narratives and as an account of God as modeling the mutuality and equality of love, not the hierarchy of power.

After these conclusions about God, some of the contemporary issues already mentioned can get more direct attention. Chapter 4 will consider the interpretation of scripture. The story of Jesus the rejected one ought to remind us to pay attention to oppressed peoples, to try to hear voices too often silenced. But does a theology that reads the biblical narratives as an account of God's identity inevitably use the Bible in a way that drowns out diverse voices and imposes a master narrative that silences alternatives? No, the argument will run: The complex, rich, jumbled character of these texts means that readers understand them best and learn most from them by acknowledging and wrestling with diversities and ambiguities in which many voices surface and questions that at the beginning are about the narratives end up being about our own lives. Chapter 5 then considers three particular questions posed by the theology here developed: Does a theology with a male savior inevitably contribute to the oppression of women? Does a theology with a suffering savior valorize suffering in a way that only makes it more likely to continue? Is a theology that identifies one human figure as the self-revelation of God, the unique savior, somehow intrinsically unfair to and oppressive of adherents of other religious traditions?

As already noted, the kind of God in whom one believes has implications for the kind of life one tries to live. The final two chapters turn to such questions. Chapter 6 claims that one properly follows the God revealed in Jesus Christ as a member of a Christian community and considers what sort of community followers of Jesus Christ ought to form. Chapter 7 begins by considering the particular vocation of Christian theologians. Like any other Christians, they are first of all members of Christian communities, but their work also addresses a wider public and, in particular, academic audiences. How should that fact shape theological work, and what sort of relations should Christians generally have to the wider societies in which they live?

Theologians of liberation, and many contemporary philosophers as well, have emphasized that each of us writes from a particular point of view, and authors ought to be honest about their contexts and even their prejudices. A few notes about the author of this book seem therefore in order.

1. I write from a position of privilege. I am a white male, with a tenured position at an excellent academic institution in a wealthy and powerful nation. That privilege makes a difference to what follows. I am often deeply moved when Latin American theologians, who risk getting murdered because of their work with the poor, or African American theologians, who have struggled all their lives against racism, write about their solidarity with the oppressed, but such language can ring false when I use it myself. I cannot pretend to be what I am not; I find myself struggling with the responsibilities of those who have worldly advantages rather than with the challenges of those without them. While the world's disadvantaged may often need to reflect first and foremost on how to empower themselves, I find myself thinking more about the dangers and ambiguities of power. But one can never say such things without qualification. Pastors know how much pain may be hidden behind a comfortable-looking face in a prosperous congregation. Even those of us who live in privilege, if we take seriously the task of following Jesus Christ, may find ourselves called upon to make unexpected sacrifices, suddenly placed at risk among the despised and oppressed in surprising ways.

2. I write as a Presbyterian. It does not follow that I am trying to write "Presbyterian theology." It would be unfaithful to the Reformed tradition itself to attempt such an enterprise self-consciously: Calvin would have thought that one should aim at Christian theology or biblical theology. Still, the way I think about the church, and the texts that shape my thought, owe much to my Presbyterian heritage. That does not seem cause for apology. "Each of us," David Tracy has written, "contributes more to the common good when we dare to undertake a journey into our own particularity . . . than when we attempt to homogenize all differences in favor of some lowest common denominator."[4] Presbyterianism is part of my particularity. Even as I struggle, sometimes ironically, sometimes angrily, with its problems, I try to bring some of its resources as part of my contribution to theological conversation.

3. My theological work grows out of a particular intellectual context. Those familiar with recent developments in theology in the United States will recognize some patterns of thought variously labeled "narrative theology," "postliberal theology," or "the new Yale school." As is often the case, those so described, myself among them, dislike the labels. But much of what follows—concern about the shape of the biblical narratives, about the God whose identity they render, and about their implications for the patterns of our lives—draws on themes developed by Hans Frei, who taught me during my graduate work at Yale, and by others of his colleagues and students.[5]

I pursue those interests while also trying to learn from, among other sources, theologies of liberation and a variety of new approaches to hermeneutics and literary criticism. Trying to listen to all these voices poses some hard questions. Does a theology of biblical narrative impose one story in a way that silences other voices? Do contemporary theorists show that the very ideas of coherent narrative or the clear identity of a person make no sense? As I move out into these conversations, has my own starting point been enriched or has it simply collapsed behind me?

I am also conscious of how rarely theologians reflecting on the Bible actually get around to looking in detail at particular biblical texts. Even Hans Frei described his masterly *The Eclipse of Biblical Narrative* as falling "into the almost legendary category of analysis of analyses of the Bible in which not a single text is examined, not a single exegesis undertaken."[6] What follows will nervously encroach on the territory of biblical exegetes, looking rather closely at some of the Gospel narratives, and thereby no doubt put its theological approach under further strain.

In an earlier book on theological method,[7] I drew some analogies with the conclusions of contemporary philosophers of science such as Thomas Kuhn and Imre Lakatos. Lakatos, for instance, argued that a scientific theory sets a program for research and that it is worth holding onto the theory as long as it continues to generate interesting and fruitful research.[8] This book, then, could be seen as one exercise in testing a particular theological research program. One could no doubt develop many of the same conclusions by way of other approaches. To take one approach is not necessarily to issue implicit condemnations of any other, so much as to say, "Let us see where this takes us, how much it can help us put together, what it can help us see." As it engages in its own development and in dialogue with other points of view and other disciplines, does it keep generating insights and raising questions worth exploring? Or does it stultify or just disintegrate? To use a phrase that Hans Frei employed in a different context: "Does it stretch or will it break?"[9] For a theological approach, as for a scientific theory, the only way to find out is to try it and see what happens.

NOTES

1. "Of all the doctrines of the church," Elizabeth Johnson writes from a feminist perspective, "Christology is the one most used to suppress and exclude women. At root the difficulty lies in the fact that Christology in its story, symbol, and doctrine has been assimilated to the patriarchal world view, with the result that its liberating dynamic has been twisted into justification for domination. . . . Thus coopted, the powerful symbol of the liberating Christ lost its subversive, redemptive significance" (Elizabeth A. Johnson, *She Who Is: The Mystery of God in Feminist Theological Discourse* [New York: Crossroad, 1992], 151).
2. John Hick, "The Non-Absoluteness of Christianity," in *The Myth of Christian Uniqueness*, ed. John Hick and Paul F. Knitter (Maryknoll, N.Y.: Orbis Books, 1987), 17.
3. John Hick, *God Has Many Names* (Philadelphia: Westminster Press, 1982), 124.
4. David Tracy, "Defending the Public Character of Theology," *The Christian Century* 98 (1981): 353.
5. See George A. Lindbeck, *The Nature of Doctrine: Religion and Theology in a Postliberal Age* (Philadelphia: Westminster Press, 1984), esp. chap. 6.
6. Hans W. Frei, *The Eclipse of Biblical Narrative: A Study in Eighteenth and Nineteenth Century Hermeneutics* (New Haven: Yale University Press, 1974), vii. This would not be true of Frei's *The Identity of Jesus Christ* (Philadelphia: Fortress Press, 1975), which draws on particular biblical texts with great sensitivity.
7. William C. Placher, *Unapologetic Theology: A Christian Voice in a Pluralistic Conversation* (Louisville, Ky.: Westminster/John Knox Press, 1989), chap. 3.
8. Imre Lakatos, "Falsification and the Methodology of Scientific Research Programs," in *Criticism and the Growth of Knowledge*, ed. Imre Lakatos and Alan Musgrave (Cambridge: Cambridge University Press, 1970), 91–196.
9. Hans W. Frei, "The 'Literal Reading' of Biblical Narrative in the Christian Tradition: Does It Stretch or Will It Break?" in *The Bible and the Narrative Tradition*, ed. Frank D. McConnell (New York: Oxford University Press, 1991), 36–77.

Part 1
God

1 The Vulnerable God

The assumption that God means, first of all, power runs through-out much of history, and it carries a great deal of accompanying baggage. God can do anything to anyone, but no one can cause pain to God—such an account of omnipotence often seems central to the very definition of deity. God is perfect, and, if we want to be perfect, it follows that we ought to try to be as powerful as possi-ble. The Christian gospel, however, proclaims the God self-revealed in Jesus Christ, and that God is very different—a God, in Leonardo Boff's phrase, "weak in power but strong in love,"[1] a God willing to be vulnerable to pain in the freedom of love.

Yet most Christians so take for granted the traditional models of divine omnipotence that they fail to notice just what a radical idea of God the gospel proposes. Later sections of this chapter will work through that interrupted, disturbing text, the Gospel of Mark, to develop the picture it provides of a vulnerable, loving God. What follows, therefore, carries through on the promises made in the Introduction as to both content and method: in con-tent, some claims about divine vulnerability; in method, the use of the narrative shapes of the Bible for the doing of theology.

When contemporary theologians turn to the Bible, the temp-tation is often to emphasize the contrasts between the world of the first century and that of our time, and on many issues such con-trasts deserve attention. On these questions about divine power, however, the gospel challenges assumptions that our own society shares with much of the ancient world. Most people today, whether or not they believe in God, think that God is about power and think that power is about the domination of others, through violence if necessary, just as human success is about wealth and career advancement and national greatness is about military triumph.

The ancient Greeks also believed in divine power, and power pure and simple, with a frankness that can make a modern reader cringe. In *Prometheus Bound*, Aeschylus told how Zeus condemned Prometheus to horrible torment because he had dared to show compassion for humankind and how he drove Io off to a life of dreadful suffering mostly just to cover up the fact that he had raped her.

The opening chorus asks,
> Who of the Gods is so hard of heart
> that he finds joy in this . . . —
> save only Zeus? For he malignantly,
> always cherishing a mind
> that bends not, has subdued the breed
> of Uranos, nor shall he cease
> until he satisfies his heart,
> or someone take the rule from him—that hard-to-capture rule.[2]

Yet Aeschylus, in many ways a traditionalist, writing plays still performed as part of a religious festival, did not question that Zeus, the king of the gods, deserves worship, for he yet retains "that hard-to-capture rule." "Might and violence," Hephaestus says early in the play, "in you the command of Zeus has its perfect fulfillment,"[3] and might and violence—power—in sufficient measure sufficed to define divinity.

Such power meant invulnerability, both literally and metaphorically. In Aristophanes' comedy *The Frogs*, Dionysius and Xanthias the slave, at one point in their trip through Hades, both claim to be gods. They devise an empirical test: Both will be flogged, and "Whichever of us squeals first or even bats an eyelid isn't a god at all."[4] Freedom from pain and suffering here defines divinity.

Greek philosophers mistrusted the idea of God as arbitrarily violent, but they reinforced the idea of invulnerable divine power. Plato warned against the teachings of the poets and playwrights, against those myths of Zeus's sexuality and vengeance. We must teach our children, he wrote in the *Republic*, that the gods are without passion and wholly good.[5] His student Aristotle picked up

4

and developed that theme of divine impassibility. A god without passion, he concluded, must be indifferent to, indeed unaware of, the joys and sorrows of our changing world, lost in an eternal and unchanging thinking about thought.[6] Divine impassibility served two functions. It ruled out vulgar passions: no more rapes, no more private vengeance. At the same time, it preserved divine power. Part of what power seemed to mean, after all, is that one can affect others for good or ill but yet remain unthreatened by them, invulnerable. It is the most powerful ruler who is safe and secure from external threat, and we all, at least in some moods, seek power so that we can be in control, without any risks from outside. For God, then, impassibility guarantees omnipotence.

The God of Israel represents a more complicated case, and we Christians should not, as too often we do, indulge in wrongheaded contrasts between the vindictive God of the Old Testament and the loving God of Christian faith. Such an interpretation distorts both sides. Yahweh, after all, spoke to Hosea of a tortured, never-ending love affair with the people Israel. But, as Israel remembered it, their God had also hardened Pharaoh's heart and punished Saul for failing to slay the Amalekites. Such a deity seems to be a God of power and might, and even brutality. By the time of Jesus, Philo had tried to do for Yahweh what Plato had done for Zeus—explain away the stories that caused ethical scandal to a philosopher. But his doctrines likely had little appeal to ordinary folk in occupied Palestine, where the memory that Yahweh had destroyed Babylon led more than the Zealots to hope that a similar fate might await imperial Rome. In that first-century world, when it came to questions about the power and passion of God, Judaism could offer, at best, mixed signals—just as, after all, the Christian church has offered, at best, mixed signals throughout its history.

In these matters, early on, Christian theology often sought alliances with the philosophers. At least as early as Justin Martyr, theologians were distinguishing the disgraceful, mad passions of pagan deities from the "impassible" God of Christian faith,[7] and much of the Christian tradition has portrayed God as unaffected and unaffectable. The Council of Chalcedon dismissed the view that the divine nature could be passible as "vain babblings" and condemned those who held it.[8] The two natures, human and divine, were so united in Christ's one person that one could say, in a manner of speaking, that the divine nature "suffered" when Christ died on the cross—but only in a manner of speaking, for it is really power and impassibility that characterize the divine nature.[9] Jaroslav Pelikan

5

even maintains that "the impassibility of God was a basic presupposition of all Christological doctrine."[10]

Mystics and theologians issued minority reports from time to time; one cannot generalize too quickly about "the Christian tradition." Even Aquinas, although he notoriously insisted that the nature of God's relations to the world is such that things in the world are affected by God, but "being related to creatures is not a reality in God,"[11] proves to be in this, as in most things, a complicated story.[12] But the language of impassibility came to dominate. Protestant scholasticism picked up much of it. The Westminster Confession of Faith explicitly affirms that God is "without body, parts, or passions, immutable."[13]

Such images of God comport well with many of the values that contemporary society still holds. We admire success and strength and being number one. "To possess power," as Carter Heyward puts it, "is to be on top—of someone else. . . . It is to be above the common folk—to flex the muscles of our brains, bodies, or ideologies—and to win."[14] A deity who most instantiates what much of society most admires, one could argue, would precisely be a powerful, invulnerable God. As Eberhard Jüngel has written, "This is the earthly way of thinking of a lord: first he has all power and then perhaps he can be merciful—but then again, perhaps not."[15] This is the sort of God to whom speakers at political conventions appeal or pray to bless America, victor in the cold war. For theologians who begin with such a picture of God, Christology can only take the form of a series of radical paradoxes, because a God so described has little in common with the crucified Jesus.

Given the long history just sketched so hastily, it is a fairly remarkable phenomenon that so many theologians of our own century have emphasized the vulnerability of God. Ronald Goetz can even speak with some accuracy of the emergence of a "new orthodoxy" of a suffering God.[16] The theme appears prominently in German theologians from Barth and Bonhoeffer to Moltmann and Jüngel, in process theologians from Whitehead on, in some of the most creative Asian theology, and in liberation thought from Latin America to feminists in the United States. It could be interesting to speculate on the reasons for this trend—the ways, perhaps, in which a century that has seen the optimism of previous generations so shattered by tragedy finds it harder to accept a God distanced from the sufferings of the world. The project immediately at hand, however, is not to explore the cultural factors that might be at work in this theological development but to argue that, in writing of a God who is vulnerable in love, Christian theologians are only reclaiming their own birthright, for it is just such a God that is encountered in the biblical narratives.

The Bible contains law codes, poems, prophecies, wise and not so wise sayings, and much else besides, as well as stories. The stories themselves are varied, and sometimes they are even mutually inconsistent. As chapter 4 will explain in greater detail, one cannot simply talk about "*the* biblical narrative." Still, stories, some of them interconnected, are surely an important part of scripture, and one of their functions is to narrate God's identity.[17] That is, in a world, whether in the first century or in the twentieth, with competing assumptions about the divine nature, one can take the Bible and say, "You want to know who God is, what God is like—well, here are some stories."

Some of the stories seem pretty brutal and at odds with the picture of God presented in others. An honest reader has to wrestle hard with whether one can somehow fit these pieces together. How can this seemingly violent God be the God of love encountered in different parts of what seems to be the same story? Many of the stories may not be historically accurate. The Gospels, as Calvin himself said, were not written, "in such a manner, as to preserve, on all occasions, the exact order of time."[18] "We know that the Evangelists were not very exact as to the order of dates, or even in detailing minutely everything that Christ said or did."[19]

Amid all the inconsistencies, whether of historical detail or of the moral character of the God portrayed, does the portrait of an identity for God emerge? Such a question permits no quick response but can be answered only in detail, by attempting to tell the biblical stories in a way that brings out such a picture and yet in general holds the elements of these varied texts somehow together. One way of thinking about an identity description is that individual biblical stories may, even if untrue as to detail, function as anecdotes that reveal a person's character[20]—in ways that get lost, as is often the case with a good anecdote, if one tries to summarize the point of the stories in nonnarrative fashion. The Gospel stories may do this most clearly, for they show the sort of person Jesus was, and in Jesus, God was revealing God's own self in human form.

Individual episodes can thus render personal identity, but the shape of a whole narrative can do so as well. The way a story presents a character—the first scene in which the reader meets this person, the way different themes gradually emerge, the dramatic turning point of the story, the feelings with which readers are left as

7

the story ends—often provides keys to the identity that a character has in a story. Newly popular hermeneutical methods such as rhetorical analysis, reader-response theory, and political and literary approaches to the Bible, it turns out, can often help us to understand such matters, although admittedly some of the insights they generate turn out to look like a careful reader's common sense.

Consider, for instance, the book of Revelation, a book that is hardly anyone's idea of a "realistic narrative." Yet there is certainly, even here, a kind of story line: On the island of Patmos, the narrator has a vision, first of "one like the Son of Man" (Rev. 1:13), who dictates messages to the seven churches of Asia. Then the narrator passes through a door to see a vision of the heavenly throne (Rev. 4:1–2).

> Then I saw in the right hand of the one seated on the throne a scroll written on the inside and on the back, sealed with seven seals; and I saw a mighty angel proclaiming with a loud voice, "Who is worthy to open the scroll and break its seals?" And no one in heaven or on earth or under the earth was able to open the scroll or to look into it. And I began to weep bitterly. (Rev. 5:1–4a)

The opening of the seven seals generates the rest of the story, so the crisis of whether anyone can be found to open the scroll constitutes the turning point of the whole narrative. But it is resolved in a very odd fashion. As the narrator weeps, one of the elders reassures him: "See, the Lion of the tribe of Judah, the Root of David, has conquered, so that he can open the scroll and its seven seals" (Rev. 5:5). But then, in the very next verse, the narrator sees not a conquering Lion but a Lamb who has been slaughtered, and it is the Lamb who opens the seals—and the rest of the story unfolds. The text offers no explanation. At least one commentator chalks it all up to confusion, "a quick and somewhat incongruous shift from one type of animal imagery to another," which may confusedly conflate an earlier tradition "in which a lion is the helper of the Messiah, who is a lamb."[21]

But is this shift of image a confusion or the very point of the story? The imagery earlier in the book consistently presents the language of power. The Son of man in Revelation 1 has feet like burnished bronze, carries a two-edged sword, "and his face was like the sun shining with full force" (Rev. 1:16). The messages to the seven churches speak the language of power and even of threat.

8

And the vision of the throne of God in Revelation 4 parades every imperial attribute discoverable by the author's quite considerable imagination. What could be more natural than to expect the arrival of that conquering royal beast, the Lion?

Instead, we get a slaughtered Lamb. Commenting on the passage, G. B. Caird writes that it is "as if John were saying to us . . . 'Wherever the Old Testament says *Lion*, read *Lamb*.' Wherever the Old Testament speaks of the victory of the Messiah or the overthrow of the enemies of God, we are to remember that the Gospel recognizes no other way of achieving these ends than the way of the Cross."[22] Caird grasps the basic contrast but puts it in a context all too common in the Christian tradition, setting the threatening God of the Hebrew scriptures off against the gentle deity of the New Testament. Stating the issue in those terms both oversimplifies the two parts of the Christian Bible and misses the more general point of this text. The lesson of this narrative turning point is a more fundamental and general one: to contrast the ideologies of power, *wherever* they are found—in Babylon, Israel, Rome, Beijing, Washington, or Christian community—with the challenge of the gospel of the crucified One, the crucified One who came to reveal the God already known as the Lord who agonized in ongoing covenant with Israel.[23]

From this moment on, at any rate, the Lamb never long leaves the story. The narrative returns to imagery of power, even of warfare, but the victories are victories of the Lamb who has been slaughtered. As Jacques Ellul puts it, for the book of Revelation,

> The one who . . . unravels the secret of history, who holds it, and allows it to unfold as history is clearly not the All-Powerful Lord: he is the immolated Lamb. In the same way the one who presides at the "Last Judgment," at the separation of the good and the evil, at the condemnation, at the ultimate combat, is not the powerful athlete, muscular and majestic, of the admirable Sistine . . . ; it is not the "chief of the heavenly militia"; it is not the Lord of Lords; it is the Lamb, the crucified, the stripped, the annihilated, the weakest of all . . . , the one who has neither beauty, nor honor, nor power.[24]

In the cultures in which the New Testament was written, as in our own, few expected a messenger, much less a self-revelation, of God, to take such a form. In the Hellenistic world, it was powerful heroes and mighty emperors who were deified. Celsus, indeed,

9

contrasted the "plainly evident" appearances of the pagan deities with the "stealthy and secretive manner" of "the fellow who deceived the Christians."[25] He knew what a divine epiphany ought to look like, and Jesus hardly fit the requirements. Many among Jesus' Jewish contemporaries understandably hoped for a triumphant Messiah who would defeat the hated Romans, and they too could only find this crucified teacher a disappointment, if they took him seriously at all.[26] The first century, like the twentieth, expected deity to triumph through power.

But suppose God is not like that. Suppose God, more than anything else, freely loves, and in that love is willing to be vulnerable and to risk suffering. Although stories provide a good way of presenting a person's identity, the task of narrating the identity of a human being who is the self-revelation of such a God poses great problems. On the one hand, one has to make it clear that the story of this human person really is the story of God. After all, as Kierkegaard once remarked, "God did not assume the form of a servant to make a mockery of us; hence it cannot be his intention to pass through the world in such a manner that no single human being becomes aware of his presence."[27] On the other hand, one needs to challenge many of the assumptions readers will bring as to the nature of God. So how does one present the story of a human life as the self-revelation of God without falling into the imagery of power and might that shaped the thinking about God in Jesus' day and continues to shape it in ours? How does one tell a story that shows readers the divinity of this wandering rabbi while at the same time rejecting the assumptions they will have about the nature of divinity?

The difficulties such problems raise for narrative strategy may be suggested by the fact that Paul did not attempt to solve them. The story he told was primarily one of the eternal Christ self-emptying into human likeness. In Paul's gospel, Jesus of Nazareth is born, shares the bread and cup on the night when he is betrayed, and suffers and dies on a cross. In Paul, there are no other stories of Jesus' earthly life, no references, ever, to a single miracle Jesus performed. There is nothing that would manifest this human life as the self-revelation of God by trading on the imagery of divine power— very little at all, in fact, about this human life. It has become customary to note that, after all, Paul had not known Jesus' life at first hand, and yet on one occasion he seems to have spent fifteen days with Peter, and he had other contacts with the Jerusalem community. Would he not have known stories about Jesus' life, stories unknown to his readers, stories that might have illustrated points of concern to him with a particular authority?

It is dangerous to infer from silence, but at least reflecting about what Paul left unsaid provides an entry point for thinking about what the Gospel of Mark does say. Through narratives, it presents an extended account of Jesus' identity as God's self-revelation: so far as we know, this was the first time anyone had ever tried to do that. For all the common condescending remarks about the quality of Mark's Greek and the awkwardness of his prose, considered as a solution to these narrative problems, the text stands as a work of genius.

Many of the scholarly studies of Mark over the last twenty-five years, from Theodore Weeden's *Mark: Traditions in Conflict* in 1971 to recent works like Ched Myers's *Binding the Strong Man* and Mary Ann Tolbert's *Sowing the Gospel*, have emphasized the contrast the Gospel makes between the twelve disciples' misguided dreams of power and Jesus' willingness to suffer.[28] Weeden argues that the author wrote with the quite specific purpose of refuting a party within his own community that had developed a divine-man Christology and ecclesiology. Jesus was, for them, the powerful wonder-worker who manifested God, and they, like the Corinthian group Paul attacked in Second Corinthians, saw themselves as simply continuing the power of Jesus in their own lives, through pneumatic gifts, ecstatic experiences, and miraculous feats.[29] By contrast, Weeden says that Mark wrote for a community of Palestinian Christians who, "separated from their Lord, . . . found themselves in a cruel period of suffering and misery while evil forces still abounded in the world," and who followed a suffering, humble Christ.[30] Therefore the disciples, who represent the ideology of power, become the villains of the story, with Jesus as the humble, suffering hero.

Weeden's historical conclusions continue to be controversial. Many scholars would still reject his location of the writing of the Gospel in Palestine. While agreeing with Weeden on the centrality of Mark's polemic against the disciples, Werner Kelber has argued that the real issue was historical rather than christological. After the destruction of the Jerusalem church in the Jewish War of A.D. 66–70, Christians needed an explanation of this tragedy, and the author of Mark provided an anti-Jerusalem, anti-twelve-disciple polemic to explain the fall of the Jerusalem church as divine punishment.[31] For Weeden, Mark is attacking a Christology that identifies Jesus as a divine man, a *theios anēr*, one of those Hellenistic

11

wonder-workers who constituted a sort of human epiphany of God, but Dieter Georgi argues that Mark still presents a divine man Christology and Jack Dean Kingsbury maintains that *theios anēr* was actually such a rare and variously used term in classical culture that it does not provide a useful category for thinking about the background of Mark, one way or the other.[32] Whatever the historical details, however, the basic theme remains: a contrast between ideologies of power and suffering that consistently undercuts the language of power and the authority of those who claim it.[33]

The Gospel's title, in most manuscripts, declares that the story before us is "the good news of Jesus Christ, the Son of God," but the narrator's own voice never refers to Jesus as the Son of God again. "Good news," *euangelion* in the Greek, would often have been the term used for the news of victory in battle or an amnesty on the accession of a new sovereign, but in this story no sooner does the Spirit descend upon Jesus and a voice from heaven proclaim him, "My Son, the Beloved" than "the Spirit immediately drives him out into the wilderness" (Mark 1:11–12). This will not be a story, we as readers gather, of easy triumphs or of the usual sort of monarch.

To be sure, this Jesus heals and performs other miracles, but he silences those he has healed, almost as if the act were one of shame (Mark 1:44; 5:43; 7:36; 8:26). In the act of healing, moreover, he touches lepers (Mark 1:41) and spits on the tongue of a deaf man (Mark 7:33)—the very forms of his healing would have been, to his contemporaries, both ritually polluting and physically disgusting.[34] When the leader of the synagogue asks for his help in curing his daughter, Jesus makes Jairus wait while he tends to a woman who has been suffering from menstrual hemorrhaging. For the business of wonder-working, this gets every priority wrong: Jesus postpones raising a child from the dead for a comparatively trivial cure whose results both their physical character and the cultural taboos of the time would have kept invisible; he turns from the socially important male to heal a nameless woman; and he responds to the woman's polluting touch with praise of her faith.[35] Then he turns to the really dramatic miracle and nearly renders it into farce, insisting, in the face of all the evidence, that the child is not dead but merely sleeping, so that onlookers burst into laughter (Mark 5:40).

What sort of miracle worker is this? The professional wonder-workers of that age, or of ours, know how to milk the dramatic moment. Jesus seems to keep undercutting the wonders; Mark, indeed, never uses the usual Greek word for "miracle" in describing these events. Little surprise, perhaps, that such acts seem to do Jesus more harm than good: after healing the leper, he can no longer go into a town openly (Mark 1:45); the Gerasenes' reaction to his cure of the demoniac is to beg Jesus to leave their neighborhood (Mark 5:17); and immediately after the dramatic resuscitation of Jairus's daughter comes the fiasco at Nazareth. Jesus walks on the water of the sea, but the narrator's immediate comment is that the disciples did not understand his miracles, for their hearts were hardened (Mark 6:51).

This Jesus calls disciples, but the narrative "paints them as obtuse, obdurate, recalcitrant men who at first are unperceptive of Jesus' messiahship, then oppose its style and character, and finally totally reject it."[36] The story ends without their rehabilitation. Yet the blame seems not to rest entirely with them.[37] Jesus speaks to the multitudes in deliberately mysterious parables, yet even the disciples to whom he offers explanations of a sort consistently fail to understand, and on one level the explanations of the supposedly opaque parables seem obvious enough to make us wonder whether we are missing the real point too. As Frank Kermode says, it feels like a narrative designed to turn every insider into an outsider.[38] The Jesus who emerges is as oddly paradoxical a teacher as he is a wonder-worker.

Who is this Jesus of Nazareth? At a kind of climax in the story, Jesus appears dazzlingly to Peter, James, and John, with Moses and Elijah beside him. The obvious thing to say would be, "Look!" but the voice from heaven, in literary terms a kind of privileged voice from outside the narrative world which speaks only here and at Jesus' baptism, says, not "Look," but "Listen to him"—although Jesus, in the scene at hand, does not speak (Mark 9:7). When he does next speak, however, he tells of the suffering the Son of Man must undergo—so that the point of the voice from heaven is to attend not to the dazzling epiphany but to the teaching about suffering. No sooner does Peter proclaim Jesus' identity as the Messiah than he starts to contradict Jesus,[39] and Jesus shifts from an already ominous command to silence to a stern rebuke. Peter expects a Messiah and thinks he knows what that means, but he has it all wrong, just as anyone with the usual expectations about wandering miracle workers would have it all wrong. And readers, with expectations set by the opening identification of this text as the gospel of the Son of God, find those expectations subverted at every step.

Mark uses every strategy to say two things at once: yes, this is the Messiah, the greatest of miracle workers, the Son of God, but, no, that does not mean at all what you thought it meant. Irony is the rhetorical device best suited for saying, "Yes, but no," and the ironies grow as the story progresses.[40] Jesus enters Jerusalem on a little colt: it is at once a humble and slightly silly ride and the fulfillment of a messianic prophecy. He is anointed as were the kings of old, as the Messiah ought to be, but by an unnamed woman,[41] and in a context where the act only generates controversy and presages his death. Through most of the Gospel, Mark has presented wonders in ways that undercut our expectations. Now the irony reverses, and he presents tragedy in a way that hints at wonder. Jesus sorrowfully ascends the Mount of Olives, accompanied by three followers who protest their loyalty, only to be betrayed by a trusted associate. It is a story of defeat, but it exactly parallels the story of David at the time of Absalom's rebellion—David the greatest king, the source of so much messianic imagery.[42]

Peter, the rock, betrays him, just as Jesus had prophesied. The cock crow brings that realization home to Peter just as the bullying soldiers are calling on Jesus to prophesy. Jesus remains silent, but we readers know his prophecy has just been fulfilled.[43] He receives a purple cloak and a crown; the soldiers bow down before him, and it is all intended as humiliating mockery. We, recognizing the irony, see that he really is a king, but his coronation takes the form of a scourging. Only in the midst of his trial does he proclaim himself the Messiah, the Son of the Blessed One. Only as he dies on the cross does a human voice at last recognize him as the Son of God.[44]

The cross, moreover, does not just represent a painful way to die. It is the humiliating penalty assigned to the lowest of criminals, the fate of the rankest of outsiders, full of shame and perhaps—although here the historical evidence is ambiguous, and Mark does not make the point—subject to curse in Jewish tradition. One might think of those who have AIDS as the equivalents in our society to one who suffers crucifixion, victims not only of great pain but also of degradation and humiliation from the dominant values of the culture. A few chapters earlier, when Jesus talked most vividly of times of crisis ahead, he had said it would be impostors claiming to be messiahs who would work signs and wonders, while disciples would suffer floggings and arrest, betrayal and hatred. In that context, as bystanders call on him to work a miracle and come down from the cross, it is his silent suffering that paradoxically confirms his identity as the true Messiah.[45]

14

And then: some women find Jesus' tomb empty, and a young man with an enigmatic message that serves only to terrify them, and at that point, notoriously, the Gospel ends, with an abruptness that extends even to the grammar of the last sentence. Jesus proclaimed himself the Messiah in the midst of a criminal trial, and a military officer recognized him as the Son of God as he died on a cross. We do not see a triumphant divine Jesus, pulling away the mask of suffering like a magician at the end of a trick. Mark's Gospel invites us to see Jesus' divinity precisely as he dies on the cross, for, after that, we never see him at all.[46]

For Christology, Hans Frei maintained, the doctrine is not the meaning of the story but rather the story is the meaning of the doctrine.[47] In other words, the hermeneutical goal should not be to find a series of doctrinal propositions that constitute the "real meaning" of the stories, such that we could then discard the stories themselves. Rather, conceptual formulations in the form of doctrines serve as heuristic aids that serve us best when they thrust readers back to the stories themselves with new understanding.[48] So in this case, to understand the story is to recognize, when it has reached its enigmatic ending, that it has been a story about God, and that it is oddly a story of triumph. As the story progresses, Jesus becomes more and more powerless, less and less free—able perhaps to raise a following in Galilee, still with a chance to escape in the garden, then a bound prisoner, then nailed to a cross. Yet the telling of the story implies an odd inverse proportion, for that moment when it seems that Jesus can do nothing at all is the culmination of his work as savior of the world. Traditional theology— Calvin's theology in particular—talked about this pattern of exchange under the category of Christ's obedience. In obediently surrendering his freedom, Jesus becomes more and more identified with God, who has complete freedom, and in that freedom takes all the risks of vulnerability.[49] The pattern of the story thus shows (not tells, but *shows* in the narrating of the story) both something about being human and something about God. In this story Jesus shows what it is to be most human, most like what a human being is supposed to be, living in full obedience to God. Such obedience turns out to mean the truest kind of freedom, in which one has chosen the life that meaningfully fulfills one's destiny. And in this story God is most God, for in coming vulnerably into creation God is not giving up the characteristics of divinity but most fully manifesting them. God is not essentially impassible and omnipotent, so that divine self-revelation in the vulnerable Jesus would be utterly

15

paradoxical, but God is most fundamentally of all, in Karl Barth's phrase, the one who loves in freedom, the one whose essence these stories reveal.[50]

Christological doctrine should not replace the narrative but rather help us understand it in just this way. The story begins by identifying itself as "the good news of Jesus Christ, the Son of God." As the narrative moves to its climax, the obedient Jesus becomes most fully one with God in increasing human powerlessness. By the end of the story, it turns out to have been an account of God's self-revelation that helps us know who God is. Yet in the story Jesus prays to one he calls his Father, and the category of "obedience" itself implies a differentiation between Jesus and that "Father." Moreover, Jesus' work begins only when the Spirit descends upon him—a Spirit from God, of God, yet somehow not the same as Jesus. The God whose identity a reader learns from this narrative is therefore not simply incarnate in Jesus but somehow more complex—a fact whose full implications chapter 3 will explore in discussing the Trinity.

Putting such questions aside for the moment, it is at least clear that the God about whom we learn in Mark's Gospel is not a God defined first of all in terms of power. "For responsible Christian usage of the word 'God,'" Eberhard Jüngel has written, "the Crucified One is virtually the real definition of what is meant with the word 'God.'"[51] If we take the Gospel of Mark as one trajectory toward understanding the God whose self-revealed identity it narrates, then we encounter a God defined by perfect love and perfect freedom. Love means a willingness to take risks, to care for the other in a way that causes the other's fate to affect one's own, to give to the other at real cost to oneself, to chance rejection. In Barth's words, God "does not forfeit anything by doing this. . . . On the contrary," precisely in showing willingness and readiness "for this condescension, this act of extravagance, this far journey," God is marked out from all the false gods. "They are not capable and ready for this. In their otherworldliness and supernaturalness and otherness," the deities of human manufacture are a reflection of the human pride which will not unbend, which will not stoop to that which is beneath it.[52] Such is not the God we come to know in Jesus. To quote a very different theologian, Carter Heyward, "Jesus did not come to reveal God's power, God's might, God's victory. Rather, Jesus came . . . into the pain, the passion, and the wonder of creation itself. Jesus accepted the vocation of being truly human in the image of an enigmatic God."[53] "The power of

16

the God depicted by Scripture," as Daniel Migliore says, "is strange power. It is not the power of force but the power of Spirit . . . , and it is made known above all in the weakness of the cross of Jesus."[54]

In forming conceptual language by which to reflect on Mark's Gospel, and the identity of God that it narrates, we quickly face a problem about the use of the word "power"—the quotations in the preceding paragraph reflect the difficulty. On the one hand, the "strange power" of God *is* a kind of power. Dying on the cross, Christ does transform the world. On the other hand, our culture, like the culture in which the Gospel was written, has a set of assumptions about power utterly at odds with the "power" of the cross—power based on fear, power seeking domination, power always edging toward violence. To abjure the language of power altogether risks one set of dangers: theologically, it might imply that God is not the creator, sustainer, and redeemer of all things; ethically, it might provide a fine excuse for fleeing the moral ambiguities of political activity. But positive Christian talk about power risks another set of dangers: cultural definitions are so apt to pervade our thinking that, within five minutes of radically redefining what power means, we unconsciously fall back into the old connotations.

In the face of such dilemmas, it seems best to say, with Barth, that God *is* the one who loves in freedom. It is love freely given that defines God, and that love then implies a certain kind of power. Whereas, if it is power that defines God, then at best one could hope it will be tempered by mercy—but then again, maybe not. Christian talk about God ought to start with love, not power, and introduce the language of power only in the context of love and only in a way that keeps challenging and subverting it by way of reminder of how easily it might be misunderstood.

If all that seems excessively paradoxical, it may be worth reflecting on how paradoxical is the way our society tends to think about power—a celebration of the sort of power that rests on a kind of weakness and insecurity. Nations proclaim their military power, but only enemy threat justifies the vast expenditures and potential loss of life, and so the power turns out to rest on fear. No matter how great the power of an armed nation-state, Augustine wrote of that of Rome, "the happiness arising from such conditions is a thing of glass, of mere glittering brittleness. One can never shake off the horrible dread that it may suddenly shiver into fragments."[55] Similarly, in individual relations, the impulse to dominate others rests in large part on feeling a need to protect oneself. In Reinhold Niebuhr's eloquent phrase, "there is no level of greatness

17

and power in which the lash of fear is not at least one strand in the whip of ambition."[56] Even with those we love most, as when parents love their children, love resists risking freedom, wants to keep in control. Human beings seek power because they are afraid of weakness, afraid of what might happen should they be vulnerable, and so the drive for power that looks like the purest expression of freedom proves in significant degree inspired by an enslaving fear that dares not risk vulnerability.[57]

What is really paradoxical is the celebration of such enslaving fear as if it were the triumph of power and freedom. Christian faith teaches that God is not powerful like that. The God who loves in freedom is not afraid and therefore can risk vulnerability, absorb the full horror of another's pain without self-destruction. God has the power to be compassionate without fear; human beings now as in the time of Jesus tend to think of power as refusal to risk compassion. But God's power looks not like imperious Caesar but like Jesus on the cross.

"Christ helps us," Dietrich Bonhoeffer wrote from his prison cell, "not by virtue of his omnipotence, but by virtue of his weakness and suffering. . . . Only the suffering God can help."[58] Particularly if "omnipotence" turns out to imply the inability to risk love, that certainly makes sense. Yet Joan Northam has a point too, when she writes that if she found herself at the bottom of a pit with a broken arm, "what I want and urgently need is a Rescuer with a very bright light and a long ladder, full of strength, joy and assurance who can get me out of the pit, not a god who sits in the darkness suffering with me."[59]

How can a suffering God help? The next chapter will consider the question as it relates to God and time, and chapter 5 will return to it in asking some questions about the valorization of suffering. But for a start, a suffering God can help, first of all, by being, in Alfred North Whitehead's famous phrase, "the fellow-sufferer who understands."[60] To know in the midst of the isolation that rejection and suffering often generate that someone always understands is in itself to be significantly empowered "to bear the pain, to resist the humiliation, to overcome the guilt."[61] Beyond that, God suffers because God is vulnerable, and God is vulnerable because God loves—and it is love, not suffering or even vulnerability, that is finally the point. God can help because God acts out of love, and love risks suffering. A God defined in terms of power is precisely not a reliable rescuer, because power provides no guarantee of concern, and power, in the way most cultures have most often used

18

the word, too often grows out of a fear of vulnerability that makes really reaching out in love, with all the risks entailed, impossible.

Sheer power, Barth says, "is not merely neutral. Power in itself is evil. It is nothing less than freedom from restraint and suppression."[62] Sheer power in that sense is not the adult's thoughtful command of the situation but the infant's worst willfulness grown beyond restraint, mad Caligula made emperor of Rome. "It is blasphemy to ascribe this kind of power to God."[63] But God's power is the power of love, which does not seek to dominate, which does not act arbitrarily (as if such willfulness were the greatest form of freedom), but acts consistently in love which authentically concerns itself for others.[64]

> God has a heart. He can feel, and be affected. He is not impassible. He cannot be moved from outside by an extraneous power. But this does not mean that He is not capable of moving Himself. No, God is moved and stirred, yet not like ourselves in powerlessness, but in His own free power, in His innermost being.[65]

Love and the unexpected moment can catch us into risking vulnerability almost in spite of ourselves, but God does not need to be pushed into the full consequences of living out love, for in freely loving, God is most of all who God is, most exemplifying the kind of power God has. When power means, as so often in human affairs it does, the uneasy quest for domination, then to be moved by another, wounded by another's pain, is experienced as a form of powerlessness, and love is trapped between inaction and the risk of impotence. But the strange power of God reveals such quests for power as a kind of weakness. It would be a weak, poor God, Jürgen Moltmann says, who could not love or suffer.[66] Such a God would be caught in a prison of impassibility.

The title of this chapter refers, however, not to God's suffering but to God's vulnerability. It seemed important to resist the claim that suffering itself is a good, an idea that the language of Moltmann and others sometimes suggests. The freedom of love is good, and that freedom risks suffering and, in a sinful world full of violence and injustice, will always encounter it sooner or later. Love does not regret the price it pays for making itself vulnerable, but to speak of paying a price is in itself to acknowledge that the suffering itself is an evil. Vulnerability, on the other hand, is a perfection of loving freedom.

Such loving freedom offers us a model for the living of our

19

own lives, but none of us is God. Our insecurities about the risks of compassion are not entirely illusory. Open ourselves to the suffering of others without limit and we can destroy ourselves, taking on more pain than we can bear. There is, however, no such thing as more pain than God can bear, and part of what it means to trust in God is to know that God can and will bear whatever cost in suffering faithfulness in love may require. To know that such a God loves us enables us to take risks of a kind we could not otherwise dare. "To love at all," C. S. Lewis once wrote,

> is to be vulnerable. Love anything, and your heart will certainly be wrung and possibly be broken. If you want to make sure of keeping it intact, you must give your heart to no one. . . . It will not be broken; it will become unbreakable, impenetrable, irredeemable. The alternative to tragedy, or at least to the risk of tragedy, is damnation. The only place outside Heaven where you can be perfectly safe from all the dangers and perturbations of love is Hell.[67]

If God will be with us in our suffering, and God's love sustains us, however, then we can dare to love and live the risks entailed in the realm between heaven and hell where we dwell and to which God freely came. The kinds of risk that the security of knowing God's love permits, therefore, are not just a kind of bonus but part of what it means to be fully human, just as the capacity for vulnerable love without limit is part of what it means to be God.

Our society, like most societies, does not think of power in this way. "Under the conditions of human life," Hannah Arendt observed, "the only alternative to power is . . . force, . . . of which one or a few can possess a monopoly by acquiring the means of violence. But while violence can destroy power, it can never become a substitute for it."[68] Force and violence are, in Arendt's terms, the *alternatives* to real power, they are where one turns when one is too weak to dare risking vulnerability. In that sense, it is the "powers and principalities" that seem to dominate our world that lack real power and the vulnerable God encountered in the biblical narratives who most manifests it. In the Fourth Gospel, Jesus wins his argument with Pilate about power; Pilate is so impotent that all he can do is turn to the violence of crucifixion.[69]

Most people today, however, like the ancient Greeks, still tend to think of power, and of divinity, on the model of Zeus, triumphant, in control, with Prometheus firmly chained to his rock. It is easy to forget the secret of the play: that only Prometheus knows the way to save Zeus from the eventual disaster that awaits him.

20

> So let him confidently
> sit on his throne and trust his heavenly thunder
> and brandish in his hand his fiery bolt.
> Nothing shall all of this avail against
> a fall intolerable, a dishonored end.[70]

Probe violence and the quest for domination far enough, and one always finds the fear of weakness.

Only a God "weak in power but strong in love" can be strong enough to take on all the world's pain and die on a cross. Trust in such a God can give human beings the strength to risk following on the path of compassion and vulnerability, to think what it means to live lives whose first priority is love. In a broken and complex world, we Christians may sometimes find ourselves driven to force and even violence in spite of our best intentions, but we need to acknowledge that to choose such alternatives is always to admit a failure of imagination, a concession to weakness, always to have betrayed the image of the power of love we have encountered in the powerless Jesus on the cross.

In his lament for his son Eric, killed at age twenty-five in a mountaineering accident, Nicholas Wolterstorff remarks that it was only in the midst of his own suffering that he saw that God suffers. He reflects on the old belief that no one can behold God's face and live. I always thought, Wolterstorff says, that this meant that no one could see God's splendor and live. A friend said perhaps it means that no one could see God's sorrow and live. Or perhaps, he reflects, the sorrow is the splendor.[71]

NOTES

1. Leonardo Boff, *Jesus Christ Liberator: A Critical Christology for Our Time*, trans. Patrick Hughes (Maryknoll, N.Y.: Orbis Books, 1978), 27.
2. Aeschylus, *Prometheus Bound*, lines 160–67, trans. David Grene, in *Greek Tragedies*, ed. David Grene and Richmond Lattimore, vol. 1 (Chicago: University of Chicago Press, 1991), 71.
3. Ibid., line 12, p. 65.
4. Aristophanes, *The Frogs*, trans. David Barrett (London: Penguin Books, 1964), 179. I am indebted to a Wabash student production of the play, directed by Christopher Doerr, for reminding me of this scene.
5. Plato, *Republic*, bk. 2, 379b, trans. G. M. A. Grube (Indianapolis: Hackett Publishing Co., 1974), 47.
6. Aristotle, *Metaphysics* 12.9.1074b, trans. Richard Hope (Ann

Arbor, Mich.: University of Michigan Press, Ann Arbor Paper-books, 1960), 266.

7. Justin Martyr, *First Apology* 25, in *Early Christian Fathers,* ed. Cyril C. Richardson (New York: Macmillan Co., 1970), 257–58.

8. J. Stevenson, *Creeds, Councils, and Controversies: Documents Illustrative of the History of the Church A.D. 337–461* (London: SPCK, 1966), 336.

9. "To hunger, to thirst, to be weary, and to sleep," Pope Leo wrote in a key document in the development of theological orthodoxy, belong to human nature, and so does feeling pity and weeping over the death of Lazarus. "It does not belong to the same nature to weep with feelings of pity over a dead friend and, after the mass of stone had been removed from the grave where he had lain four days, by a voice of command to raise him up to life again" (The Tome of Leo, in *Christology of the Later Fathers,* ed. Edward Rochie Hardy and Cyril C. Richardson [Philadelphia: Westminster Press, 1954], 365). Cyril of Alexandria even claims that in the cry from the cross, Jesus was speaking for others, not for himself. See Paul S. Fiddes, *The Creative Suffering of God* (Oxford: Oxford University Press, 1988), 28.

10. Jaroslav Pelikan, *The Emergence of the Catholic Tradition* (Chicago: University of Chicago Press, 1971), 270.

11. Thomas Aquinas, *Summa Theologiae* 1a, q.13, a.7, vol. 1, ed. Thomas Gilby, trans. Herbert McCabe (Garden City, N.Y.: Image Books, 1969), 215.

12. For a revisionist interpretation, see David Burrell, *Aquinas: God and Action* (Notre Dame, Ind.: University of Notre Dame Press, 1979), 85. Catherine LaCugna argues that the denial of real relations to creation in God means only that God's relations to the world are all freely chosen. See Catherine LaCugna, "The Relational God: Aquinas and Beyond," *Theological Studies* 46 (1985): 655–56.

13. Westminster Confession of Faith, chap. 2, *Book of Confessions,* Presbyterian Church (U.S.A.), 6.011.

14. Carter Heyward, *Our Passion for Justice* (New York: Pilgrim Press, 1984), 117.

15. Eberhard Jüngel, *God as the Mystery of the World,* trans. Darrell L. Guder (Grand Rapids: Wm. B. Eerdmans Publishing Co., 1983), 21.

16. Ronald Goetz, "The Suffering God: The Rise of a New Orthodoxy," *Christian Century* 103 (April 16, 1986): 385–89.

17. Hans W. Frei, *The Identity of Jesus Christ* (Philadelphia: Fortress Press, 1975), 87. "When one regards the biblical canon as a whole, the centrality to it of a narrative element is difficult to overlook: not only the chronological sweep of the whole, from creation to new creation, . . . but also the way the large narrative portions interweave and provide a context for the remaining materials so that

they, too, have a place in the ongoing story, while these other materials—parables, hymns, prayers, summaries, theological exposi-
tions—serve in different ways to enable readers to get hold of the
story and to live their way into it" (Charles M. Wood, *The Formation of Christian Understanding: An Essay in Theological
Hermeneutics* [Philadelphia: Westminster Press, 1981], 100).
18. John Calvin, *Commentary on a Harmony of the Evangelists*, trans.
William Pringle, vol. 1 (*Calvin's Commentaries*, vol. 16) (Grand
Rapids: Baker Book House, 1989), 216.
19. Ibid., 2:89.
20. David Kelsey uses this term to describe what Karl Barth does in
the "Royal Man" section of the *Church Dogmatics*. See David H.
Kelsey, *The Uses of Scripture in Recent Theology* (Philadelphia:
Fortress Press, 1975), 43.
21. Martin Rist, "Revelation: Introduction and Exegesis," *The Interpreter's Bible*, vol. 12 (New York: Abingdon Press, 1957), 407.
22. G. B. Caird, *The Revelation of St. John the Divine* (New York:
Harper & Row, 1966), 75.
23. See Abraham J. Heschel, *The Prophets*, vol. 2 (New York: Harper
& Row, Harper Torchbooks, 1971), 1–11 on the theology of
pathos in the prophets of Israel.
24. Jacques Ellul, *Apocalypse: The Book of Revelation*, trans. George W.
Schreiner (New York: Seabury Press, 1977), 117.
25. Origen, *Contra Celsum* 7.35, trans. Henry Chadwick (Cambridge:
Cambridge University Press, 1953), 422–23.
26. The evidence concerning violence and military imagery in messianic expectations is mixed. *The Psalms of Solomon* and *4 Ezra*,
e.g., say that the Messiah will not use military weapons; *2 Baruch*
says he will carry a sword (J. H. Charlesworth, "From Messianol-
ogy to Christology," in *Judaisms and Their Messiahs*, ed. Jacob
Neusner, William Scott Green, and Ernest Frerichs (Cambridge:
Cambridge University Press, 1987), 248. Green's introduction to
this helpful volume (pp. 2–3) surveys some of the complexities of
first-century references to messiahs.
27. Søren Kierkegaard, *Philosophical Fragments*, trans. David Swenson
(Princeton: Princeton University Press, 1962), 69, translation altered.
28. Theodore J. Weeden, *Mark: Traditions in Conflict* (Philadelphia:
Fortress Press, 1971); Ched Myers, *Binding the Strong Man: A
Political Reading of Mark's Story of Jesus* (Maryknoll, N. Y.: Orbis
Books, 1988); and Mary Ann Tolbert, *Sowing the Gospel* (Minneapolis: Fortress Press, 1989).
29. Weeden, *Mark: Traditions in Conflict*, 60–61.
30. Ibid., 132.
31. Werner H. Kelber, *Mark's Story of Jesus* (Philadelphia: Fortress
Press, 1979), 88–95.
32. Dieter Georgi, *Die Gegner des Paulus im 2 Korintherbrief*

(Neukirchen-Vluyn: Neukirchener Verlag, 1964); Jack Dean Kingsbury, "The 'Divine Man' as the Key to Mark's Christology— The End of an Era?" *Interpretation* 35 (July 1981): 248. See also Morton Smith, "Prolegomena to a Discussion of Aretalogies, Divine Men, the Gospels and Jesus," *Journal of Biblical Literature* 90 (June 1971): 174–99.

33. Norman Perrin said Weeden's work offered a "catalytic agent" for thinking about Mark's Christology (Norman Perrin, *A Modern Pilgrimage in New Testament Christology* [Philadelphia: Fortress Press, 1974], 110).

34. Myers, *Binding the Strong Man*, 153, 205.

35. Ibid., 200–202.

36. Weeden, *Mark: Traditions in Conflict*, 50–51.

37. Here I would disagree with Weeden, who insists that "Mark is assiduously involved in a vendetta against the disciples" (ibid.). For a more positive interpretation of Mark's picture of the disciples, see Robert C. Tannehill, "The Disciples in Mark: The Function of a Narrative Role," *Journal of Religion* 57 (1977): 386–405; and Elizabeth Struthers Malbon, "Fallible Followers," *Semeia* 28 (1983): 29–48.

38. "Being an insider is only a more elaborate way of being kept outside" (Frank Kermode, *The Genesis of Secrecy: On the Interpretation of Narrative* [Cambridge, Mass.: Harvard University Press, 1979], 27). "A 'gospel' is a narrative of a son of god who appears among men as a riddle inviting misunderstanding" (Jonathan Z. Smith, *Map Is Not Territory* [Leiden: E. J. Brill, 1978], 204).

39. "Peter's next actions in relation to Jesus are shocking in the extreme. When Jesus starts to teach the disciples about the inevitability of suffering, rejection and death that he faces, Peter rebukes him (8:31–32). . . . What degree of pride or arrogance must exist to allow one to refute the Messiah?" (Tolbert, *Sowing the Gospel*, 201).

40. See Wayne C. Booth, *A Rhetoric of Irony* (Chicago: University of Chicago Press, 1974), 28–29. For an approach that deals with different issues, but in a way complementary to mine, see Jerry Camery-Hoggatt, *Irony in Mark's Gospel* (New York: Cambridge University Press, 1991).

41. The ways in which, at a number of places in the story, women get the point while the male disciples fail to do so subverts the patriarchal power structures of Mark's society. As a rhetorical device, praiseworthy characters are often anonymous, while those who, in one way or another, fail are named. See Tolbert, *Sowing the Gospel*, 274, 292–93.

42. John R. Donahue, "Temple, Trial, and Royal Christology," in *The Passion in Mark*, ed. Werner H. Kelber (Philadelphia: Fortress Press, 1976), 76.

43. Robert M. Fowler, *Let the Reader Understand: Reader-Response Criticism and the Gospel of Mark* (Minneapolis: Fortress Press, 1991), 159.

44. Calvin, I fear, got this one wrong. "When Mark says that *the centurion* spoke thus, because Christ, *when he had uttered a loud voice, expired,* some commentators think that he intends to point out the unwonted strength which remained unimpaired till death; and certainly, as the body of Christ was almost exhausted of blood, it could not happen, in the ordinary course of things, that the sides and the lungs should retain sufficient vigour for uttering so loud a cry. Yet I rather think that *the centurion* intended to applaud the unshaken perseverance of Christ in calling on the name of God. Nor was it merely the *cry* of Christ that led *the centurion* to think so highly of him, but this confession was extorted from him by perceiving that his extraordinary strength harmonized with heavenly miracles" (John Calvin, *Commentary on a Harmony of the Evangelists,* vol. 3, *Calvin's Commentaries,* vol. 17 [Grand Rapids: Baker Book House, 1989], 327). The whole point is precisely that this is *not* a moment of miraculous or extraordinary strength.

45. Tolbert, *Sowing the Gospel,* 261.

46. See Neill Q. Hamilton, *Jesus for a No-God World* (Philadelphia: Westminster Press, 1969), 62–63; Donald Michie and David Rhoads, *Mark as Story* (Philadelphia: Fortress Press, 1982), 61–62; and John Dominic Crossan, "Empty Tomb and Absent Lord," in Kelber, *The Passion in Mark,* 152.

47. Hans W. Frei, *Types of Christian Theology* (New Haven: Yale University Press, 1992), 126.

48. Paul Ricoeur makes an analogous point about understanding myths. See Paul Ricoeur, *The Symbolism of Evil,* trans. Emerson Buchanan (Boston: Beacon Press, 1967), 348–52.

49. Frei, *The Identity of Jesus Christ,* 112–15.

50. Karl Barth, *Church Dogmatics,* 2/1, trans. T. H. L. Parker et al. (Edinburgh: T. & T. Clark, 1957), 257–321.

51. Jüngel, *God as the Mystery of the World,* 13.

52. Ibid., 159.

53. Heyward, *Our Passion for Justice,* 28.

54. Daniel L. Migliore, *Faith Seeking Understanding* (Grand Rapids: Wm. B. Eerdmans Publishing Co., 1991), 52.

55. Augustine, *The City of God* 4.3., ed. Vernon J. Bourke, trans. Gerard G. Walsh et al. (Garden City, N. Y.: Image Books, 1958), 87.

56. Reinhold Niebuhr, *The Nature and Destiny of Man,* vol. 1 (New York: Charles Scribner's Sons, 1941), 194.

57. Nietzsche is the classic case of this kind of quest for power. I am indebted to a conversation with Thomas Tracy about Nietzsche for many of these reflections.

58. Dietrich Bonhoeffer, *Letters and Papers from Prison*, trans. Reginald H. Fuller et al. (New York: Macmillan Publishing Co., 1972), 360–61.
59. Joan Northam, "The Kingdom, the Power and the Glory," *Expository Times* 99 (1988): 302.
60. Alfred North Whitehead, *Process and Reality* (New York: Free Press, 1969), 413.
61. Wendy Farley, *Tragic Vision and Divine Compassion: A Contemporary Theodicy* (Louisville, Ky.: Westminster/John Knox Press, 1990), 81.
62. Barth, *Church Dogmatics*, 2/1, 524.
63. Ibid., 525. I am therefore not persuaded by the case made against Barth, that, "although Barth does make efforts in the direction of modifying the *scope* of divine power, he leaves the *meaning* for power underlying the term 'omnipotence' unaltered," in Anna Case-Winters's thoughtful book *God's Power: Traditional Understanding and Contemporary Challenges* (Louisville, Ky.: Westminster/John Knox Press, 1990), 97.
64. "The freedom to be able and to be required to choose between good and evil is a lesser freedom than the freedom to will and to do the good. . . . Whoever is truly free, does not have to choose any longer" (Jürgen Moltmann, "Antwort," in *Diskussion über Jürgen Moltmanns Buch "Der gekreuzigte Gott*," ed. Wolf-Dieter Marsch [Munich: Chr. Kaiser Verlag, 1967], 173).
65. Barth, *Church Dogmatics*, 2/1, 370. "We may believe that God can and must only be absolute in contrast to all that is relative, exalted in contrast to all that is lowly, active in contrast to all suffering, inviolable in contrast to all temptation, transcendent in contrast to all immanence. . . . But such beliefs are shown to be quite untenable, and corrupt and pagan, by the fact that God does in fact be and do this in Jesus Christ" (Karl Barth, *Church Dogmatics*, 4/1, trans. G. W. Bromiley [Edinburgh: T. & T. Clark, 1956], 186).
66. Jürgen Moltmann, *The Crucified God*, trans. R. A. Wilson and John Bowden (New York: Harper & Row, 1974), 253.
67. C. S. Lewis, *The Four Loves* (New York: Harcourt, Brace & Co., 1960), 169.
68. Hannah Arendt, *The Human Condition* (Chicago: University of Chicago Press, 1958), 202. I am indebted to Reinhard Hütter for reminding me of Arendt's insights on this topic.
69. "Do you not know that I have power to release you, and power to crucify you?" (John 19:10).
70. Aeschylus, *Prometheus Bound*, lines 917–21, p. 98.
71. Nicholas Wolterstorff, *Lament for a Son* (Grand Rapids: Wm. B. Eerdmans Publishing Co., 1987), 81.

2 The Eternal God

God's vulnerability in love is only one side of what Christians believe about God. Even if we concede what was argued in the previous chapter—that the capacity to risk vulnerability is a sign of strength rather than of weakness—still, just being involved, at risk, vulnerable, does not answer every question about God as the object of faith. Can we be sure that a free God will not turn away from creatures and stop loving? Can we be sure that God will not be engulfed, overpowered by vulnerability? If God is with us in love today but perhaps not tomorrow or the next day, then God cannot be, in the words of the Scots Confession, the one "whom only we must worship, and in whom alone we put our trust."[1] It is therefore important that the God encountered in the biblical narratives *remains* trustworthily loving, even amid the risks of vulnerability.

> The grass withers, the flower fades;
>   but the word of our God will stand forever. (Isa. 40:8)

The theological tradition has affirmed this quality in God with adjectives such as "faithful," "constant," "unchanging," and "immutable."

Those words carry differing implications, particularly about God's relation to time, and those differences point to a significant tension in Christian theology. That tension emerges not only in the use of these various adjectives but in how Christians understand "eternity." What does it mean to say that God is "the high and lofty one who inhabits eternity"? (Isa. 57:15). Theologians have often given one of two answers, and both pose problems for thinking about God as both vulnerable and trustworthy in love.

According to one definition, eternity means timelessness, the very opposite of time, and God as eternal is not in time at all. But how can such a God really care about temporal creatures, really be vulnerable in love? According to another definition, eternity means just time like ours, but infinitely extended in both directions. But is God then caught in the uncertainties of time? Is God time's prisoner, just as we are, and not therefore ultimately trustworthy?[2]

This chapter will turn to a third way of thinking about eternity, drawing on Boethius's classic definition of it as "perfect possession all at once of limitless life," on Karl Barth's accounts of time and eternity in his *Church Dogmatics*, and on the Gospel of John's modeling of eternal temporality. Eternity understood in this way involves full engagement with all the joys and sorrows of temporal life, open therefore to love and all its mischances. But it also brings time into a stable and coherent whole such that the love of one who is eternal can be trusted unconditionally, because existing in eternity means not being shaken by the problematics of time as we experience it. The key to this third way of thinking about eternity turns out to lie in examining more carefully exactly how we experience time. If one thinks about time simply as a geometrical line, then one is either moving down the line or not—either in time as we are or else timeless. But if one realizes that time has character, has varying qualities, then one can be "in time" in a variety of different ways—among them, a way called "eternally" which permits of simultaneous vulnerability and trustworthiness. An analysis of eternity will therefore require a substantial digression on the philosophy of time.

First, though, something needs to be said about those two alternative ways of defining "eternity." The first was to say that eternity is the very opposite of time, timelessness. "The doctrine of God's timelessness," Richard Swinburne writes, "seems to have entered Christian theology from neo-Platonism, and there from Augustine to Aquinas it reigned."[3] Its reign did not end with Aquinas; Schleiermacher held roughly this view,[4] and it informs many current discussions of God and eternity.[5] Aquinas, to take a classic example, pictured a circle, in which time flows along the circumference and God occupies the center, in exactly the same relation with every temporal point, but not on the line of time at all.[6]

Alternatively, Aquinas proposed that God is like someone on a high tower overlooking a road. Those on the road see their immediate companions. "If, however, there were someone outside of the whole order of those passing along the road, for instance, stationed in some high tower, he would at once see all those who were on the road . . . all at the same time."[7] The created world exists in the flow of time, but God does not, and so God can be simultaneous with every moment in time, and thus in relation with every temporal creature, but not at all in time—in the tower looking down, but not ever at any point on the road.

A vast literature has debated the problems and strengths of this position.[8] In the context of this argument, two problems seem worth particular attention. First, its most persuasive forms appeal, explicitly or implicitly, to images that describe time in spatial terms: the circle, the passing roadway. But do such spatial images take time's character *as time* seriously enough? Space exists all at once, laid out before us. Time passes. As long ago as the fourteenth century, Duns Scotus criticized Aquinas's image of the circle on the grounds that "time is not a standing circumference, but a flowing one, of which circumference there is nothing except the actual instant."[9] The points on the circle, the travelers on the road, do not exist all at once, so in what sense can one draw simultaneous lines to them or see them simultaneously? The metaphors that are intended to clarify the issue turn out only to disguise the problems.[10]

Second, a personal God vulnerable in love of changing creatures presumably does at least some of the following things: remembering, anticipating, reflecting, deliberating, deciding, intending, hoping, sympathizing. God may well do such things differently from human beings, but it is hard to imagine *any* sense in which such intrinsically temporal activities could be done by a timeless being. "Hence no eternal being, it would seem, could be a person."[11] Certainly the kind of vulnerable person whom God was described as being in the previous chapter could hardly remain so disengaged from the world of changing times.

A generation ago, in his influential *Christ and Time*, Oscar Cullmann offered a very different account of eternity. The biblical understanding of "eternity," he maintained, was not timelessness but simply time like ours, indefinitely extended. "In the New Testament field, it is not time and eternity that stand opposed, but limited time and endless time."[12] He analyzed the Greek and Hebrew words usually translated as "eternity" and concluded that they were regularly used to mean just "a long stretch of time." In the

29

Bible, he said, "eternity" refers to a length of time—perhaps an indefinitely long one—not to something opposite to time. To think of timeless eternity is to import categories foreign to the Bible from Greek philosophy.

In the years since Cullmann wrote, many scholars have grown skeptical both of his particular conclusions and of the kind of etymological analysis that produced them. James Barr, for instance, notes that it is only because there is a "very serious shortage within the Bible of the kind of *actual statement* about 'time' or 'eternity' which could form a sufficient basis for a Christian philosophical-theological view of time" that writers like Cullmann turned to analysis of Greek and Hebrew words.[13] But most of the key words, Barr argues, were used in a number of different ways, and it proves hard to draw any general conclusions simply from their etymologies.[14] Barr finds little evidence for consistent Greek or Hebrew "patterns of thought" about time, such that one could draw clear contrasts between them. After all, he remarks impatiently, Paul, who lived in the relevant cultures and who, on other topics, frequently addressed problems about "translating" from one to the other, never said anything to a Gentile audience like, "You think that eternity is timelessness, but we think it is the totality of time," or "You think time is a circle, but we think it is a straight line."[15] Paul never made such contrasts, according to Barr, because they were not there to be made. Hebrew, Greek, and early Christian folk all had many different, perhaps rather jumbled, ways of thinking about time and eternity. A Hebrew word that we might translate as "eternity" could indeed mean just "a long stretch of time," but Genesis seems to think of time as "beginning" with creation in a way that implies God's "timeless" existence before creation.[16] In short, cultural or etymological analysis does not generate "*the* biblical concept of eternity," and certainly not a consistent picture of it as simply indefinitely extended time.

The real issues, however, do not depend on etymology. As one reads the biblical stories, it is clear that the God here rendered is related to time in ways different from God's creatures. If our time is finite but God's has no limits, that in itself makes for a qualitative as well as a quantitative difference. The sense that time is running out, that every decision leaves less time for alternatives, is crucial to our experience of existing in time. If God's case is different, then so is the way God is in time. God also presumably sees the future and understands the past in ways different from creatures. A God in time in just the same way creatures are would be trapped in many of the same ambiguities that afflict creatures—only for a much longer period—captive to time's uncertainties in just the ways we are, inadequate as an object of trust.

A loving but trustworthy God can thus be neither timeless nor in time in the same way we are. But those are the only options for thinking about God's relation to time or the meaning of "eternity" only if we think of time purely in geometrical terms, so that one is either traveling along the line of time or else off it. If time can have different characteristics as well as different lengths, then perhaps "eternity" could be the name for a kind of time, a way of being really temporal but a way different from our own.

The classical definition of eternity, quoted almost universally down the centuries, comes from Boethius's *The Consolation of Philosophy*, written in the early sixth century. "Eternity," he wrote, is "a perfect possession all at once of limitless life" (*interminabilis vitae tota simul et perfecta possessio*).[17] Much of the contemporary philosophical discussion of eternity interprets this as one more vote for timelessness, but that flies in the face of Boethius's actual wording.[18] "Life" seems to be an obviously temporal category, for living things have properties that can exist only temporally. The "possession" of life therefore cannot be timeless. "Life must at least involve some incidents in time and if, like Boethius, we suppose the life in question to be intelligent, then it must involve also awareness of the passage of time."[19]

Boethius's eternity therefore is neither simply time like that of creatures indefinitely extended nor a timelessness altogether unrelated to temporal duration. It is "life," but "limitless life" possessed "all at once." At first glance, of course, this poses more problems than it solves, because the only kind of life that human beings experience is human life, lived in time as humans know it. Thinking about a different kind of time requires asking just what "time" means, in order to distinguish time itself from the features it has in human, and for that matter sinful, experience.

"What then is time?" Augustine asked at the beginning of what remains the most famous discussion of the topic. "I know well enough what it is provided that nobody asks me; but if I am asked what it is and try to explain, I am baffled."[20] The problem about which he worried most can be stated quite simply. We talk about "a long time" or "a short time" as if time existed in varying lengths and could be measured.[21] But the future does not yet exist, the past no longer exists, and the present is an instant without duration, so there do not seem to be any existing lengths or durations

31

of time "out there" such that one could measure them.[22] Augustine considered the possibility that one could measure time against the movement of the sun, moon, and stars, but he quickly rejected it: "It is by time that we measure the movement of bodies," and not vice versa.[23] After all, it at least makes sense to imagine all the heavenly motions slowing down, but that would be incoherent if those motions provided the scale that defined time.

"I begin to wonder," Augustine wrote, whether time "is an extension of the mind itself."[24]

> It is in my own mind, then, that I measure time. I must not allow my mind to insist that time is something objective. . . . I say that I measure time in my mind. For everything which happens leaves an impression on it, and this impression remains after the thing itself has ceased to be. It is the impression that I measure, since it is still present, not the thing itself, which makes the impression as it passes and then moves into the past. When I measure time it is this impression that I measure. Either, then, this is what time is, or else I do not measure time at all.[25]

In my mind I remember the past and anticipate the future, and these memories and anticipations have presently existing "length" which it is therefore possible to measure. If time is, as Augustine assumed, something that comes in measurable lengths, it must therefore be these mental phenomena that constitute time.

Exploring the phenomenology of time at the beginning of this century, Edmund Husserl followed in Augustine's path.[26] Considering a musical note heard over a "length of time," he concluded that the length we measure is the length of a presently experienced "retentional consciousness" and not the "time" of actually sensing the sound, which does not exist at any one time and therefore could not be measured.[27] Husserl even offered a helpful diagram of a horizontal line of "now points" with a vertical line dropping down from the present now point and constituting the retained and hence measurable past.[28] The twentieth-century phenomenologist concludes that Augustine was right and that time is, first of all, time-as-experienced.

Contemporary physicists, interestingly enough, reach much the same conclusion. Reflecting on the implications of quantum mechanics, Bernard d'Espagnat concludes that "what philosophers often call 'physical' or 'mathematical' time . . . the variable t which figures in the mathematical expression of the elementary laws of physics . . . is not an element of independent reality." By contrast, experienced time has "a 'density of reality' which cannot be denied. . . . So it is not absurd to speak (albeit loosely) of it as being 'more real' than the first kind. And that, after a fashion, provides reason after the fact for those philosophers who, sometimes implicitly and not fully aware of what they are doing, identify 'true time' with the consciousness human beings have of time."[29] The physicist's concession to the insight of philosophers is a bit grudging, but the substantive point gets made. Clock time, and the time of the physicists' equations, have their significance only as they can be related to experienced time.

If thinking about eternity requires getting clear about time, then it has to look at time as humanly experienced, the starting point for what we mean by time. Whatever his considerable flaws as a person, much less a political thinker, Martin Heidegger offered a quite remarkable account of human temporality that addresses just the relevant issues.[30] It was a theme central to his philosophy. "The central problematic of all ontology," he wrote, "is rooted in the phenomenon of time."[31] He announced his intention to interpret human existence "in terms of temporality."[32] It is time, he insisted, that serves "as the transcendental horizon for the question of being."[33] What is particularly significant in Heidegger's analysis is his understanding that time as humanly experienced is not a featureless line of duration. Time has particular characteristics shaped by our concerns for its particular moments, so that a poet or an artist might be more help in describing it than a geometer.

Specifically, Heidegger says that to exist as a human being is to exist temporally in a very particular way, as "ahead-of-itself-Being-already-in-as-being-alongside."[34] That is, to be human is, (1) first of all, to exist "ahead-of-itself"—to make plans, to worry about coming dangers, to have hopes, in short, to have concern for the future. If one literally never gave a thought to what comes next, one would neither exist temporally nor be human.[35] (2) But being human also means "Being-already-in," what Heidegger sometimes calls "thrownness." By the time they are self-conscious, human beings always find themselves with a past already behind them—relationships established, good and bad memories, debts incurred, satisfactions and regrets. To exist humanly means "*never* to have power over one's ownmost Being from the ground up,"[36] never to be starting with a completely clean slate. (3) Finally, being human means "being alongside," being in a world with other humans, with physical objects that get in one's way or serve as useful tools, with a whole environment.

33

Human temporal experience therefore is not of an undifferentiated continuum of clock time, and Heidegger thought that starting with such a model will inevitably botch one's thinking about human temporality.[37] Instead, human beings experience particular relationships of concern to future, past, and present. How are humans to live in the context of such a temporal experience? Heidegger saw two options, which he called authentic and inauthentic existence.

To exist authentically means (with respect to the future) facing the fact that one is going to die, not in the sense of worrying about the pain of dying but acknowledging the finitude of life. Every moment means that much less time left; temporal finitude is a basic fact of human existence. With respect to the past, it means acknowledging that, however much I have been "thrown" into it, the past that lies behind me is *my* past, and taking responsibility for it. Therefore, with respect to the present, authentic existence means, among other things, knowing that decisions really matter, because they are irreversible and always involve further limits on a finite future, and accepting one's own responsibility for those decisions. To go to law school is, for many an undergraduate, to decide irrevocably not to go to graduate school straight out of college—returning to graduate school at the age of thirty being a very different option—and thereby to end up having become a different person. So it is with all our decisions and their consequences.

To exist inauthentically is to hide from all this. The inevitable human reality of death recedes from the mind. One accepts the roles proposed by others. "My parents wanted me to go to law school, my adviser said I'd do well there, and I even won a scholarship. Lots of my friends are going to law school." Somehow the decision never quite gets claimed as one's own, one never quite faces the momentous consequences of such a choice in a finite existence, and one's existence falls into a kind of blending in with one's social surroundings. One "gets dragged along," one loses oneself, one flees in the face of oneself.[38] Relations with past, present, and future get fundamentally transformed.

To exist inauthentically is to lose one's individuality. It is in some deep sense to live a lie, for each human being is going to die, each human being does have her or his particular past, and inauthentic existence rests on avoiding the facing of such basic realities. It would be pleasant to find that the turn to authentic existence leads to a happy, fulfilled life, but Heidegger has a kind of bleak forthrightness in such matters. "*Authentic* Being-towards-death can

34

not evade its ownmost non-relational possibility, or *cover up* this possibility by thus fleeing from it."[39] Facing one's temporal finitude does not make that hard fact go away. Claiming one's past, with all its mistakes and all its unrealized possibilities, as one's own does not suddenly lift its burdens. It simply leaves one stuck with the reality of one's past, staring into a finite future, and conscious of the irrevocable consequences of each present decision, "thrown," "unsupported," facing up to the lack of any meaning above or beyond.[40] No wonder that Heidegger's key adjective for authentic existence is "anxious."[41]

The problem, then, lies not with either inauthentic or authentic existence but with human temporality as we have come to experience it. The way human beings find themselves existing in time, it is as if time keeps flying past us—every moment that much less of a finite future ahead of us, more of a past irrevocably ours even if we never quite sensed having chosen it, an always fleeting present, the pieces neither coherently fitting together nor deriving meaning from their place in some larger whole. As Paul Fiddes writes in reflection on Heidegger:

> We are unable to bring our past, present, and future into a whole. We cannot integrate our present with our past because we either regret the loss of the past in nostalgia, or we try to obliterate our memory of it in guilt. We cannot integrate our future with our present, because we either try to escape into it in wish-fulfilment dreams, or feel threatened by it.[42]

To live in time like that is to live torn. The demands of a future faced or the reality of a past accepted in responsibility can feel only like a burden; the only alternatives seem hiding, fleeing, or a kind of grim resoluteness.

But suppose there were another way of existing temporally. At this point a number of the threads of this discussion begin to come together. The chapter began by asking about the meaning of eternity, and eternity, on Boethius's account, seemed to involve neither timelessness nor simply indefinitely extended time but a different kind of time. So understanding eternity meant getting a better understanding of time, and inquiry into the nature of time revealed that time means, first of all, the human experience of time. Heidegger's analysis suggests the bleak, fragmented character of human temporality as we know it. Could there be an alternative form of temporality, a different way of experiencing time in which one could live and love fully, vulnerable in relation to a changing world, and yet remain somehow free of entrapment in the anxious uncertainties of time, and therefore trustworthy and faithful? Might that kind of time turn out to be "eternity"?

The relation of time and eternity has often been acknowledged as one of the central themes of Barth's *Church Dogmatics*.[43] Yet as George Hunsinger has observed, "No topic in Barth interpretation is more in need of clarification."[44] A number of factors contribute to the difficulties. Barth's most interesting remarks on the topic tend to pop up almost in passing through the many volumes of the *Dogmatics*. They are not always consistent.[45] Beyond that, however, Barth's views just seem at first or even second glance very peculiar. Part of the point of the rather wide ranging discussion so far in this chapter has been to try to set a context for them.

In his Romans commentary, Barth tended, under Kierkegaardian influence, to contrast divine eternity with creaturely time in the most radical way. "Time is nothing when measured by the standard of eternity,"[46] and the only connection between them comes at a durationless instant, the equivalent to the geometric point where a tangent touches a circle: "Between the past and the future . . . this is a 'Moment' that is no moment in time. This 'Moment' is the eternal Moment—the *Now*—when the past and future stand still."[47] But in the *Church Dogmatics*, Barth extends that geometric point to thirty years or so. It is, he says, in the human life of Jesus that eternity touches time.[48] If discussions of time, as argued earlier, need to begin with the human experience of time, and Jesus Christ, as Barth insists, defines what it is to be truly human, then a proper understanding of time needs to begin with Jesus Christ.

This looks very odd. To find out what "time" means, it might seem plausible to turn from physicists to phenomenologists, but the idea of turning to the particular history of Jesus Christ in order to understand time in general is surely a strange one. Yet Barth insists firmly: "We must let ourselves be told what time is by revelation itself," and, for Barth, revelation means, first of all, Jesus Christ.[49]

Barth often talks about human temporality in language at least as grim as Heidegger's.

> For us the past is the time which we leave and are in no longer. . . . It may almost be thought of as though it had never been. . . . We do not even know whether we will have a future.

As for the present, where

we think we can take our ease and enjoy in impregnable
security . . . , we find that we are wholly and utterly inse-
cure. . . . It is the moment we can never prevail upon to
stay, for always it has already gone or not yet come. . . . In
the present in which we think we have it most securely we
have no time.

This is our being in time.[50]

However, "what we have been describing is *sinful* man in time."[51]
Christ lives human time as it is meant to be, and the result is a very
different kind of temporality—a temporality that turns out to fit the
definition of eternity, so that Christ's human time reveals not only
what human temporality could be but what divine temporality is.
Jesus Christ's time differs from sinful time in at least two respects.
For the sake of having convenient labels, they can be called "sub-
jectively" and "objectively," although these are not Barth's terms
and it would be dangerous to push their implications very far. Sub-
jectively (that is, in his human experience of time), Jesus experiences his life as a whole, in which past, present, and future are not
at war with one another but cohere. Objectively (that is, as known
by God), Jesus' life is anticipated before it comes and treasured in
God after its completion, so that it is in significant relation with all
moments of time. Each of these points requires, clearly, further
explanation.

Boethius defined eternity as "a perfect possession all at once
of limitless life." But in sinful life, past, present, and future are at
odds, opposed to one another. As the momentarily present rushes
by, the future feels like a threat and the past like a burden, unless
we simply repress thoughts of them. But in the "sea of the incom-
plete and changeable and self-changing" that makes up human history, a "completed event, fulfilled time," the life of Jesus, has
occurred, a "self-moved being in the stream of becoming."[52]

Jesus' life was fully in time. As with the rest of us, what he did
and said and what happened to him during his life define his identity, so that for him as for anyone else moments were irretrievable
and decisions were irreversible. He too was stuck with his past. Like
the rest of us, he lived moving toward death, so that at each moment he had less time left in which to do things he wanted to do.
For him too the present was but a fleeting instant.

However, Jesus' life "does not extinguish but integrates and
to that extent overcomes the differences between what we call past,
present and future. For even as human life, it shares the sovereignty
of the life of the divine Subject over these distinctions."[53] Jesus

37

obediently accepted his past as at once fully his own and a gift from God and felt no need either to repress or to regret it. He trustingly moved toward a future that, whatever tragedies might befall, moved him ultimately toward God. Thus he did not need to try desperately to grasp the fleeting present but could live each moment to the full. "There is in Him no opposition or competition or conflict, but peace between origin, movement and goal, between present, past and future."[54]

While there may be these differences in Jesus' experience of time, it might seem that they do not constitute any difference in time itself. But if time is, first of all, experienced time, and that experience is not an undifferentiated line of duration but shaped by the concerns that one brings to it, then Jesus' subjective relation to time really makes time different. Specifically, since future, past, and present cohere in his life without conflict, he possesses the whole of his life as a whole at every moment of it, thereby instantiating both the reality of eternity and an escape from the problematics of sinful time.

> Eternity is not merely the negation of time. It is not in any way timeless. On the contrary, as the source of time it is supreme and absolute time, i.e., the immediate unity of past, present and future.[55]

Jesus lived in just that kind of time. He really lived *in time*, experiencing the joys and sorrows of each moment to the full and in the moment. But he also experienced his life as holding together in a kind of unity such that he was who he was from start to finish. He did what he had to do in order to be who he was and is in the time he had in which to do it, so that the finitude of life was no burden but gave to his life just its appropriate shape. "The fact that the Word became flesh undoubtedly means that, without ceasing to be eternity, in its very power as eternity, eternity became time."[56]

Jesus' life also has a special relation to time in the mode I have cautiously called "objectively." As a human lifetime, it has a particular temporal location and limits—from somewhere around 4 B.C. to somewhere around A.D. 30. Yet before and after that time—indeed before the foundation of the world and for all eternity—God has always been and always will be the self-revealing God self-revealed in this human life. Therefore we cannot say of Jesus "that He was 'not yet' in this time before His time, just as we cannot say of the time after His earthly life, the time of the apostles and the community, that He is 'no longer.'"[57] Christ remains able to be present as our contemporary centuries after his death; his time does not cease to exist when it is past.[58] "His past history, His yesterday, cannot be understood as a thing of the past, a thing of yesterday. The yesterday of Jesus is also today."[59]

Just as the human course of Jesus' life has a special kind of experienced unity, so Christ's human life has a unity with God—coming from God, destined to God, and always with God. In the time of King David, God already was the God who would be revealed in the life of Jesus Christ, and God now continues to be the God who was revealed in that life. The particular time of that human life is thus in God at every time. The human life of Jesus, anticipated, lived, and remembered in God, and lived as such by Jesus, thus also in this way achieved the kind of time that is eternity, and therefore, in the human life of Jesus, eternity existed in a particular time. The vulnerable God fully in time is thus in this way too the trustworthy God free of the traps of sinful time.

Part of the promise of the gospel is that a human being can share in the kind of unity of life characteristic of "eternal life" in a way "proper to it in its creatureliness."[60] In communion with Jesus Christ, Christians can find healing of life's fragmentation, such that their lives become more nearly meaningful wholes. In communion with Jesus Christ, Christians can begin to live their lives with, from, and toward God, such that life's fleetingness is no longer a burden or a terror.

The hope of "eternal life," then, is hope neither for a life of unending duration nor somehow for escape from time. Heidegger is simply right that human existence is "Being-towards-death."

> There is no human greatness and grandeur which is not exceeded, overshadowed and fundamentally called in question by death: not even that of the promised and manifested Messiah and Son of Man; not even that of the incarnate Son of God. . . . Death must show what it can do on Him supremely, as in a masterpiece. No place must be left for foolish dreams, as though everything were bound to come right in the end.[61]

To be human is to be finite and mortal. Someday one "will only have been," as once one had not been. A human being "as such, therefore, has no beyond. Nor does he need one, for God is his beyond."[62] To be human in Christ is not only to begin to have the temporal course of one's earthly life cohere in a kind of whole but to look back to one's origin as from God, and therefore purposed, and forward to God as one's goal. Therefore one's beginning becomes not a shadow but a promise,[63] and "Death now wears a guise in which we can look it in the face."[64]

Such a life opens up possibilities for love and vulnerability. One can take the risks of love sustained by a vision of one's life as providentially originated, destined to God, and coherent. No longer need the past seem only a burden, the future a cause of anxiety, and the present a fleeting moment. One can move from sinful time toward eternal life, an eternity that is neither timeless nor simply duration infinitely extended.

Readers of Rudolf Bultmann will recognize a good many similarities here to the account he derived a generation ago from reflection on the New Testament and on Heidegger. For Bultmann, faith is "*transition into eschatological existence.* In the midst of the world the believer is lifted out of secular existence—though he is still 'in the world,' he is no longer 'of the world.' . . . He already has Death *behind* him; . . . he already *has* Life. . . . *Freedom* is promised to the possessor of this faith-knowledge. From what? From the world, from sham 'reality,' from both its seductiveness and its open enmity."[65] Christian life is a joyous sort of authentic existence, and, according to Bultmann, only faith in Jesus Christ makes such life possible.

The interpretation presented here differs in a number of details, but the most important difference is that, for Bultmann, narrative, and thus real temporality, gets lost, both for Jesus and for the Christian believer. Notoriously, Bultmann did not think that Christian faith required any historical content about Jesus—the mere fact *that* God did act in history sufficed.[66] The shape of Jesus' human life, whether as lived historically or as narrated in the Gospels, therefore does not matter. Similarly, what matters for the life of a Christian is a moment of decision for faith, not the developing of virtues over the course of a Christian life.[67] What is odd is that a theology that drew so much from Heidegger's analysis of temporality as central to human existence should so ignore the temporal extension of human life, whether Jesus' or the believer's.

The way to capture the temporality of a life is through narrating it. The previous chapter quoted Hans Frei's remark that in Christian theology the story is the meaning of the doctrine, not the other way around: that is, Christians do not figure out the "real meaning" of the biblical narratives in some doctrinal formulation and then discard the stories, but doctrines serve as aids for reflection on the biblical narratives. The theme of this chapter illustrates that point even better, because the best way to present a way of existing temporally is to display it narratively. Chapter 1 traced the theme of divine vulnerability through the Gospel of Mark. Eternity and time seem to be themes particularly characteristic of the Gospel of John. The opening phrase concerns time ("In the beginning . . ."). John 1:1 includes three static verbs of being in reference to God: "In the beginning *was* the Word, and the Word *was* with God, and the Word *was* God."[68] Then John 1:3 has three verbs of temporal becoming: "All things *became* through him, and without him not one thing *became*. What *has become* in him was life, and the life was the light of all people."[69] Right at the start, the text contrasts the divine and creaturely ways of existing with respect to time: God is; creatures become. John 1:8 emphasizes the contrast: John the Baptist "*came* to testify to the light" ("*became* a man sent from God whose name was John," one might translate with ponderous literalness), but he "*was* not the light." Creatures cannot cross over into divine temporality. But then in 1:14 the Logos, subject of all these "was" verbs, suddenly "*became* flesh." The divine *can* cross into creaturely temporality. One could develop rather a good basic theology out of the verbs of the first few verses of this Gospel. As John's Gospel shifts from prologue to narrative, time keeps coming up as an issue. At Jesus' baptism, John identifies him by saying, "This is he of whom I said, '*After* me *comes*[70] a man who ranks ahead of me because he *was before* me'" (John 1:30). In human time, Jesus comes after John, for John's ministry has already begun. John leaves his listeners with a puzzled sense of some other kind of time in which Jesus precedes. The whole temporal structure of this section is wonderfully complex, in a way that can best be explained with the introduction of a bit of technical terminology.

The literary critic Gerard Genette defines an "analepsis" as "any evocation after the fact of an event that took place earlier than the point in the story where we are at any given moment" and a "prolepsis" as "any narrative maneuver that consists of narrating or evoking in advance an event that will take place later." Analepsis and prolepsis can be either internal (pointing backward or forward to a time within the time narrated by the story) or external (pointing to a time before the primary story begins or after it ends).[71] John 1:19–34 begins with an internal analepsis: the narrator recalls what John had said to the priests and the Levites from Jerusalem. John responds to their questions with an external analepsis, recalling what the prophet Isaiah said (although, just to make things really complicated, if we take the opening of the prologue to be the

41

beginning of John's narrative with the beginning of all things, then no analepsis can really be "external" to this narrative). Then John gives proleptic accounts of Jesus' activity, and the section ends with his affirmation, "This is the Son of God," which, with reference to God and the language of unchanging being, pulls back out of the language of creaturely temporality altogether.[72] This passage is doing on a small scale what the whole Gospel of John does: particular events are really happening in time, but the narration of them so connects past, present, and future that they become a single whole rather than separate elements at odds with one another. Creaturely time turns into divine eternity.

In the first of Jesus' miracles, he initially resists his mother's insistence that he cope with the shortage of wine for the marriage feast by saying, "My *time* has not yet come."[73] After Cana, Jesus goes to Jerusalem and cleans out the Temple. In the face of protest, he proclaims, "Destroy this temple, and in three days I will raise it up." His puzzled critics respond, "This temple has been under construction for forty-six years, and will you raise it up in three days?" (John 2:20). The narrator explains, "He was speaking of the temple of his body"—an anticipation of the resurrection—but in the immediate context of the story, what is clear is that Jesus is somehow operating in time differently from anyone else. In the next episode, Nicodemus is similarly puzzled. How can he be "born from above"? He has already "grown old." "Can one enter a second time into the mother's womb and be born?" (John 3:3–4). Like so many of those who encounter Jesus, Nicodemus cannot make sense of Jesus' way of thinking about time.

Readers of John's Gospel already have a clue. We know from the prologue about two different forms of time at work here; we have a context for making sense of it when Jesus explains to Nicodemus that the Father "gave his only Son, so that everyone who believes in him may not perish but may have eternal life" (John 3:16). Divine eternity has entered human temporality and brought with it the possibility for a new kind of life. So in the next chapter Jesus explains to the Samaritan woman—the well where she is drawing water is enmeshed in creaturely time: "Everyone who drinks of this water will be thirsty again" (John 4:13). Jesus offers her a different kind of water—living water, of eternal life. In the Greek, he describes drinking from the well with a present participle, generally used of an action that is repeated, but drinking the living water with an aorist subjunctive, generally used of a completed, self-contained act.[74] He promises her, in an odd mixture of future and present, "The hour is coming, and is now here,[75] when the true worshipers will worship the Father in spirit and truth" (John 4:23). She seizes on the future tense: "I know that Messiah is coming" (4:25). That makes sense in terms of creaturely time: things are bad now, but they will get better later. But Jesus returns to the present verb, the part she failed to understand. "I am he." She is intrigued by what he says about temporal matters. "Come and see," she calls to her neighbors, "a man who told me everything I have ever done!" But she remains puzzled. "He cannot be the Messiah, can he?" (4:29).

Puzzles about time continue in succeeding episodes. Jesus encounters people who are the victims of Heideggerian temporality, trapped by their pasts and ever threatened by a constantly pressing future. The royal official in John 4:49 urges Jesus to hurry to his son's bedside in order to effect a cure, but Jesus tells him the boy is already cured, and the text makes a point of time: the father checks and establishes that the cure occurred at the very moment Jesus spoke. In the next scene the invalid at the pool of Bethzatha is clearly a victim of time: he has been ill for the specified time of thirty-eight years, and he now lies near a pool that supposedly has miraculous power of healing for the first person who can enter it when the waters have been stirred up (by the sudden flow of an underground spring, Raymond Brown suggests[76]), but because of his condition he is unable ever to be first off the mark and into the pool: "While I am making my way, someone else steps down ahead of me" (John 5:7). Jesus, however, just does not share others' anxieties about time. Whether he can get to the child's bedside in time, or how this invalid can move quickly enough to the pool does not worry him. "Stand up," he says, "take your mat and walk" (5:8). And the man does so, "at once" (5:9).

As early as his encounter with the Samaritan woman, Jesus responds to her reference to the Messiah with one of the most problematic phrases in the Gospel: *egō eimi,* "I am (he)." The phrase keeps repeating: "I am the bread that came down from heaven" (John 6:41), "I am the light of the world" (John 8:12), and so on. One could read this as just standard, first person singular pronoun and verb, but it is also the Septuagint's translation of God's self-revelation to Moses in Exodus: "I AM WHO I AM. . . . Thus you shall say to the Israelites, 'I AM has sent me to you'" (Ex. 3:14). By the climax of John 8, the phrase clearly means more than a standard subject and verb. Jesus tells his opponents, "Abraham rejoiced that he would see my day; he saw it and was glad" (John 8:56), and

43

they, firmly rooted in sinful time, demand, "You are not yet fifty years old, and have you seen Abraham?" (8:57). "Jesus said to them, 'Very truly, I tell you, before Abraham was, I am.' So they picked up stones to throw at him" (8:58–59). *Egō eimi* here points back to Exodus and to the verbs of divine time at the beginning of John's prologue. Particularly in conjunction with the following reference to stoning, it points forward toward the moment of Jesus' arrest in Gethsemane, when the soldiers say they are looking for Jesus of Nazareth, and he replies, "*Egō eimi*," "I am he" (18:5). The soldiers step back and fall to the ground, as if in the face of a theophany— here the reference back to Exodus is unmistakable. As in John 1:19–34, analepsis and prolepsis are combining past, present, and future, with a verb of eternal being laid, as it were, overtop the whole, so that past, present, and future in their coherent wholeness turn, in the narrative, into eternity. By the end of John 8, the dramatic tension of rising conflict has reached a kind of climax, and there is really nothing to happen but for the tragedy to move to its conclusion.

Before that, however, the Gospel of John presents, among other things, Jesus' long farewell discourse (John 13—17), and here too time behaves in strange ways. "The temporal perspectives of the farewell discourse," Alan Culpepper admits in a thoughtful recent book, "are notoriously difficult to sort out."[77] Jesus seems to be speaking from a temporal perspective in which the crucifixion, resurrection, and ascension have already happened. At the beginning of John 17, for instance, Jesus seems to look back on the whole of his work: "I glorified you on earth by finishing the work that you gave me to do" (17:4). "I have made your name known to those whom you gave me from the world" (17:6). "And now I am no longer in the world" (17:11). The farewell discourse is, in Gail O'Day's phrase, "a narrative out of place, a narrative discourse that is paradoxically . . . a remembrance of things hoped for."[78]

References to the Paraclete get particularly complex. Jesus consistently refers to the Paraclete in the future tense (John 14:15, 26; 15:26; 16:13), yet the presence of the Paraclete is narrated in the present tense: "You know him, because he abides with you" (14:17).

> Careful delineation of temporal boundaries breaks down at Jesus' words about the Paraclete. . . . No present moment can consume the Paraclete. On the contrary, each present moment is reopened to the future through the presence of the Paraclete. That the Paraclete crosses temporal boundaries within the narrative structure of the farewell discourse provides literary confirmation of a theological reality.[79]

As Jesus pulls out of the narrative time frame, the language of the text pulls out of the sinful time of creatures. "The voice of the risen Jesus (17:12) draws together past, present, and future in one narrative moment."[80]

It is significant that the attempt to narrate the relation of past, present, and future in eternity draws the Paraclete so prominently into what had been a story of the Logos and the Father. As the next chapter will argue, exploring the identity of the eternal God— and the vulnerable God—narrated in the Bible leads to thinking about that God in Trinitarian terms. Before we turn to that topic, however, a tentative word of conclusion is in order.

The only kind of time we know in our own experience is sinful time, with past, present, and future at discord and human existence trapped among them, so that, too often, the only alternative we can imagine to such time is a timelessness that escapes all the concreteness of temporal joys and sorrows. Jesus Christ manifests a different kind of temporality, that of eternal life, in which past, present, and future come together in a meaningful whole, moving from, to, and always in, God, a kind of time that fits Boethius's classic definition of eternity. He is really in time, open to love and all the risks that go with it, but in time in the mode of eternity, not trapped but free, not vacillating but constant in love.

In the very way it narrates Jesus' story, John's Gospel shows that sort of time, as past, present, and future keep so intertwining that the perspective of temporal process merges with the perspective of eternal being. This sort of eternity, the possession of limitless life all at once, is not timeless but fully and coherently temporal. It is therefore related to time in a way that makes all the actions and relations of love and freedom possible, but it is also at peace in time in a way that leaves the believer secure in God's faithful constancy. Eternity, as God knows it and as human creatures can come to approximate it, is a "time" neither of invulnerable changelessness nor of shifting and unreliable relations but the "time" where fully vulnerable love can be trustworthy.

NOTES

1. *Book of Confessions*, Presbyterian Church (U.S.A.), 3.01.
2. The term "time's prisoner" comes from Richard Swinburne, who nevertheless defends this definition of eternity. See Richard Swinburne, "God and Time," in *Reasoned Faith*, ed. Eleonore Stump (Ithaca, N.Y.: Cornell University Press, 1993), 218.

3. Richard Swinburne, *The Coherence of Theism* (New York: Oxford University Press, 1977), 217.
4. Friedrich Schleiermacher, *The Christian Faith,* trans. H. R. Mackintosh and J. S. Stewart (Edinburgh: T. & T. Clark, 1928), 205–6.
5. In most nuanced form in Brian Leftow, *Time and Eternity* (Ithaca, N.Y.: Cornell University Press, 1991). When Leftow writes (p. 3), "Today the claim that God is temporal enjoys nearly as universal an acceptance among philosophers and theologians," he seems to me to be considerably overstating his position as a member of an embattled minority.
6. Thomas Aquinas, *Summa contra Gentiles* 1.66.7, trans. Anton C. Pegis, vol. 1 (Garden City, N. Y.: Image Books, 1955), 219. Aquinas's position is actually more complicated than this account acknowledges. I am using one theme in his work by way of example.
7. Thomas Aquinas, *Commentary on Aristotle's "On Interpretation"* 1.14.19, trans. Jean T. Oesterle (Milwaukee: Marquette University Press, 1962), 117.
8. Leftow's *Time and Eternity* both surveys the literature and stands as a most important contribution to it.
9. John Duns Scotus, *Ordinatio* 1, d.39, q.5, sec. 35; quoted in Alan G. Padgett, *God, Eternity, and the Nature of Time* (New York: St. Martin's Press, 1992), 51. This is another form of Augustine's worry about whether lengths of time "exist" (discussed below).
10. Swinburne persuasively argues that something analogous is true of Stump and Kretzmann's account of what it means for something eternal to be "simultaneous" with something temporal: it appeals to an analogy it never really explains. See Eleonore Stump and Norman Kretzmann, "Eternity," *Journal of Philosophy* 78 (1981): 439; idem,"Eternity, Awareness and Action," *Faith and Philosophy* 9 (1992): 463–82; and Swinburne, "God and Time," 217–18. Paul Fitzgerald makes a similar case for the incoherence of Stump and Kretzmann's concept of eternity as an "atemporal duration" (Paul Fitzgerald, "Stump and Kretzmann on Time and Eternity," *Journal of Philosophy* 82 [1985]: 260–69). I have a similar problem with Leftow's proposal that "God is temporally omnipresent and omnicontiguous, as if eternity were a higher dimension in which He and temporal beings coexist" (Leftow, *Time and Eternity,* 267). He regularly refers to the "time" of eternity (the quotation marks are his) and invites us to think of eternity as like a higher dimension. He gives us a set of logical rules for how to operate with the concept as he defines it, and some analogies or metaphors ("as if eternity were a higher dimension") whose status remains unclear, but I am left without a feel for what Leftow's version of eternity means, what it would be like. ("Thus I have called eternity logically a 'time' even though it has no temporal properties," ibid.,

72). Later parts of this chapter will sketch an alternative. Rather than thinking of time as an undifferentiated continuum and then of eternity as "a mode of being midway between temporality and the absolutely durationless existence of an instant" (ibid., 146), I will propose that time as experienced has varied texture and that eternity can therefore be a kind of time. Leftow begins with the fact that God has life (and thus ought to have a kind of extension) but is simple (and thus ought to exist at a point) and tries to fit those two conclusions together (ibid., 149). Perhaps our difference comes in part from the fact that I am beginning with the triune life of God rather than a doctrine of divine simplicity.

11. Robert C. Coburn, "Professor Malcolm on God," *Australasian Journal of Philosophy* 41 (1963): 155. See also J. R. Lucas, *A Treatise on Time and Space* (London: Methuen, 1973), 3, 309. Leftow argues that a timeless being can understand (*Time and Eternity*, 285–90) and engage in intentional actions (pp. 295–97). Even granting those arguments, there remain a range of predicates that seem necessary to the character of the loving God identified in the Bible which are intrinsically temporal. See Swinburne, *The Coherence of Theism*, 214, for such an argument; for Leftow's reply, see *Time and Eternity*, 307. Leftow describes a kind of interaction in which the order of response and counterresponse is "*solely* logical" (i.e., not temporal). It just doesn't sound like interaction to me.

12. Oscar Cullmann, *Christ and Time*, trans. Floyd V. Filson (Philadelphia: Westminster Press, 1951), 46.

13. James Barr, *Biblical Words for Time* (London: SCM Press, 1962), 131.

14. Ibid., 22–23.

15. Ibid., 155.

16. Ibid., 152.

17. Boethius, *The Consolation of Philosophy* (New York: G. P. Putnam's Sons, 1918), 400; my translation. I should acknowledge that in what follows I am exploring implications of Boethius's definition, which has come to have a life of its own in these discussions, and not trying to recover Boethius's own views about time in their original context.

18. The point is made by Wolfhart Pannenberg, *Systematic Theology*, vol. 1, trans. Geoffrey W. Bromiley (Grand Rapids: Wm. B. Eerdmans Publishing Co., 1991), 405. Even a careful scholar like Alan Padgett simply asserts that, "for Boethius eternity is non-durational as well as timeless" (Padgett, *God, Eternity, and the Nature of Time*, 46). Others claim that he was unclear or inconsistent. See, e.g., Robert Cook, "God, Time, and Freedom," *Religious Studies* 23 (1987): 81; or Swinburne, *The Coherence of Theism*, 218–21. Stump and Kretzmann, and Leftow, argue for a considerably more

complex reading of Boethius's position. See Eleonore Stump and Norman Kretzmann, "Atemporal Duration," *Journal of Philosophy* 84 (1987): 214–19; and Leftow, *Time and Eternity*, 112–46.

19. William Kneale, "Time and Eternity in Theology," *Proceedings of the Aristotelian Society* 61 (1961), 99.
20. Augustine, *Confessions* 11.14, trans. R. S. Pine-Coffin (London: Penguin Books, 1961), 264.
21. "We are aware of periods of time. We compare them one with another and say that some are longer and others shorter. We even calculate how much longer or shorter one period is than another" (ibid., 11.16, p. 266).
22. Ibid., 11.18, p. 267.
23. Ibid., 11.23, p. 271.
24. Ibid., 11.26, p. 274.
25. Ibid., 11.27, p. 276.
26. Ricoeur speaks of "the stroke of genius of Book 11 of Augustine's *Confessions*, in whose wake will follow Husserl, Heidegger, and Merleau-Ponty" (Paul Ricoeur, *Time and Narrative*, vol. 1, trans. Kathleen McLaughlin and David Pellauer [Chicago: University of Chicago Press, 1984], 16).
27. Edmund Husserl, *The Phenomenology of Internal Time-Consciousness*, trans. James S. Churchill (Bloomington, Ind.: Indiana University Press, 1964), 53–54.
28. Ibid., 49. I have drastically simplified a story made complex by both the difficulty of Husserl's position and the fact that the text of *The Phenomenology of Internal Time-Consciousness* as we have it combines several manuscripts with probably different positions on these matters. See Robert J. Dostal, "Time and Phenomenology," in *The Cambridge Companion to Heidegger*, ed. Charles Guignon (Cambridge: Cambridge University Press, 1993), 146–49.
29. Bernard d'Espagnat, *Reality and the Physicist: Knowledge, Duration, and the Quantum World*, trans. J. C. Whitehouse (Cambridge: Cambridge University Press, 1989), 217–18.
30. It is disappointing that the rich discussion among analytic philosophers on time and eternity so generally ignores Heidegger's analysis.
31. Martin Heidegger, *Being and Time*, trans. John Macquarrie and Edward Robinson (New York: Harper & Row, 1962), 40.
32. Ibid., 63.
33. Ibid.
34. Ibid., 237.
35. "Being futural gives time, cultivates the present and allows the past to be repeated in how it is lived. With regard to time this means that *the fundamental phenomenon of time is the future*" (Martin Heidegger, *The Concept of Time*, trans. William McNeill [Oxford: Basil Blackwell Publisher, 1992], 14E).

36. Heidegger, *Being and Time*, 330. An old Peanuts cartoon captures the point. Charlie Brown: "I think the whole trouble is that we're thrown into life too fast. . . . We're not really prepared." Linus: "What did you want. . . . A chance to warm up first?" (quoted in Robert L. Short, *The Gospel according to Peanuts* [Richmond: John Knox Press, 1964], 36–37). There are certainly analogies here to a doctrine of original sin, but I suspect it is dangerous to push them too far.

37. Heidegger, *Being and Time*, 374; and idem, *The Concept of Time*, 18E–19E.

38. Heidegger, *Being and Time*, 400, 229.

39. Ibid., 304–5.

40. Ibid., 311.

41. Ibid., 228–35.

42. Fiddes, *The Creative Suffering of God*, 103, with reference to Heidegger, *Being and Time*, 236–37, 279–80.

43. "The so-called 'inner logic' of the *Church Dogmatics* is the axis of eternity and time unfolded through the motif of the 'analogy of faith'" (Robert H. Roberts, "Karl Barth's Doctrine of Time," in *Karl Barth*, ed. Stephen Sykes [New York: Oxford University Press, 1979], 88). In almost Heideggerian language, Barth at one point declares, "Humanity is temporality. Temporality, as far as our observation and understanding go, is humanity" (Karl Barth, *Church Dogmatics*, 3/2, trans. Harold Knight et al. [Edinburgh: T. & T. Clark, 1960], 522). The best discussion of the topic I know in English is John Colwell, *Actuality and Provisionality: Eternity and Election in the Theology of Karl Barth* (Edinburgh: Rutherford House Books, 1989).

44. George Hunsinger, *How to Read Karl Barth: The Shape of His Theology* (New York: Oxford University Press, 1991), 14.

45. "Time has nothing to do with God" (Karl Barth, *Church Dogmatics*, 2/1, trans. T. H. L. Parker et al. [Edinburgh: T. & T. Clark, 1957], 608. "God . . . is supremely temporal" (Barth, *Church Dogmatics*, 3/2, 437).

46. Karl Barth, *The Epistle to the Romans*, trans. Edwyn C. Hoskyns (London: Oxford University Press, 1933), 43.

47. Ibid., 497.

48. "The decisive temporal source (the 'Now' moment of *Romans*) is given temporal and historical extension as it becomes identified with God's act in Jesus Christ" (Roberts, "Karl Barth's Doctrine of Time," 109). "The eternity of Jesus . . . is the human history of Jesus which is eternity, without becoming something other than the temporal event in Palestine. The meaning of Barth's doctrine can, at least, be that the history of Jesus has taken over the place in the structure of reality which 'eternity' had in religious

Christianity" (Robert W. Jenson, *God after God: The God of the Past and the God of the Future, Seen in the Work of Karl Barth* [Indianapolis: Bobbs-Merrill Co., 1969], 70).

49. Karl Barth, *Church Dogmatics*, 1/2, trans. G. T. Thomson and Harold Knight (Edinburgh: T. & T. Clark, 1956), 45. For Barth, "There is neither a general divine nor a general human temporality which takes ontological precedence over the particular temporality of Jesus" (Hunsinger, *How to Read Karl Barth*, 17).

50. Barth, *Church Dogmatics*, 3/2, 513–14.

51. Ibid., 517.

52. Karl Barth, *Church Dogmatics*, 1/1, trans. G. T. Thomson (Edinburgh: T. & T. Clark, 1936), 116.

53. Karl Barth, *Church Dogmatics*, 4/3, trans. G. W. Bromiley (Edinburgh: T. & T. Clark, 1961), 45. See also Barth, *Church Dogmatics*, 1/2, 52; Jenson, *God after God*, 171; and Hunsinger, *How to Read Karl Barth*, 58, 240.

54. Barth, *Church Dogmatics*, 2/1, 612.

55. Karl Barth, *Church Dogmatics*, 3/1, trans. J. W. Edward et al. (Edinburgh: T. & T. Clark, 1958), 67. Ricoeur's brilliant project in the three volumes of *Time and Narrative* deserves a far more detailed analysis than it can receive here. As I understand it, Ricoeur thinks the narration of a story can give passing time a kind of unity in roughly the way that Barth sees happening in the life of Jesus. See also Paul Ricoeur, "Narrative Time," *Critical Inquiry* 7 (1980): 188. But some life stories (fictional or not) as narrated surely leave readers principally with a sense of the incoherence and lack of unity of the lives they narrate. To bring the pieces together into a narrative whole is to see even more vividly their sad discordance. It is the particularity of Jesus' life as narrated, not simply the fact of the narration of a life, that makes for its coherence. I do not understand (I mean that not as criticism but just literally: I do not understand) why *Time and Narrative* never turns to any lengthy discussion of biblical narratives.

56. Barth, *Church Dogmatics*, 2/1, 616.

57. Ibid., 3/2, 475.

58. Ibid., 463–64.

59. Ibid., 467. Barth illustrates the point in his discussion of the three forms of the parousia. In Hellenistic sources, he reminds his readers, "parousia" means "effective presence," so that the "three forms of the parousia" are the three forms of Christ's effective presence in creation. At a particular date now in the past, Jesus was raised from the dead. He is now present in the power of the Spirit. He will return in glory. We naturally see these as three separate temporal events, but for Barth they are three forms of one event (Barth, *Church Dogmatics*, 4/3, 292). Christ's presence now "is

no less genuinely His own direct and personal coming, His *parousia*, presence and revelation, than was His coming there and then to His disciples in the Easter event, or than will be one day His coming in its final and conclusive form as the Judge of the quick and the dead" (ibid., 356).

60. Ibid., 4/3, 311. See also 4/1, 111.
61. Ibid., 3/2, 601–2.
62. Ibid., 632.
63. Ibid., 576
64. Ibid., 638.
65. Rudolf Bultmann, *Theology of the New Testament*, vol. 2, trans. Kendrick Grobel (New York: Charles Scribner's Sons, 1955), 78.
66. The clearest statement I know is in "An Interview with Rudolf Bultmann," trans. Carol Fellows, *Christianity and Crisis* 26 (1966): 253.
67. "The new people of God has no real history, for it is the community of the end-time, an eschatological phenomenon. . . . Therefore neither the Christian community nor the individuals within it have any responsibility for the present world and its orders, for the tasks of society and the state. . . . All this means that in early Christianity history is swallowed up in eschatology" (Rudolf Bultmann, *The Presence of Eternity* [New York: Harper & Brothers, 1957], 36–37).
68. As early as the fourth century, John Chrysostom noted the oddity of the imperfect tense, as opposed to a straightforward present. Of human things, he said, such verbs refer to past events, but when used of God they signify eternity (*Patrologia Graeca* 59.40; quoted in Frank Kermode, "John," in *The Literary Guide to the Bible*, ed. Robert Alter and Frank Kermode [Cambridge, Mass.: Harvard University Press, 1987], 443).
69. See ibid., 445–47. I have modified the NRSV to make clearer the threefold repetition of *egeneto* (become). Translators differ on which clause belongs to which sentence here, in ways that do not matter to my argument. For a summary of the debate, see Rudolf Schackenburg, *The Gospel according to St. John*, vol. 1, trans. Kevin Smyth (New York: Seabury Press, 1980), 239–40. The point here is not to explore the etymologies of particular words as Cullmann did but to trace the whole pattern of talk about time in the gospel.
70. *Egeneto* again.
71. Gerard Genette, *Narrative Discourse: An Essay in Method*, trans. Jane E. Lewin (Ithaca, N.Y.: Cornell University Press, 1980), 40.
72. See R. Alan Culpepper, *Anatomy of the Fourth Gospel: A Study in Literary Design* (Philadelphia: Fortress Press, 1983), 55, for a more elaborate account.
73. The NSRV translates *time* as *hour*. The text keeps playing with

being/becoming: the water *becomes* wine; the wine simply *is* (Kermode, "John," 449).

74. Gail R. O'Day, *Revelation in the Fourth Gospel* (Philadelphia: Fortress Press, 1986), 63.

75. Charles Talbert argues that this is an authorial aside to the reader. Jesus said, "The hour is coming when true worshippers . . ." and the author interrupts to tell us that that hour has now already arrived, an allusion, presumably, to the destruction of the Second Temple as well as to the resurrection of Christ (Charles H. Talbert, *Reading John: A Literary and Theological Commentary on the Fourth Gospel and Johannine Epistles* [New York: Crossroad, 1992], 114). The Greek admits of either possibility. Raymond Brown reads the "and now is," as does the NSRV, as part of Jesus' speech (Raymond E. Brown, *The Gospel according to John* [Garden City, N.Y.: Doubleday & Co., 1970], 172). It would be too much to see the ambiguity between Jesus speaking and narrator commenting as intentional, but it does point to the way in which Jesus' time is never quite the narrative time of the story.

76. Brown, *The Gospel according to John*, 207.

77. Culpepper, *Anatomy of the Fourth Gospel*, 36.

78. Gail R. O'Day, "I Have Overcome the World," *Semeia* 53 (1991): 157. For earlier passages, note John 13:19; 14:29; 15:11; 16:1; 16:4; 16:33. See also O'Day, *Revelation in the Fourth Gospel*, 85.

79. Ibid., 161.

80. Ibid., 163.

3 The Triune God

The Perichoresis of Particular Persons

The last two chapters have both approached issues that have to do with the Trinity. To speak, as Mark does, of the "Gospel of Jesus Christ, the Son of God," or to talk about the obedience of Christ, as the Reformed tradition has done so prominently, raises obvious questions: What does it mean for "God" to have a "Son"? To whom is Christ obedient? Similarly, thinking about the relations between time and eternity leads to questions about the incarnation: Should one simply say that "God" was born in the first century? If not, what sorts of distinctions need to be introduced?

The natural way in which such issues arise indicates that it makes no sense to pose a sharp dichotomy between biblical narratives and Trinitarian metaphysics, as if issues about the Trinity were foreign to a biblical, narratively oriented theology. The argument of this chapter, indeed, will be that precisely reflecting on the identity of the God revealed in the biblical narratives leads to the realization of God's triunity.

Twenty-five years ago, when as an undergraduate I was just embarking on the study of theology, devoting a chapter to the doctrine of the Trinity might well have seemed an enterprise so eccentric as to require initial explanation, if not apology. Some more conservative types would simply have declared it unbiblical. For more radical theologians, it just served as a good example of the sort of dogma thoroughly irrelevant to contemporary life. All in all, it seemed hard enough back then to argue that God was alive, without tackling the claim that God was triune.

At one level, everything has changed. The three most significant living German Protestant theologians, Wolfhart Pannenberg, Jürgen Moltmann, and Eberhard Jüngel, have all come to make the Trinity the organizing principle and central theme of their theologies. The last decade has seen important books on the Trinity from Latin American liberationists such as Leonardo Boff and Eastern Orthodox theologians such as John Zizioulas.[1] The corporately written Roman Catholic and Lutheran doctrinal theologies recently published in this country feature prominent chapters on the Trinity early on, and the authors of those chapters, Catherine LaCugna and Robert Jenson, have also published major books of their own on the topic.[2] The Presbyterian Church (U.S.A.)'s 1991 A Brief Statement of Faith uses the Trinity as both starting point and structural principle.

But at other levels, has anything really changed very much? In the average congregation, or even ministerial gathering, or even seminary classroom, does not the Trinity often still come as bad news rather than good? Just when a Christian or a new theological student was dealing with struggles to believe in God, it emerges that Christians have to believe not only that God exists but that God is, in some complicated way, both one and three. Dorothy L. Sayers wrote a generation ago that, to the average churchgoer, the mystery of the Trinity means,

> The Father is incomprehensible, the Son is incomprehensible, and the whole thing is incomprehensible. Something put in by theologians to make it more difficult—nothing to do with daily life or ethics.[3]

So perhaps it is best not to bother with it very much. Pastors out in the parish can hope that Trinity Sunday will fall on either Father's Day or Flag Day, or that they can find some way to finesse the topic as long as no one ever asks them to explain it. As Karl Rahner frankly put it,

> We must be willing to admit that, should the doctrine of the Trinity have to be dropped as false, the major part of religious literature could well remain virtually unchanged. . . . The catechism of head and heart (as contrasted with the printed catechism) . . . would not have to change at all if there were no Trinity.[4]

Even of Calvin, after all, Karl Barth could say that, while he gave "indeed a thoroughly correct and respectful exposition of the

54

doctrine of the Trinity . . . it is noteworthy that the author's interest in this matter is not exactly burning."[5]

The doctrine of the Trinity needs to be reclaimed, not just among theologians but in the faith and life of Christian people, for the catechism of the head and even the catechism of the heart, and for at least two reasons. First, as chapters 1 and 2 have argued, Christian theology should not begin with a concept of God—perhaps a concept of God as first of all powerful or as timelessly eternal—derived from some set or other of cultural or philosophical assumptions but from the vulnerable God fully immersed in life who is revealed in Jesus Christ. If Christians begin with the biblical narration of God's self-revelation, however, and consider its implications, they will find themselves thinking about a triune God. It is not that Christians know God first, and then have to add something about the Trinity, but that Christians come to know God precisely as triune: the Logos incarnate in Jesus, the one whom Jesus called Father, and the Holy Spirit.[6]

Second, there is the issue of practical import. In his dismissal of the doctrine of the Trinity, Immanuel Kant argued the same point that Dorothy Sayers imagined the average churchgoer making. In his words, this doctrine "has no practical relevance at all, even if we think we understand it. . . . Whether we are to worship three or ten persons in the Divinity makes no difference" for our "rules of conduct."[7] But Kant was wrong. If we Christians understand the doctrine of the Trinity aright, we will realize that it implies that God is not about power and self-sufficiency and the assertion of authority but about mutuality and equality and love. Moreover, in thinking about a God with an internal "life" that exists independent of creation, we will not think of timeless immutability as the highest ideal. If we think of God as perfect, such reflections change our model of perfection. That in turn can transform not only the way we think about God but the way we think about Christian communities and our own lives as Christians. "The doctrine of the Trinity," as Robert Wilken has written, "reaches to the deepest recesses of the soul and helps us know the majesty of God's presence and the mystery of his love. Love is the most authentic mark of the Christian life, and love among humans, or within God, requires community with others and a sharing of the deepest kind."[8] The doctrine of the Trinity is the account of that community and sharing in the life of God.

This chapter will not develop a theology of the Trinity, a task far too great for a short book, let alone for a single chapter.[9] The chapter will focus on two issues already mentioned: the relation of Trinitarian theology to the biblical account of God's self-revelation in Jesus Christ—the "particular persons" of the chapter's subtitle; and some of the implications of the Trinity for thinking about the nature of God—a topic that will lead to perichoresis and back to the vulnerable God strong in love rather than power, discussed above in chapter 1.

The first of these topics picks up a methodological theme prominent in several of the recent books on the Trinity, namely, that one should begin, not with abstract ideas of threeness and oneness, but with the concrete three persons we encounter in scripture.[10] In the first volume of his *Systematic Theology*, Pannenberg even criticizes Barth and Jüngel for starting their Trinitarian thinking with abstract concepts of revelation and love rather than "from the data of historical revelation of God as Father, Son, and Spirit."[11] Whether or not the comment is fair as a criticism of Barth and Jüngel, the basic instinct behind it seems correct. Christians did not start talking about the Trinity because of some fondness for the number three. They did so because they found they had to, in order to say what they needed to say about the particular God they had come to know in three particular ways.

To move from the data of God's self-revealing work to a doctrine of the Trinity is to presuppose the principal thesis of what may be the most influential book on this topic in this century, Karl Rahner's *The Trinity*. "The 'economic' Trinity," Rahner wrote, "is the 'immanent' Trinity, and the 'immanent' Trinity is the 'economic' Trinity."[12] In traditional terminology, the immanent Trinity is the threefold character that God has within God's own nature. The economic Trinity is what gets described in the biblical accounts of God's self-revelation—Jesus Christ the Son, the Father to whom he prayed, and the Holy Spirit at work in our hearts and in the world.

In the theological tradition, these two Trinities, economic and immanent, had tended to move farther apart. The argument began with the idea that all of God's works are the works of all three Persons of the Trinity.[13] At most, one "appropriated" various particular works to various persons—creation to the Father, redemption to the Son, sanctification to the Spirit, for instance—but this was just a kind of heuristic fiction: all the works of the Trinity *ad extra* were equally the works of the whole triune God. Therefore it followed that there was no correspondence between the instances of activities of God in the world and the intradivine persons, and one therefore could not make any moves from the economic Trinity to the immanent Trinity. Rahner said that was wrong. First of all,

> Jesus is not simply God in general, but the Son. The second divine person, God's Logos, is man, and only he is man. Hence there is at least *one* 'mission,' *one* presence in the world, *one* reality of salvation history which is not merely appropriated to some divine person, but . . . proper to him. . . . At any rate, this *one* case shows up as *false* the statement that there is nothing in salvation history, in the economy of salvation, which cannot equally be said of the triune God as a whole and of each person in particular.[14]

Moreover, the separation of economic and immanent Trinities defeats the whole point. The issue is God's self-revelation, but, if the triune way in which we know God does not disclose the triune way in which God really is, then God has not revealed God's own self, and a hidden God remains unknown behind the revealed God.[15]

One note of caution does seem in order: God's self-revelation implies a created world to which revelation can be directed, and the Christian tradition has wanted to hold that God can be God even without a created world—so that creation is an act of freedom and grace, not some sort of necessity. Therefore the economic Trinity cannot be "who God is" in the same essential sense in which the immanent Trinity is. God could be God without an economy of revelation.[16] But the economic Trinity does indeed *reveal* who God is and in that sense corresponds to the immanent Trinity. God could be God without revelation to the world, but the revelation to the world is God's authentic *self*-revelation and therefore reveals who God really is. All three persons are at work in all of God's works, but in different manners which we come to know in a way that reflects actual distinctions within the triune God.

The distinctions, after all, keep emerging in the language of the biblical narratives. A brief summary may serve as a useful reminder. The Gospel of Mark declares itself to be, right at the start, "the good news of Jesus Christ, the Son of God." "It is God the only Son, who is close to the Father's heart, who has made him known," the Fourth Gospel says (John 1:18): the Word of God who in the beginning was with God and was God. Christ is "the image of God," Paul writes to the Corinthians (2 Cor. 4:4),[17] and the Letter to the Hebrews speaks of Christ as "the exact imprint of God's very being" (Heb. 1:3). The terms vary, but part of the

57

message, at least, seems clear enough: if you want to know who God is, attend to these stories about Jesus Christ.

What do we learn from these stories? We learn that Jesus Christ is one

> who, though he was in the form of God,
>> did not regard equality with God
>> as something to be exploited,
> but emptied himself,
>> taking the form of a slave,
>> being born in human likeness.
> And being found in human form,
>> he humbled himself
>> and became obedient to the point of death—
>> even death on a cross. (Phil. 2:6–8)

This is what God is like, not as mere message from God, information passed on, but as God's own self come among us as the revelation of who God is.

Then in addition, in the Gospel accounts, Jesus consistently speaks of one he calls his Father. He bears witness to the Father (John 8:18, 50) and serves the Father's will (John 10:36–37). The Father, he says, is greater than he (John 14:28), and the word he speaks is "not mine, but is from the Father who sent me" (John 14:24). When someone calls him good, he insists that only the Father is good (Mark 10:18).[18] He subjects his will to the will of the Father (Mark 14:36), and prays to the Father. On the other hand, Jesus says that to know the Son is to know the Father (John 8:19). "The Father and I," he says, "are one," using the strong Greek word *hen*, meaning one and the same thing, sharing one reality (John 10:30).

The word "Father" of course raises a good many complex issues today, and the Christian tradition has, to put it mildly, given mixed signals about how this particular symbol functions. The Council of Toledo, in A.D. 675, spoke of the Son as "begotten or born out of the Father's womb,"[19] the paradoxical language opening up the symbol and challenging any literal interpretation of the male language. Aquinas, on the other hand, appealed to the teaching of Aristotelian biology that the father actively imposes form on the offspring, while the mother passively contributes only the matter, and concluded that only a Father, as pure act, could singularly beget the Word.[20] On this interpretation, the maleness of the Father really mattered.

Faced with this complicated tradition, a good many recent theologians have tried to return to Jesus' own example. Beginning with Joachim Jeremias, biblical scholars and theologians have argued that Jesus himself used the word "Abba" and that this was an informal, family term rarely if ever otherwise used of God, something like the equivalent of calling God "Daddy."[21] Jesus' own references to his "Abba" were therefore not the reaffirmation of stern and distant patriarchy but shocking, revolutionary language of intimacy with God.[22]

Unfortunately, all three of the historical claims implied by this line of thought seem problematic. (1) Talmudic references to God as "Abba" show that this usage would not have been unique or necessarily revolutionary in the Jewish context.[23] (2) As Jeremias himself came to admit, "Abba" was in common use among adults, sometimes as a mark of respect for old men and teachers; "Daddy," with its childhood connotations, is simply a misleading translation.[24] In fact, the New Testament itself always follows the word with the Greek translation, *ho patēr*, the rather formal "the father." More informal Greek translations were available—the diminutive *pappas,* for instance—but neither Paul nor Mark used them.[25] (3) Most important, it is simply not clear that Jesus used the term "Abba." The word appears, after all, only three times in the New Testament. In Paul's two uses (Rom. 8:15 and Gal. 4:6) it refers to the practice of the community—it is Christian believers who cry, "Abba, Father"—without reference to what Jesus himself did. The one Gospel passage (Mark 14:36) refers to a scene in which Jesus is praying to God without any human witnesses. True enough, the use of this Aramaic word untranslated in a Greek text may point backward to something in Jesus' own practice or the life of the earliest Christian communities, but the scanty evidence simply does not warrant historical claims about the centrality of "Abba" in Jesus' own talk about God.[26]

The debate about "Abba" illustrates the dangers of putting too much theological weight on particular historical claims about details of Jesus' life or ministry. The next chapter will return to the general issue of historical claims concerning the biblical narratives and argue for a significantly more complex relation between theology and history. In thinking about God as "Father," the moral indeed seems to be that theologians should not rest too much on any one foundation but should consider the issue in the context of a variety of historical, textual, and theological conclusions.

Historically, for instance, Elisabeth Schüssler Fiorenza and others have made a good case that the very earliest Christian communities embodied more equality between women and men than subsequent periods during which the later New Testament books, at least, were written.[27] A cumulative case that does not depend too much on just two or three passages indicates that the gospel created initial communities that in important ways challenged the patriarchal social structures of their time.

In the New Testament texts themselves, moreover, Jesus is, with some consistency, bringing into question what contemporary American politicians would call "traditional family values." "Call no one your father on earth," Matthew's Gospel has him say, "for you have one Father—the one in heaven" (Matt. 23:9). Following the Jesus who does the will of this Father means abandoning the usual family obligations—not even worrying about your duty to bury your own human father (Matt. 8:21–22). Faithfulness to Jesus' Father in heaven means the abolition or radical relativizing of every human form of patriarchy, and therefore the symbol of the Father in heaven, in this particular context, may oddly challenge patriarchal social structures that embody power in earthly fathers.[28]

Phyllis Trible, among others, makes an important counterargument: "To the extent that Jesus disavowed the earthly father in the name of the heavenly father, . . . to that extent Jesus re-enforced patriarchy by absolutizing the rule of the father. To transfer male dominance from earth to heaven is not to eliminate but to exacerbate it."[29] But does that argument cast the issues too much in either/or terms? Exclusively male language about God does reinforce patriarchal structures. If we speak of God only as "Father," then fathers will seem a bit like God. On the other hand, a radical challenge to earthly fathers on behalf of a heavenly father can subvert those structures. If there is a God, Moltmann once remarked, then at least human beings cannot play god over each other.[30] Analogously, one might argue, if God is really our Father, then at least no man can play ultimate patriarch. It is surely possible for the same symbol to function in some degree in both ways at once. If it does so, then a contemporary Christian theology sensitive to some of the concerns of feminism might want to introduce diverse images, including female ones, for God into the life of the church—including images already present in the Christian tradition—while also learning from and celebrating the antipatriarchal messages embodied in the New Testament language about God the Father.

Theologians—and preachers and hymn writers and liturgists—

THE TRIUNE GOD

need to explore alternative terms for the Persons of the Trinity that
remain faithful to the logic of Trinitarian thought. Elizabeth Johnson cites a number of possibilities: primordial Being/expressive
Being/unitive Being (John Macquarrie); God's absoluteness/
humaneness/present presence (Gordon Kaufman); love as creative
source/self-expressive act/responsive movement (Norman Pittenger); divine being/divine Logos/divine love (Langdon Gilkey).[31]
These possibilities may seem a bit cumbersome, but they have at
least the advantage of not dividing up the work of the Trinity, with
one job per person, as does the all-too-common "Creator, Redeemer, Sustainer." Both the logic of the tradition and contemporary practice seem to incline toward maternal symbols, "Mother"
among them, for the whole triune God rather than the first Person
of the Trinity—God as "like a mother," or the formula "Father,
Son and Holy Spirit, one God, Mother of us all"[32]—and it will be
interesting to see how such usage develops.

The language of "Father" and "Son" will surely continue to
be important in the Christian tradition, and in a more diverse linguistic context perhaps "Father" can function in more complex
ways. Anne Carr remarks that women find that the "official language for God" in the Christian tradition gives them "an image of
God as authoritarian, as a judge 'over against' the self, humankind,
the world. It is an image of God as power in the sense of control,
domination, even coercion."[33] If Christians think of God as vulnerable in love, then "Father" language itself may become less problematic.

In any event, Christians will be most faithful to the biblical
narratives if "Father" functions, when used, primarily as a symbol
of love rather than of power.[34] Theologically, and for reasons that
go beyond these issues of gender too, it is important not to picture
the Trinitarian Father purely as the impassible Judge to whom the
Son offers sacrifice in obedience. That way of telling the story does
foster a picture of father as distant tyrant that carries unhealthy
lessons about family structure but also distorts the biblically narrated relations within the Trinity. The "Son" does not win over the
love of a reluctant "Father." "*God* so loved the world that he gave
his only Son" (John 3:16). "In this is love, not that we loved God
but that he loved us and sent his Son to be the atoning sacrifice for
our sins" (1 John 4:10). God as parent, so willing to be vulnerable
in love as to send off a beloved child to die for a sinful creation, is
also fully engaged in the risks of love. As Calvin put it, "It was not
after we were reconciled to him through the blood of his Son that

61

he began to love us. Rather, he has loved us before the world was created."[35]

If the New Testament indeed presents us with the narratives of a vulnerable God, then the "Father" to whom they refer is at least an unusual sort of patriarch. Perhaps even the use of the word "Abba" can, by its very foreignness, call Christians' attention to the special characteristics here embodied, without making specific claims about the usage of the historical Jesus. The One called Abba in the biblical narratives overflows in love. The sending of the Christ and the Spirit manifests this divine love (Rom. 8:39). The Jesus vulnerable in love is the image of this One, the exact imprint of this One's very being; indeed, Paul identifies the love of Christ with the love of God expressed in sending the Son (Rom. 8:35).[36] This Abba calls us to turn away from obedience to the lords of this world to a new kind of intimacy based on love. We did not "receive a spirit of slavery to fall back into fear," Paul wrote to the Romans, but "a spirit of adoption. When we cry, 'Abba! Father!' it is that very Spirit bearing witness with our spirit that we are children of God, and if children, then heirs, heirs of God and joint heirs with Christ" (Rom. 8:15–17). Heirs do not grovel before intimidating powers but feel at home on the family estate, do not let anybody push them around, and joyfully obey in love the One whose love they have come to know. In most human situations such joy is always tempered by the contrast between the heirs who inherit and the servants and others who get left out, but in this case status as heirs is open to all, and to prodigal children especially. The Middle Eastern patriarch walks through the village in his long robe at a stately pace; Jesus' Abba, indifferent to dignity, runs to greet every returning prodigal.

When we cry, "Abba! Father!" Paul says, it is the Spirit bearing witness. The Spirit too is part of the story of this God. Mary was found to be with child from the Holy Spirit, two of the Gospels tell us (Matt. 1:18; Luke 6:27–35). The Spirit descended on Jesus at baptism and then led him into the wilderness, Luke says (Luke 4:1), from which he returned "filled with the power of the Spirit" (Luke 4:14). The Spirit provided Jesus with the power and authority with which to perform his works (Mark 3:20–30). The Spirit is the Paraclete—the advocate, the comforter, the defender, the one who makes urgent appeals—whom Jesus promised his Father would send (John 14:16, 26).

This Spirit seems in some ways the most mysterious part of the story. Yves Congar puts it this way:

> The incarnate Word has a face—he has expressed his personality in our human history in the way persons do, and the Father has revealed himself in him. The Spirit does not present such personal characteristics. He is, as it were, buried in the work of the Father and the Son, which he completes.[37]

Having quoted Congar's references to the Holy Spirit as "he," one should acknowledge that pronouns are a particular problem here. The word for "spirit" is feminine in Hebrew, neuter in Greek, and masculine in Latin; Jerome once cited this as evidence that gender does not apply to God at all.[38] It is tempting to make the Spirit the feminine side of God and thus begin, as it were, to even out gender representation within the godhead, but here Rosemary Radford Ruether seems correct: a Trinity with two male and one female persons does not exactly manifest equality, and the traditional image of the Spirit as the Person who perfects and completes the Trinitarian work while glorifying the Father and Son would invite thinking of a feminine Spirit as "a subordinate principle underneath the dominant image of male divine sovereignty,"[39] thus if anything reinforcing gender stereotypes.[40] Questions of gender in reference to God need to be addressed in other ways.

What is important, in regard to the Holy Spirit, is to preserve personhood. However problematic "she" or "he" may be, "it" is just wrong. The temptation to move to impersonal language in connection with the Spirit is not one to which contemporary concerns about gender gave rise for the first time. Barth proposes that there is a reluctance in us to affirm the Spirit's personhood, since part of the particular work of the Spirit lies in the nurturing of our response to revelation, and therefore the full acknowledgment of the divinity of the Spirit involves conceding that even our response to God is not our work but God's, so that we are not, as it were, even masters in our own house.[41] The work of God for us is not something simply external we observe as interested spectators, nor is it something we do for ourselves. Rather, it achieves completion only when it transforms us from within, and even that transformation is the work of the triune God. We acknowledge that when we affirm the coequal personhood of the Holy Spirit. Barth may have been right, incidentally, to say that Calvin was not very enthusiastic about the Trinity, but he was irreproachable on the topic of the work of the Spirit.

As noted above in chapter 1, Barth regularly referred to God as "the one who loves in freedom." That phrase could be used of any of the Persons of the Trinity.[42] Christ breaks the bonds of the law, sits at table with outcasts and sinners, and freely risks everything in love. The One he called "Father" overflows with love for creation, challenges every human definition of authority, and so loves even a world of sinners as to send a beloved only child to redeem it. But the Spirit bears a special relation to freedom and love. In describing living by the Spirit in his letter to the Galatians, Paul writes of being called to freedom (Gal. 5:13) and lists love as the first of the fruits of the Spirit (Gal. 5:22). Above all, in those grand discourses which begin in John 14, Spirit and love and truth keep intertwining, with the memory hovering over them of that earlier word that the truth will make us free (John 8:32). As Walter Kasper puts it,

> Everywhere that life breaks forth and comes into being, everywhere that new life as it were seethes and bubbles, and even, in the form of hope, everywhere that life is violently devastated, throttled, gagged and slain—wherever true life exists, there the Spirit of God is at work.[43]

The Spirit manifests God's love in freedom, and when the Spirit has sealed God's work in us, then we ourselves live in love and freedom.

Christ, the very image of God, according to the passage from Philippians already quoted, "did not regard equality with God as something to be exploited." Such generosity, such mutual deference, characterizes all the Persons of the triune God. Philippians 2 continues by telling of God's exaltation of Christ Jesus

> so that at the name of Jesus
>   every knee should bend,
>   in heaven and on earth and under the earth,
> and every tongue should confess
>   that Jesus Christ is Lord,
>   to the glory of God the Father. (Phil. 2:10–11)

The Father's glory lies not in any honors directly given the Father but in this grand, universal adulation of the Son. Yet Christ, as we have seen, subjects his will to the will of the one he calls Abba or Father and serves that One's will in obedience (Mark 14:36; John 10:36–37). He asks that he might be glorified only that he might in turn glorify the One whom John's Gospel has him call simply "God." The Spirit in turn glorifies the Christ and claims nothing from individual authority but speaks of the Son from the Father (John 16:14–15; 14:26).[44]

We all live in human communities, from nation-states to college campuses to churches to corporations, full of jockeying for position and all kinds of competitiveness. Even within ourselves, we often find the part of us most committed to career at war with the part of us most interested in family, and so on. The triune God, the Bible intimates to us, is not like that. In this unity in diversity mutual love and deference wonderfully yield mutual glorification.

Christians, then, do not believe in just any Trinity but in the Triunity of these three Persons—the Christ who does not grasp at equality but humbles himself, even to death on a cross, the One he called Abba or Father, outpouring love, challenging human assumptions about hierarchy, the Holy Spirit of love, truth, and freedom, all one God glorifying each other. That said, the old question remains as to whether Christians are just shockingly bad at arithmetic and unable to realize that three does not equal one.

The answer to that question lies in reflecting on the relation of the three and the one in Christian theology, and at some level that relation remains a mystery. But the word "mystery" should not be an excuse for intellectual sloppiness. Christians should try to understand what they can, and in this case the theological tradition has offered to explain quite a lot. As we try to understand these matters today, however, analysis of the traditional terminology may not offer a very helpful starting point. The Greek *hypostaseis* and *ousia* notoriously do not translate very well into the Latin *personae* and *subsantia*, and the English "persons" and "substance" may not render either version with much precision. "I do not know," even Augustine frankly admitted about the Greek theologians, "what different meaning they wished to give *ousia* and *hypostasis*."[45]

Moreover, sometime between the ancient world and the world of post-Kantian philosophy and post-Einsteinian physics, the meaning and context of "person" and "substance" changed radically in the intellectual tradition of the West. Personhood has come most generally to refer above all to individual self-consciousness, the Cartesian *ego cogito*, and philosophers and physicists alike think of the "substances" of the world as shaped and defined by the thinking of such "persons." That alters both the meaning of "person" and the relation of person and substance in fundamental ways. The moral is not that we ought to give up the traditional terminology but only that the terms themselves do not initially give us much help in understanding. As a supplement to the terms used of the Trinity, the theological tradition has often appealed to analogies. Two of the analogies most often used in the tradition for the

Trinity, the psychological and the social, may provide a more useful starting point.

In the first half of his great book on the Trinity, Augustine laid out the elements of the church's teaching on the Trinity as he understood it. Then in the later books he began to explore various analogies to the Trinity in human experience. The order of his procedure is worth noting. He is not saying that we find a threefoldness in various aspects of our experience and can therefore infer to a triune God. Rather, his discussions offer an instance of *fides quaerens intellectum*, the great Augustinian tradition of faith seeking understanding. He begins with the faith he has received, and then he struggles, with analogies among other devices, to understand it more fully.

If we are made in the image of God, as our faith assures us, and God is triune, then there ought to be some analogy to that threefoldness within us. In book 9 of *On the Trinity*, Augustine therefore considers the human mind. My mind exists, and it exists in knowing and loving. At first glance, Augustine's model might seem to imply subordinationism, for existence sounds like the substance of the mind, with knowing and loving only its activities. Augustine, however, insists that the mind exists *only in* knowing and loving, and therefore existing has no priority. The mind is not like a knife that can sit there on the shelf being a knife, waiting to start cutting. In his terminology, "love and knowledge are not in the mind as in a subject, for they are there substantially as the mind itself is."[46] The mind's very existence, for Augustine, inheres in its activities of knowledge and love. If nothing else, in isolation it would know and love itself.

But there is also a relation, Augustine thinks, between knowing and loving. One cannot love something without knowing it— that part may be obvious. If you say, "Don't you love Hong Kong?" or "Don't you love skiing?" my answer is, "I don't know— I've never been there, I've never done it, how can I talk of love?" Augustine thinks the relation works the other way too. I cannot know what I do not love. Often enough, one hears a remark like, "You've been around my family, my church, my school, and I suppose you know a lot of information, but you don't really understand, you can't have a certain kind of empathetic feel—because you don't love them." There are, to be sure, things that "we rightly disapprove of."[47] To know them is not to love them. But even then there is a relation between knowledge and love, for we are glad to have censured evil, glad therefore to have recognized it, glad to have known it. We love our knowledge even as we do not love the thing we know.[48]

So the mind exists and knows and loves. And this existence and knowledge and love are not three parts, like the back and the seat and the legs of a chair. The whole mind exists and knows and loves. Nor is this trinity of the mind like a single drink made of water and wine and honey. In that case, even though each of them extends through the whole drink, still each is also a separate substance, a different kind of thing. No, mind and love and knowledge are three things, yet one thing.[49] Moreover, in knowing something, we produce an image of the thing known, as a parent begets a child and as the Logos is the image of the Father. And love unites subject and object in love just as the Holy Spirit for Augustine unites the Father and the Son in love. "And so there is a certain image of the Trinity: the mind itself, its knowledge, which is its offspring, and love as a third; these three are one and one substance."[50] One can trace that psychological analogy for the Trinity through the history of Western Christendom from Augustine to Anselm to Aquinas to Barth.

But another analogy, the social, appears in various forms particularly in the Eastern church and was expounded and elaborated in the Latin West in the twelfth century by Richard of St.-Victor. Richard began with love. God is perfect love, perfect charity, and perfect love needs an object. To be sure, God can love the creation, but it would be disorderly to love it supremely, for the creation is not supremely good. "However, as long as anyone loves no one else as much as he loves himself, that private love which he has for himself shows clearly that he has not yet reached the supreme level of charity. . . . Therefore, so that fullness of charity might have a place in that true Divinity, it is necessary that a divine person not lack a relationship with an equally worthy person, who is, for this reason, divine."[51] But the highest kind of love is mutual love, and "in mutual love it is absolutely necessary that there be both one who loves and one who returns love. . . . Therefore, the showing of love freely given and the repayment of love that is due prove without any doubt that in true Divinity a plurality of persons cannot be lacking."[52]

This analysis yields only a duality. Richard thinks, however, that even two persons in mutual love still do not encompass perfect love. If you were deeply involved in a mutual love, it would still be an imperfection of that love if you were not willing to share it. "Nothing is rarer or more magnificent than to wish that another be loved equally by the one whom you love supremely and by whom you are supremely loved. . . . So a person proves that he is not perfect in charity if he cannot yet take pleasure in sharing this excellent joy." The perfection of love requires therefore not only an object of love whose object I am in turn but a third person with whom I am willing to share the perfection of this mutual love. "Thus you see how the perfection of charity requires a Trinity of persons, without which it is wholly unable to subsist in the integrity of its fullness."[53] Something like this social analogy of the Trinity runs down the history of Eastern Christianity from the time of the Cappadocian Fathers and has drawn increasing interest in our time in the West. Indeed, many of the last decade's works on the Trinity seem to cast Augustine as the villain of the story and some version of a social Trinity as the collective hero.[54]

The adherents of these two analogies, indeed, find themselves regularly in conflict. To those who favor the psychological analogy, drawing the analogy of three human beings sharing mutual love seems to imply the existence of three gods. To those who favor the social analogy, the psychological one seems to imply a God who is one person, albeit with a complicated internal life.[55] Moltmann, who favors the social analogy, says that Barth's Trinity is "a late triumph for the Sabellian modalism which the early church condemned,"[56] and George Hunsinger, writing with sympathy to Barth, says that the form of the social analogy in Moltmann's *The Trinity and the Kingdom* "is about the closest thing to tritheism that any of us are ever likely to see."[57]

Conceding that any account of such matters involves the risky application of human analogies to a divine mystery, still, the psychological and social analogies for the Trinity may not point in quite such different directions as first glance suggests, if one reflects a bit more deeply about the nature of human self and human community. Indeed, the point of the preceding discussion of these analogies is in part that it leads to such reflection.[58]

The human self, to use a bit of jargon that has become a philosophical cliché, is socially constructed. In important ways, I do not find out who I am by introspection in isolation but by how other people define me and how I define myself in interaction with them.[59] In Buber's phrase, "I become through my relation to the Thou."[60] Narcissus, after all, who fell in love with his reflection in a pool, and thus, Ovid says, "with an insubstantial hope, mistaking a mere shadow for a real body," lacks an authentic other and therefore can only die: that is somehow the point of the story.[61] We all know tragic stories of children whose parents keep telling them they are worthless—of course they come to believe it. The expectations and responses of those around us shape all of us; indeed, we become selves, persons, in interaction with others, in a social context.

Something within us resists this human reality. I want to be self-sufficient; I want to define who I am. I want to be in control. Yet interaction with an other is basic to my very identity as a person. Hegel's *Phenomenology* is, among many other things, the story of the pathos of trying to define oneself in relation without losing control of one's identity. It is interesting that one of Hegel's early images for the process is of mortal combat, an image that may suggest just how terrifying Hegel found the issue. If you and I challenge each other to a fight to the death, then whoever wins has established an identity—as victor—in relation with another and yet succeeded in achieving control, for now the opponent is safely dead. Such an ontological achievement seems almost worth the risk of the consequences of losing.[62] But victory in such combat is always Pyrrhic: no sooner do I triumph and thereby affirm myself than I have killed the other and find myself again in an isolation that threatens even my own identity.

So do not kill off your other, but turn to enslavement, and keep a handy other around the house to affirm your identity. Trouble is, what you really want is a slave who will reliably tell you how wonderful you are, in a way that you will really believe. But a slave knows what it is safe to say, and so after a while the slave's praise of the master no longer works. It comes to be like a teacher asking students on the day before the exam how they liked the course. "It is not an independent, but rather a dependent consciousness that he has achieved. He is thus not assured of self-existence as his truth."[63] (I leave the masculine pronouns in place: Hegel's self seems to me irreducibly masculine; that may be part of the problem.) What we want is to have an other who is really other but who, we can trust, will never criticize, never threaten. We want to be Narcissus, who had, Ovid tells us, "a pride so unyielding" that no one "dared to touch him,"[64] but a Narcissus who can reach through the surface of the pool.

To speak of Hegel's pathos is to imply that Hegel was still pursuing Narcissus's dream. The object, after all, turns out to be part of the subject in the end. Contemporary philosophers such as Emmanuel Levinas have protested against the character of Hegel's enterprise. "The Other as Other," Levinas writes, "is not only an alter ego: the Other is what I myself am not. The Other is this, not because of the Other's character, or physiognomy, or psychology, but because of the Other's very alterity."[65] The Other is really other, and not, in the end of the day, only a part or projection of myself. "The solipsist disquietude of consciousness, seeing itself, in all its adventures, a captive of itself, comes to an end here: true exteriority is in this gaze which forbids me my conquest."[66] To look another person honestly in the face, Levinas insists, is to encounter someone I cannot control. In Jean-François Lyotard's elegant phrase, Levinas "attacks Hegelian alterity . . . as . . . only a caprice of identity."[67] I can really be myself only in relation, and I can be in true relation only if I fully respect the otherness of the other. That means doing a host of things Hegel's assertive self resists: becoming vulnerable, accepting that I am not fully in control, not in a position to control, or therefore to know, how the story will turn out. I would then also have to accept the limits and partiality of my understanding, thereby giving up Hegel's project of arriving at an absolute standpoint from which I can see the truth without partiality. Acknowledging my limits, making myself vulnerable in full relation to an other is the only way I can become fully myself. Such loss of self-independence in relation does not threaten individual identity but precisely creates it.

In another way too we often become most fully ourselves when we at once lose ourselves and find ourselves—the Gospel language seems the only appropriate description for the experience—in a community that transcends ourselves. In Indiana, one always starts illustrating this point with an example from basketball. In a team sport, the players who are always asking, "How am I doing? Am I getting my share of the shots? Am I going to be the star in tomorrow's paper?" never in fact play to their potential. On the other hand, we have all seen the games, and some of us maybe had the luck to take part in them, where the players lost themselves in a team effort that involved a kind of self-forgetfulness that paradoxically made them the best players, as individuals, that they had ever been. One can tell similar stories about artists lost in their work, lovers lost in their beloved, workers lost in the excitement of a common enterprise, contemplatives lost in God. Afterward, perhaps, they look back on themselves and say, "What a remarkable thing I did there," but part of what was remarkable was that at the time no such thought crossed their minds. One tossed aside the part of oneself that always stands watching on the sidelines, and, in forgetfulness of self, became most fully oneself.

There are limits to how much humans can do this sort of

thing. We are sinners, and we have bodies—for the Christian tradition these are two quite different issues, but in different ways they
both limit our capacity to find ourselves in losing ourselves. We are
sinners, and therefore we can never quite achieve forgetfulness of
self. Could even Michael Jordan make the double-backhanded basket
purely in the joy of the rhythm of the game, with no thought of
the million-dollar endorsement intruding? Perhaps for a moment,
but the thought comes back.

Even free of sin, we would still be embodied selves, with inevitable limits.[68] When you break your ankle, I tell you that I am
sharing your pain, but you know it is not really true. I may be em-
pathizing, I may feel great distress, but the pain in that ankle is
yours and not mine. As I watch you eating the omelette I have prepared for you, my pleasure in your pleasure may be even greater
than your pleasure; cooking for appreciative friends can be a greater
joy than eating. But it is a different pleasure, the particular sensa-
tion of the omelette on your taste buds is yours alone.

Suppose, however, there were disembodied agents who were
also without sin, each defining its own identity in genuine otherness, each losing itself in common enterprise pursued without jeal-
ousy or conflict, so at one that each was in the all. The classical
theological term for such a state of affairs is "perichoresis," the
"passing into one another" of the divine Persons. "The Father is in
me and I am in the Father," Jesus says in John 10—and a bit earlier, "The Father and I are one." Two or three can so pass into one
another that they become as one. Gregory of Nazianzus was probably the first to use the term "perichoresis," although he used it for
the interpenetration of the two natures, human and divine, in
Christ.[69] A text called *Pseudo-Cyril* used it of the Persons of the
Trinity in the sixth century, but it was John of Damascus who fully
developed the theme. As Daniel Migliore nicely explains the idea of
perichoresis, the trinitarian Persons "'indwell' each other . . . 'make
room' for each other, are incomparably hospitable to each other."[70]

The analysis so far presented has taken its start from the social
analogy of the Trinity, moving from plurality to unity. An exclusive
emphasis on the social analogy, however, risks suggesting that the
divine Persons are just rather like human persons, only very closely
interrelated. But John of Damascus made an interesting move that
in a way jumps to the other side and emphasizes the unity of God.
With all *creatures*, he explained, their individuality is actual, and
one can see what they have in common by reason or thought. So
Peter is actually distinct from Paul, and we have to impose some

71

uniting conceptual category in order to think that they are both human beings, or Americans, or whatever. In the case of the Trinity, however, the Damascene says, the *unity* is actual, and it is the *distinction* that has to be made conceptually. We do not encounter three Gods and determine they must be one, the way we encounter three baseball players and determine they must all be Yankees; rather, we encounter one God and determine that that God is three-personed.[71] Each human person

> is distinct and considered in itself, since it has a great many things to distinguish it from the other. For, truly, they are separated in place and they differ in time, judgment, strength, form—or shape, habit, temperament, dignity, manner of life, and all the other distinctive properties—but most of all they differ by the fact that they do not exist in each other but separately.

"With the uncircumscribed God," however, "we cannot speak of any difference in place, as we do with ourselves, because the Persons exist in one another."[72] God exists three-personedly, but none of those three Persons has independent existence, for they are what they are in relation, so that God is what God is in this interrelation.

Moreover, while the Persons undertake different tasks in enacting God's love for the world (the economic Trinity we encounter, it will be remembered, corresponds to the immanent Trinity), they never act at cross-purposes. "Every operation," Gregory of Nyssa wrote, "which extends from God to the Creation, . . . has its origin from the Father, and proceeds through the Son and is perfected in the Holy Spirit. For this reason the name derived from the operation is not divided with regard to the number of those who fulfill it."[73] In the early church, theologians often used the image of the one Sun from which different rays shone forth to make the distinction between one God and three Persons—sometimes they even treated the Father as the Sun and the Son and Spirit as rays coming forth in a way that risked subordinating the second and third Persons of the Trinity to the first. But Gregory of Nazianzus dramatically reversed the image: so perichoretically united is the work of the three Persons that it is like the light from three *Suns* shining to form one *beam*.[74] God is who God is in being God, that is, in doing what God does. And what God does, while authentically revealing the threefold way in which God is through the different roles of the three Persons, is always a unified act. It is interesting that people coming, as it were, from opposite sides,

from the context of the psychological and social analogies, such as
Barth and Moltmann, unite in finding perichoresis to be the key in
sorting out the meaning of the Trinity.[75] When we think of the
Three so united in purpose and activity, beyond all discord, when
we think of one God so rich in love, the questions of whether these
are three individuals or one melt away. Not three isolated individuals; not one without internal distinction. Each in full selfhood precisely in community; one most itself in its threeness.

Such human analogies may provide a glimpse of how God can
be at once one and three, but what does it matter beyond the solv-
ing of a puzzle? This chapter began with the proposal that the
Trinity should not be bad news, one more difficult thing to be believed, but good news of central importance to Christian faith.
First, that is so because Christians, in their lives and in scripture,
come to know God precisely as triune. We do not know an abstract God first and then have to attach this trinitarian talk, but,
from the start, we encounter God in Jesus Christ, in the one he
called Father, in the Holy Spirit. Second, knowing God as triune
tells something important about God. God is not an isolated, single
monarch whose only relation is to rule. God is a community of
equals united in mutual love, "a monarchy that is not limited to
one Person," Gregory of Nazianzus wrote, "but one which is made
of an equality of Nature and a union of mind, and an identity of
motion and a convergence of its elements to unity."[76] God, to return to the central theme of this book, is defined in terms of love
rather than power.

That matters because Christians have so often modeled hier-
archies in this world after the presumed divine hierarchy. "The one
God, the one heavenly king," declared Eusebius of Caesarea, Con-
stantine's court flunky, "corresponds to the one king on earth."[77]
Ignatius of Antioch had earlier appealed to the principle of one
God, one bishop.[78] Ephesians makes an analogous argument for
the hierarchy of male over female (Eph. 5:22–23). But the triune
God is about equality and mutual concern, a God of love. In the
Christian tradition at least, the God of monotheism, as Patricia
Wilson-Kastner observes, "has historically been imaged as a male,
patriarchal and dominating." The doctrine of the Trinity encourages us, on the other hand, "to focus on interrelationship as the
core of divine reality."[79] "Monotheism," Walter Kasper has written,
"has always been a political program as well as a religious: one God,
one realm, one emperor." But in the Christian vision of the triune

God, "God's unity is fullness and even overflowing fullness of self-less giving and bestowing, of loving self-outpouring; it is a unity that does not exclude but includes; it is a living, loving being with and for one another."[80] Christians worship that sort of God. For Christians sympathetic with feminist concerns, it can therefore be particularly important not to let the problems of the language of "Father" and "Son" stand in the way of significant attention to the implications of the Trinity. As Anne Carr has written,

> The mystery of God as Trinity, as final and perfect sociality, embodies those qualities of mutuality, reciprocity, co-operation, unity, peace in genuine diversity that are feminist ideals and goals derived from the inclusivity of the gospel message. The final symbol of God as Trinity thus provides women [and men too, one hopes!] with an image and concept of God that entails qualities that make God truly worthy of imitation, worthy of the call to radical discipleship that is inherent in Jesus' message.[81]

Writing to the Romans, Paul assured them, "If the Spirit of him who raised Jesus from the dead dwells in you, he who raised Christ from the dead will give life to your mortal bodies also through his Spirit that dwells in you" (Rom. 8:11). Paul lacked most of the categories with which the church later expressed the doctrine of the Trinity, and yet he was pointing to the Trinitarian shape of the narratives of God's work of salvation. It is the Father of Jesus who raised Jesus from the dead; it is through the indwelling of the Spirit that one comes to know the life given to Jesus in the resurrection. This chapter thus points back to previous discussions of those biblical narratives. The perichoretic love within the Trinity is a love willing to be vulnerable lying at the heart of who God is. In mutual love the Persons of the Trinity live limitlessly in a life that coheres without opposition between past, present, and future, and thus live eternal life.

But this chapter also points forward. The traditional eucharistic prayers of the church begin with praise of the Father, narrating God's mighty acts; then there is an anamnesis, remembering Jesus narratively, then an epiclesis, invoking the Spirit and the future the Spirit brings.[82] In the prayers of the sacrament of the Eucharist, Christians locate themselves within a triune pattern that gives shape to their lives (and thus—see chapter 2—connects their time with eternity). Chapter 6 will return to the question of what it means for the life of Christian communities that they worship this triune God, a God instantiating mutual love and equality. Before that, the next two chapters will return to some of the contemporary concerns that raise questions about a christological, trinitarian theology based on biblical narratives.

Perhaps this chapter needs to conclude by emphasizing yet again that Christian faith does not concern just any trinity—the point is not equality and mutual love between someone or other, fill in the blanks. The three Persons of the God in whom Christians believe are the Christ who suffered on the cross, the one whom Christ called his Father, whose outpouring love sends forth both the Christ and the Spirit, and the Spirit who makes communities of love and freedom. If we Christians are invited to draw diagrams about God, we should not begin with a pyramid with a single divine point at the top. The symbol of the Trinity, Elizabeth Johnson writes,

> indicates that the particular kind of relatedness than which nothing greater can be conceived is not one of hierarchy involving domination/subordination, but rather one of genuine mutuality in which there is radical equality while distinctions are respected. . . . At the heart of holy mystery is not monarchy but community; not an absolute ruler, but a threefold *koinōnia*.[83]

At the end of his journey through Paradise, Dante tells us, he saw "three circles of three colors and one magnitude; and one seemed reflected by the other, as rainbow by rainbow, and the third seemed fire breathed forth"[84]—interconnected circles representing the equality and reciprocity of the one triune God.

NOTES

1. Leonardo Boff, *Trinity and Society*, trans. Paul Burns (Maryknoll, N.Y.: Orbis Books, 1988); and John D. Zizioulas, *Being as Communion: Studies in Personhood and the Church* (Crestwood, N.Y.: St. Vladimir's Seminary Press, 1985).
2. Francis Schüssler Fiorenza and John P. Galvin, eds., *Systematic Theology: Roman Catholic Perspectives* (Minneapolis: Fortress Press, 1991); Carl E. Braaten and Robert W. Jenson, eds., *Christian Dogmatics*, 2 vols. (Philadelphia: Fortress Press, 1984); Catherine Mowry LaCugna, *God for Us: The Trinity and Christian Life* (San Francisco: Harper, 1991); and Robert W. Jenson, *The Triune Identity: God According to the Gospel* (Philadelphia: Fortress Press, 1982).

3. Dorothy L. Sayers, *Creed or Chaos* (New York: Harcourt, Brace & Co., 1949), 22.

4. Karl Rahner, *The Trinity*, trans. J. Donceel (New York: Herder & Herder, 1970), 10–11.

5. Karl Barth, *Church Dogmatics*, 1/1, trans. G. T. Thomson (Edinburgh: T. & T. Clark, 1936), 477.

6. I have begun these reflections on the Trinity with the traditional "second person," as does the Presbyterian Brief Statement of Faith. Barth offers a good argument: "Biblical revelation has a definite historical center, while the doctrine of the Trinity has a definite historical occasion, in biblical revelation. Historically speaking, the three questions answered in the Bible as to Revealer, Revelation, and Revealedness have not the same weight; it is rather the second of these concepts, God's action in His revelation, . . . which is the real theme of the biblical witness. . . . And so, too, the doctrine of the Trinity historically considered, in its origin and construction, has not been interested equally in Father, Son and Holy Spirit; here also the theme was primarily the Second Person of the Trinity" (ibid., 361).

7. Immanuel Kant, *The Conflict of the Faculties*, trans. Mary J. Gregor (Lincoln, Neb.: University of Nebraska Press, 1992), 66–67.

8. Robert Wilken, "The Resurrection of Jesus and the Doctrine of the Trinity," *Word and World* 2, no. 1 (Winter 1982): 28.

9. To mention just one point, the debate over the *filioque* clause in the creed which has so divided Eastern and Western Christians down the centuries will not be discussed.

10. See, e.g., Wolfhart Pannenberg, *Systematic Theology*, vol. 1, trans. Geoffrey W. Bromiley (Grand Rapids: Wm. B. Eerdmans Publishing Co., 1991), 296; Jürgen Moltmann, *The Trinity and the Kingdom*, trans. Margaret Kohl (San Francisco: Harper, 1991), 64; and LaCugna, *God for Us*, 2.

11. Pannenberg, *Systematic Theology*, 1:296, 298. Barth does begin his account of the Trinity, "In order to achieve the necessary conceptual clarification of the question of the Subject of revelation . . ." (Barth, *Church Dogmatics*, 1/1, 348). But he also says that such analysis only "brings us in a preliminary way into proximity with the problem of the doctrine of the Trinity" (ibid., 343).

12. Rahner, *The Trinity*, 22.

13. Augustine, *Enchiridion* 38, trans. J. F. Shaw (Chicago: Henry Regnery Company, 1961), 47–49; Basil, Letter 189.7, *Letters*, trans. Agnes Clare Way (New York: Fathers of the Church, 1955), 31; Aquinas, *Summa Theologiae* 3a., q.3, a.5, trans. R. J. Hennessey, vol. 48 (London: Eyre and Spottiswoode, 1976), 99–100; and Barth, *Church Dogmatics*, 1/1, 416—to cite an impressive range of authorities.

14. Rahner, *The Trinity*, 23. See also Eberhard Jüngel, "Das Verhältnis von 'ökonomisches' und 'immanenter' Trinität," *Zeitschrift für Theologie und Kirche* 72 (1975): 353–65.

15. In Rahner, "The possibility of a *deus absconditus* . . . who lurks behind *deus revelatus* is banished once and for all. There is no God who might turn out to be different from the God of salvation history" (LaCugna, *God for Us*, 211). For an extension of the implications of Rahner's identification of economic and immanent Trinities, see Piet Schoonenberg, "Trinität—der vollendete Bund," *Orientierung* 37 (May 31, 1973): 115–17. Barth anticipated Rahner's basic point: "The reality of God in His revelation is not to be bracketed with an 'only,' as though somewhere behind His revelation there stood another reality of God, but the reality of God which meets us in revelation is His reality in all the depths of eternity" (Barth, *Church Dogmatics*, 1/1, 548). In Robert Jenson's language, if "God is *our* God antecedently in himself," then God is "action and relatedness [and] . . . history antecedently in himself" (Jenson, *The Triune Identity*, 138).

16. "If . . . we can speak of the trintarian relations only as enacted and never as internal, then the only life that God has is the life that is (must be?) shared with creatures" (J. A. DiNoia, review of *God for Us*, by Catherine Mowry LaCugna, *Modern Theology* 9 (1993): 216.

17. See also Col. 1:15.

18. Jesus refuses to assign James and John places on his right and left, saying that such matters are the Father's business (Matt. 20:23). He does not, he says, know how the age will end, for only the Father knows this (Mark 13:32).

19. Quoted in Moltmann, *The Trinity and the Kingdom*, 165.

20. Thomas Aquinas, *Summa contra Gentiles* 4.11.19., trans. Charles J. O'Neil (Garden City, N.Y.: Image Books, 1957), 90.

21. Joachim Jeremias, *New Testament Theology*, trans. John Bowden (New York: Charles Scribner's Sons, 1971), 61–68.

22. This analysis, unfortunately, lies behind A Brief Statement of Faith, Presbyterian Church (U.S.A.). See William C. Placher and David Willis-Watkins, *Belonging to God: A Commentary on "A Brief Statement of Faith"* (Louisville, Ky.: Westminster/John Knox Press, 1992), 94–95.

23. See Pannenberg, *Systematic Theology*, 1:260.

24. See Joachim Jeremias, *The Prayers of Jesus*, trans. John Bowden (Naperville, Ill.: Alec R. Allenson, 1967), 57–65; and James Barr, "*Abba* Isn't Daddy," *Journal of Theological Studies* 39 (1988): 28–47.

25. Mary Rose D'Angelo, "Abba and 'Father,'" *Journal of Biblical Literature* 111 (1992): 614–16. I am indebted to Amy Plantinga Pauw for first calling my attention to this important article.

26. Ibid.
27. Elisabeth Schüssler Fiorenza, *In Memory of Her: A Feminist Theological Reconstruction of Christian Origins* (New York: Crossroad, 1983), 105–53.
28. See ibid., 149–51; see also Diane Tennis, *Is God the Only Reliable Father?* (Philadelphia: Westminster Press, 1985).
29. Phyllis Trible, "God the Father," *Theology Today* 37 (1980): 118.
30. Jürgen Moltmann, *The Crucified God*, trans. R. A. Wilson and John Bowden (New York: Harper & Row, 1974), 252.
31. Elizabeth A. Johnson, *She Who Is: The Mystery of God in Feminist Theological Discourse* (New York: Crossroad, 1992), 210.
32. There is also the medieval tradition of reference to Jesus as Mother.
33. Anne E. Carr, *Transforming Grace: Christian Tradition and Women's Experience* (San Francisco: Harper & Row, 1988), 139–40.
34. Having praised diversity of usage, I am embarrassed that, as the introductory note on language warned it would, the rest of this chapter so consistently uses the language of "Father" and "Son." As I traced complex historical arguments, it proved excessively confusing when my own commentary was using varied language different from that of the sources whose views I was tracing.
35. John Calvin, *Institutes of the Christian Religion* 2.16.4, ed. John T. McNeill, trans. Ford Lewis Battles (Philadelphia: Westminster Press, 1960), 506. See the interesting discussion of Calvin on God's compassionate Fatherhood in Brian A. Gerrish, *Grace and Gratitude: The Eucharistic Theology of John Calvin* (Minneapolis: Fortress Press, 1993), 28, 38–41.
36. See Pannenberg, *Systematic Theology*, 1:423. "The being of the obedient man Jesus can be taken up into God's own being, as the confession of his lordship would have it, only if God's being is understood as love" (Regin Prenter, "Der Gott, der Liebe ist," *Theologische Literaturzeitung* 96 [1971]: 406).
37. Yves Congar, *I Believe in the Holy Spirit*, trans. David Smith, vol. 3 (New York: Seabury Press, 1983), 5. The Spirit is "faceless" (Walter Kasper), "shadowy" (John Macquarrie), "ghostly" (Georgia Harkness), the "poor relation" of the Trinity (Norman Pittenger) (Johnson, *She Who Is*, 130).
38. Jerome, *Commentary on Isaiah* 11 (on Isa. 49:9–11), *Patrologia Latina* 24, 419b; cited in Congar, *I Believe in the Holy Spirit*, 3: 157.
39. Rosemary Radford Ruether, *Sexism and God-Talk: Toward a Feminist Theology* (Boston: Beacon Press, 1983), 60.
40. Although on the other hand: "In the divine economy it is not the feminine person who remains hidden and at home. She is God in the world, moving, stirring up, revealing, interceding. It is she who calls out, sanctifies, and animates the church" (Jay G.

Williams, "Yahweh, Women and the Trinity," *Theology Today* 32
[1975]: 240).

41. Barth, *Church Dogmatics*, 1/1, 535. That marvelous theologian
Austin Farrer, for instance, writes, "The revealed parable of the
Godhead is a story about two characters, Father and Son. . . . The
Trinity is not (in human terms) a society of three but a society of
two" (Austin Farrer, *Saving Belief* [London: Hodder & Stough-
ton, 1964], 128–29. Rowan Williams worries that even in
Barth, "the relative clarity of the treatment of Father and Son is it-
self put into question by the apparent failure of the same method
to produce an adequate theology of the Spirit," and notes that
Jüngel, following Barth on the Trinity, almost never mentions the
Spirit (Rowan Williams, "Barth on the Triune God," in *Karl
Barth*, ed. Stephen Sykes [New York: Oxford University Press,
1979], 171).

42. I find intriguing but not finally persuasive Peter Hodgson's proposal to identify (with qualifications) "One" with the Father,
"loves" with the Son, and "freedom" with the Spirit. See Peter C.
Hodgson, *God in History: Shapes of Freedom* (Nashville: Abingdon
Press, 1989), 94.

43. Walter Kasper, *The God of Jesus Christ*, trans. Matthew O'Connell
(New York: Crossroad, 1984), 202. "The Spirit appears as resistance, rising above all hatred, hoping against all hope. The Spirit is
that little flicker of fire burning at the bottom of the woodpile.
More rubbish is piled on, rain puts out the flame, wind blows the
smoke away. But underneath everything a brand still burns on, un-
quenchable. . . . The Spirit sustains the feeble breath of life in the
empire of death" (Boff, *Trinity and Society*, 217).

44. "The Trinitarian event, then, means that the Father's 'womb' is
'empty' once he has generated the Son, that the Son who is God
in receiving rather than taking is 'poor'. . . that the Holy Spirit as
mere 'breath' of the Father and Son is in some sense also 'without
being'—in other words the self-giving of the persons within the
trinitarian life of love, which includes the way in which each person allows the other two to be, involves this kind of freedom of
space, without any implication that God is less than God because
of this" (Gerard O'Hanlon, *The Immutability of God in the Theology of Hans Urs von Balthasar* [Cambridge: Cambridge University
Press, 1987], 55).

45. Augustine, *On the Trinity* 5.10., trans. Stephen McKenna (Washington, D.C.: Catholic University of America Press, 1963), 187.
"As a piece of trinitarian language, *hypostasis* is merely an item of
linguistic debris knocked from Hellenistic philosophy by collision
with Yahweh" (Jenson, *The Triune Identity*, 108).

46. Augustine, *On the Trinity* 9.5, p. 275.

47. Ibid., 9.15, p. 284.
48. Ibid., p. 285.
49. Ibid., 9.7, p. 276.
50. Ibid., 9.18, p. 289.
51. Richard of St.-Victor, *The Trinity* 3.2, p. 375; I am using Grover A. Zinn's translation from the volume on Richard of St. Victor in the Classics of Western Spirituality series (New York: Paulist Press, 1979). So far as I can tell, this is the first English translation of Richard's work on the Trinity.
52. Ibid., 3.3, p. 376.
53. Ibid., 3.11, pp. 384–85. Thus I think Moltmann is wrong to worry that in Richard the Spirit is merely a relation between two persons rather than a person. Augustine may be a more complicated case, but in Richard the analogy is to lover, beloved, and third person with whom mutual love can be shared, *not* to lover, beloved, and love. See Jürgen Moltmann, "Antwort," in *Diskussion über Jürgen Moltmanns Buch "Der gekreuzigte Gott,"* ed. Wolf-Dieter Marsch (Munich: Chr. Kaiser Verlag, 1967), 186.
54. I agree that there is a problem in Augustine's Trinitarianism, but I do not think it lies in his rather careful use of the psychological analogy. Rather, it concerns the problem that, as noted at the beginning of this chapter, LaCugna has argued afflicts the theological tradition since Athanasius: Trinitarian thought has gotten separated from the history of God's salvific activity in history. As Robert Jenson puts it in typically forceful fashion, Augustine's influence "has blighted our trinitarianism, for Augustine experienced the triune character of God himself as one thing and the history of salvation as quite another. Thus the trinitarian formulas lost their original function" (Jenson, *The Triune Identity*, 116). To put the matter in more technical fashion, the result is that the "missions" (the movements of God into the world) are completely separated from the "processions" (the internal relations among the persons). See ibid., 125. "'Being sent' and 'being given' are terms applying to God only in time; 'generation' and 'spiration,' only in eternity" (Thomas Aquinas, *Summa Theologiae* 1.43.2., vol. 7, trans. T. C. O'Brien [London: Eyre and Spottiswoode, 1976], 213).
55. William J. Hill, *The Three-Personed God: The Trinity as a Mystery of Salvation* (Washington, D.C.: University Press of America, 1983), 61.
56. Moltmann, *The Trinity and the Kingdom*, 139. For a similar claim about both Barth and Rahner, see LaCugna, *God for Us*, 254. "Augustine only gets beyond Modalism by the mere assertion that he does not wish to be a Modalist, and by the aid of ingenious distinctions between different ideas" (Adolf von Harnack, *History of Dogma*, trans. E. B. Speirs and James Millar, vol. 4 [London: Williams & Norgate, 1898], 131).

57. George Hunsinger, review of *The Trinity and the Kingdom*, *The Thomist* 47 (January 1983): 131. The "danger of tritheism is even clearer" for Moltmann's theology in *The Trinity and the Kingdom* (Kasper, *The God of Jesus Christ*, 379 n. 183).

58. "The 'imago Trinitatis' . . . can only be developed in two opposite lines of being and thought that point to each other. The one is the inner structure of the created spirit, which Augustine thoroughly explored. . . . But . . . [this] closes the created spirit in on itself and is unable to show how genuine objectification and genuine love—which is always directed toward the other—can come about. So the image of God must also lie in the opposite movement of the Spirit that compels it to go out from itself, that is, from the 'I' to the 'thou.' . . . It is inappropriate, therefore, on the basis of the strictness of the first schema, where similarity to God lies primarily in the unity of the Spirit, to ban all use of the second schema, that is, to declare it impossible for the Persons within the Godhead to say 'Thou.' Conversely it is mistaken to take a naive construction of the divine mystery after the pattern of human relationships (as Richard of St.-Victor attempted by way of a counterblast to Augustine) and make it absolute; for it fails to take into account the crude anthropomorphism involved in a plurality of beings. The creaturely image must be content to look in the direction of the mystery of God from its two starting points at the same time; the lines of perspective meet at an invisible point, in eternity" (Hans Urs von Balthasar, *Theo-Drama III*, trans. Graham Harrison [San Francisco: Ignatius Press, 1992], 526–27).

59. George Herbert Mead, "The Mechanism of Social Consciousness," *Selected Writings*, ed. Andrew J. Reck (Chicago: University of Chicago Press, 1964), 134–41.

60. Martin Buber, *I and Thou*, trans. Ronald Gregor Smith (New York: Charles Scribner's Sons, 1958), 11. Having grown up on this translation of Buber, I cannot break myself of it. John D. Zizioulas talked about how "person" means "openness of being," *ekstasis*, so that to be a person is to be open toward communion and self-transcendence (John D. Zizioulas, "Human Capacity and Human Incapacity: A Theological Exploration of Personhood," *Scottish Journal of Theology* 28 [1975]: 408).

61. Ovid, *Metamorphoses*, trans. Mary M. Innes (Harmondsworth, Middlesex: Penguin Books, 1955), 85. See also Julia Kristeva, *Tales of Love*, trans. Leon S. Roudiez (New York: Columbia University Press, 1987), 103–21.

62. G. W. F. Hegel, *The Phenomenology of Mind*, trans. J. B. Baillie (New York: Harper & Row, Harper Torchbooks, 1967), 232.

63. Ibid., 237.

64. Ovid, *Metamorphoses*, 83.

65. Emmanuel Levinas, *Time and the Other*, trans. Richard A. Cohen (Pittsburgh: Duquesne University Press, 1987), 83. "The face is, from the start, the demand. . . . It is the frailty of the one who needs you, who is counting on you. . . . It is not at all a question of a subject faced with an object" (Emmanuel Levinas, "The Paradox of Morality," in *The Provocation of Levinas*, ed. Robert Bernasconi and David Wood [London: Routledge & Kegan Paul, 1988], 171).

66. Emmanuel Levinas, *Collected Philosophical Papers*, trans. Alphonso Lingis (Dordrecht: Martinus Nijhoff, 1987), 55.

67. Jean-François Lyotard, "Levinas' Logic," trans. Ian McLeod, in *The Lyotard Reader*, ed. Andrew Benjamin (Oxford: Basil Blackwell Publisher, 1989), 276.

68. Our body "is the tragic instrument which leads to communion with others but at the same time it is the 'mask' of hypocrisy, the fortress of individualism, the vehicle of the final separation, death" (Zizioulas, *Being as Communion*, 52). I think this mixes up embodiedness and sin.

69. See Harry A. Wolfson, *The Philosophy of the Church Fathers* (Cambridge, Mass.: Harvard University Press, 1956), 421. Wolfson's discussion (pp. 418–28) remains the best survey of the historical issues about perichoresis in English. For the passage from Gregory of Nazianzus, see Letter 101, to Cledonius the Priest against Apollinaris, trans. Charles Gordon Browne and James Edward Swallow, *The Nicene and Post-Nicene Fathers*, 2d ser., vol. 7 (New York: Christian Literature Co., 1893), 439–43.

70. Daniel L. Migliore, *Faith Seeking Understanding: An Introduction to Christian Theology* (Grand Rapids: Wm. B. Eerdmans Publishing Co., 1991), 70. "Precisely through the personal characteristics that distinguish them from one another, the Father, the Son and the Spirit dwell in one another and communicate eternal life to one another. In the perichoresis, the very thing that divides them becomes that which binds them together. The 'circulation' of the eternal divine life becomes perfect through the fellowship and unity of the three different Persons in the eternal love" (Moltmann, *The Trinity and the Kingdom*, 175).

71. "That which is common and one is considered in actuality by reason of the co-eternity and identity of substance, operation, and will and by reason of the agreement in judgment and the identity of power, virtue, and goodness—I did not say *similarity*, but *identity*. . . . For there is one essence, one goodness, one virtue, one intent, one operation, one power—one and the same, not three similar one to another, but one and the same motion of the three Persons" (John of Damascus, *The Orthodox Faith* 1.8, trans. Frederic H. Chase, Jr. [New York: Fathers of the Church, 1958], 186).

72. Ibid., 187.
73. Gregory of Nyssa, *To Ablabius: On "Not Three Gods,"* trans. H. C. Ogle, *The Nicene and Post-Nicene Fathers,* 2d ser., vol. 5 (New York: Christian Literature Co., 1892), 334; I have slightly revised the translation.
74. Gregory of Nazianzus, "The Fifth Theological Oration: On the Holy Spirit," *Orations* 31.14, trans. Charles Gordon Browne and James Edward Swallow, *The Nicene and Post-Nicene Fathers,* 2d ser., vol. 7 (New York: Christian Literature Co., 1893), 322. See Jenson, *The Triune Identity,* 113. "Through this reciprocal participation the three modes of being *become* concretely united. In this concrete unity they *are* God" (Jüngel, *The Doctrine of the Trinity,* 32).
75. Barth, *Church Dogmatics,* 1/1, 425; and Moltmann, *The Trinity and the Kingdom,* 157.
76. Gregory of Nazianzus, "The Third Theological Oration: On the Son," *Orations* 29.2, *The Nicene and Post-Nicene Fathers,* 2d ser., 7: 301.
77. Quoted in Moltmann, *The Trinity and the Kingdom,* 195.
78. Ignatius, "Letter to the Magnesians" 3, *Early Christian Fathers,* 95.
79. Patricia Wilson-Kastner, *Faith, Feminism, and the Christ* (Philadelphia: Fortress Press, 1983), 122–23. "The trinitarian God is eminently God for us, whereas the unitarian God is eminently God for himself alone" (Catherine Mowry LaCugna, "The Baptismal Formula, Feminist Objections, and Trinitarian Theology," *Journal of Ecumenical Studies* 26 [Spring 1989]: 243).
80. Kasper, *The God of Jesus Christ,* 307. "God loves in freedom, lives in community, and wills creatures to live in community. God is self-sharing, other-regarding, community forming love. This is what might be called the 'depth grammar' of the doctrine of the Trinity" (Migliore, *Faith Seeking Understanding,* 64).
81. Carr, *Transforming Grace,* 156–57.
82. Jenson, *Triune Identity,* 33.
83. Johnson, *She Who Is,* 216.
84. Dante, *Paradiso* 33.116–20, trans. Charles S. Singleton (Princeton: Princeton University Press, 1975), 379. I warned at the outset that I would not be discussing the *filioque,* and I have cut the quotation off before Dante moved on to include that in his image.

Part 2

Diversities

4 Gospels' Ends

The Vulnerability of
Biblical Narratives

In A.D. 423, Theodoret of Cyrrhus, newly made a bishop, discovered that copies of Tatian's *Diatessaron* were widely available in his diocese out along the Euphrates. Horrified, he issued a vigorous denunciation and burned as many as he could find—at least two hundred. It is rather surprising that the work that inspired this outburst of pious fury was simply a compilation of the stories and sayings from the four canonical Gospels into one continuous narrative.[1]

Book burning represents the most repressive side of any tradition, yet Theodoret, however much one deplores his methods, was in an odd way striking a blow against repression and in favor of diversity, and he was doing so in a way that was characteristic of most of the Christian tradition.[2] With very rare exceptions, Christians have respected the distinctness of the four different Gospels. One should not take this for granted. Having four different stories of Jesus' ministry is at least inconvenient, and their inconsistencies lead beyond inconvenience to embarrassment and potential scandal. Moreover, this is a fixable problem; piecing together a single narrative with only quite minimal excisions is actually not that difficult. Yet with rare exceptions Christians have not done it.

This chapter will consider ways in which the Gospel narratives accept diversity, let multiple voices speak, leave ambiguities in place, and thus do not attempt to impose a neat master narrative on

Christian existence. Saying that, however, exacerbates some already complex questions about the truth of these narratives. If the church had followed Tatian in conflating the Gospels, ironing out inconsistencies in the process, then Christians would have a coherent narrative whose historical truth they could, at least in principle, affirm. But given diversities, ambiguities, and ironies, what are Christians to believe about the truth of these narratives? Perhaps their very diversity and ambiguity represent part of the meaning of these texts, one of the ways in which they function for readers by raising questions about the varied voices within the world they narrate and the relation of that world to history and to the reality of their readers. One cannot judge their truth without first having understood their complex meanings.

The fourfold Gospels exemplify a larger issue. The Christian Bible contains the most diverse miscellany of small and large pieces—nonnarrative material such as letters and laws, hymns and sayings, as well as stories. And among the stories there are connections, gaps, repetitions, apparent inconsistencies, hints of other stories left untold—the list goes on. The Bible also contains, of course, Hebrew scriptures we call the Old Testament, as well as the New Testament.[3] Paul Ricoeur has remarked that God is "intended by the convergence of all these partial discourses."[4] The narratives of this God who eschews brute force were not edited with the brute force necessary to impose a single, clear framework. Indeed, the way they talk about the relation of text, history, and reader gets lost if one tries to impose such a single perspective. As the end of this chapter will indicate, it is just in the diversity of their narrative strategies that these narratives connect their worlds to the worlds of their readers.

Even as the Christian tradition has preserved biblical diversity, however, Christian theologians have often ignored its implications. In periods when the literary tradition emphasized narrative coherence, a similar emphasis naturally developed in biblical interpretation—if the Gospels told stories and if realistic novels were the dominant form of written story in a culture, then the Gospels must be like realistic novels. Societies with clear hierarchies of power naturally looked for, and therefore found, in scripture a coherent, univocal authority. Perhaps our time, just as it has proven to be fertile ground for reflection on divine vulnerability, can provide us with the intellectual resources to see more clearly the diversity of the Bible—with Jacques Derrida or Paul de Man deconstructing texts, with Frank Kermode finding opacity and loose ends, and with

88

feminist critics calling attention to repressed voices just behind texts. Yet too often theologians still fail to attend to such lessons. Many of the traditions of biblical literalism of course treat the Bible as a seamless whole. But many of those who talk these days about the use of biblical narrative in theology also emphasize the unity of the (singular?) story.

Hans Frei's constructive proposal in Christology, *The Identity of Jesus Christ*, which has influenced this book in many ways, reads a variety of Gospel texts with great sensitivity, but it does work primarily with Luke, focusing not only on one Gospel but on the one that has the smoothest narrative coherence.[5] George Lindbeck talks about "the canonical narrative" and sometimes seems to treat it as a unified whole that rather straightforwardly provides a framework for Christian understanding.[6] To move to other authors who use terms such as "narrative" and "story," Gabriel Fackre titled his introduction to Christian theology *The Christian Story*, and he regularly uses that singular phrase, with both "Christian" and "Story" capitalized.[7] Stanley Hauerwas celebrates the virtues of a Christian community formed by a Christian story—again the nouns, both of them, are usually singular.[8]

Such voices praise the unity and coherence they claim for "the story." From another point of view, Susan Handelman, in her fascinating book *The Slayers of Moses*, contrasts a Jewish tradition in which interpretation rests on "principles of multiple meaning and endless interpretability," with the Christian claim that the incarnation of the Word makes a final, definitive interpretation possible.[9] Handelman rejoices in the recent recovery of the Jewish richness of conflicting, always unfinished interpretation from Freud to Derrida to Harold Bloom. For her, unity and coherence and singular meaning are Christian vices rather than Christian virtues, but Christian characteristics nonetheless.

But is the package of Christian scripture all that neatly tied? Can we talk about *the* Christian story, *the* biblical narrative? Not without a great many qualifications. Christians learn about a vulnerable God through complex and ambiguous narratives in which no one story overpowers all the others. Partially repressed voices make themselves heard, and honest readers have to struggle with diversity and ambiguity as they think about how these texts make sense and relate to their own worlds. To illustrate the point, consider a deceptively simple question: The Gospels tell the story of Jesus. How does that story end?

The obvious first problem, of course, is, in which Gospel?

The differences do not involve merely variation of detail. Contrast Mark's frightened women fleeing the empty tomb with Matthew's great commission from the mountaintop in Galilee with Luke's account of the disciples walking back to Jerusalem with John's mysterious final appearance by the seashore. The mood, the dramatic shape of the ending, varies radically from one to another.

But the difficulties grow worse. With at least three of the Gospels, one cannot even define what counts as the end. With Mark, there is manuscript evidence for a long ending and a short one. In purely textual terms the preponderance of the evidence supports the shorter ending, but its astonishing abruptness bewilders in its content and even grammatical structure. A mysterious young man appears to the women at the tomb. "So they went out and fled from the tomb, for terror and amazement had seized them; and they said nothing to anyone, for they were afraid" (Mark 16:8).[10] The Greek is even stranger, for there the sentence ends with *gar*, the word that gets translated "for." "They said nothing to anyone; they were scared was why," is as close a translation idiomatic English permits. It is just grammatically possible, but it is certainly an odd way to end a book, and interpreters of Mark have constantly struggled with the problem. A long tradition of distinguished scholars even posits, without any evidence except the sheer implausibility of things as they are, a lost final page of the original Gospel.[11]

John poses a different problem. Most scholars agree that John 21, the end of the Gospel, was not part of the original text.[12] But was it added by a redactor or by the original author? If by a redactor, how soon did he come along, and what else did he change? For that matter, after all these years, is it the earlier version or the redacted one that counts as "The Gospel according to John"?[13] Someone or other seems willing to defend almost every possible hypothesis. Luke seems at first to have a textually unproblematic ending, but then of course Luke also wrote the book of Acts. So does the end of the Gospel count as the end of his story, or only the middle? Matthew seems to be the only case of a Gospel with a straightforward ending,[14] although even there the apparently explicit Trinitarian language of Jesus' final words has left some scholars wondering whether this is perhaps theologically a bit too good to be true and might be a later addition.

Such textual questions are of course only preliminary. It is bad enough that "the story of Jesus" has four different endings and that at least three of the four pose textual problems. What strange endings these Gospels have. Mark offers the most dramatic case:

confronted with the empty tomb, the women flee in fear and tell no one, the male disciples long since gone—and there the Gospel ends. John ends with Jesus' mysterious appearance by the Sea of Tiberias. Jesus asks Peter some questions that neither Peter nor the reader understands very well, there are enigmatic references to the fate of the disciple whom Jesus loved, and the text concludes by reporting, in the third person, that this very disciple is the one who has written the words we have been reading—assuming, of course, that those concluding words are part of the original text, the original text, that is, of the editorial addition of John 21. This is itself a matter of some debate.[15] By comparison, the final appearances in Luke and Matthew come as a relief in their clarity, although one might have hoped for a straight answer as to whether all this happened in Jerusalem or in Galilee.

You need not deconstruct these texts. They fall apart in your hands. Gospel writers seem to be like prophets as Luther described them: they "have a queer way of talking, like people who, instead of proceeding in an orderly manner, ramble off from one thing to the next, so that you cannot make head or tail of them or see what they are getting at."[16] One feels inclined to say of the Gospels together what Frank Kermode says of Mark's Gospel: that it is, "to put the matter too simply— . . . either enigmatic or terrible, or . . . muddled."[17] Either the Gospels are a kafkaesque house of mirrors, turning every insider into an outsider, or else they are just an incoherent text, and the trick has been to sustain for nearly two thousand years the game of trying to make sense of them. But a trick either way.

"Why is this scripture so unclear?" Ludwig Wittgenstein once asked. It seemed, he said, as though someone wanted to deliver a warning about some terrible danger, but told a riddle, so that listeners failed to get the warning until and unless they figured out the riddle.[18] If the warning were urgent, what an odd procedure. Yet surely one cannot infer some lack of urgency for the biblical message. "Isn't it possible," Wittgenstein continued, "that it was essential in this case to 'tell a riddle'?" Might there be something about the content of these works such that a complex, ambiguous text—a riddle, so to speak—oddly enough provided the clearest way to convey their particular burden? If so, a hermeneutics appropriate to these texts would need to take that into account.

For one thing, the texts seem to resist certain kinds of literalism. When we read the biblical texts, it often emerges that, if we try to take them as a set of propositions whose individual and collective truth we are to believe, we find that the project does not work very well. Bultmann was right about this; "the New Testament already invites criticism."[19] The attempt to read it as a set of true propositions keeps running up against so many puzzles that it seems that either this text does not make any sense at all or else such approaches are going about reading it in the wrong way. Chronologies are inconsistent, lists of disciples vary, we find reports of events no one could have witnessed, and so on. As noted at the beginning of this chapter, the fact of four different Gospels in itself raises a host of questions. Some of the puzzles strike home so immediately that, as Wittgenstein remarked in a very different connection, for a mistake this seems too big.[20] Determined enough readers, to be sure, can stick to it, but in the face of the character of these texts, one begins to feel like Ptolemaic astronomers, balancing epicycle on epicycle, and to look for other ways of reading them.

As already noted in the Introduction and in chapter 1, Hans Frei proposed one alternative. The stories capture through narrative a person's identity. Reading these stories, one learns who Jesus is— that is, one learns both the characteristics of his human life and the fact that that human life was somehow the self-revelation of God. Many of the individual episodes serve as biographical anecdotes, "true" if they illustrate his character authentically even though the particular incident they narrate never happened, and the overall shape of the narrative portrays something of Jesus' identity.

While such an identity description need not be correct in all its particulars in order to get someone's identity right, its general themes do have to capture a person's essential features, and *some* of its particulars may be crucial. Plato may have made up most of the dialogues and still shown us who Socrates really was, but if Socrates was never ironic, or if he tried to run away at the end, then Plato was wrong about him. Similarly, if Jesus never taught about love, or if the disciples, as Reimarus argued two hundred years ago, conspired to invent the story of the resurrection so that they would not have to go back to fishing, then the Gospels are wrong about Jesus.

As a child, one sometimes hears a variety of stories about an eccentric relative. The stories may conflict with each other, or at least seem to do so, and some may turn out not to be true, but it could nevertheless be the case that, on finally getting to know Uncle John or Great-Aunt Sarah, one realizes that those stories were giving an authentic picture of this person's identity. "I had developed an idea of who she was, and I turn out to have been right." Christians believe, I am suggesting, that the Gospel narratives give such pictures of the identity of Jesus Christ. If we came to know Jesus, we would, without worrying about many of their details, say that through them we had come accurately to know who he is. Notice, incidentally, that such a claim is compatible with having significantly different pictures before us. My set of anecdotes about Great-Aunt Sarah may give an idea different from yours, and perhaps only getting to know the person herself would enable us to see how both of us can have authentic senses of her identity, fitting together in unexpected ways.

Historical evidence, on this account, can *refute* faith. Theological reflection on the logic of the narratives as identity descriptions works out what themes or particulars of the story are crucial to Jesus' identity and, if historical evidence persuasively refuted the relevant claims, one would have to give up—either give up this sort of theological project or give up being a Christian.

To say that is to rule out a certain kind of poststructuralist Christian theology. Some deconstructionist literary critics invite their readers into a world in which there are only texts, in which, in Jacques Derrida's terms, "reading . . . cannot legitimately transgress the text toward something other than it, toward a referent (a reality that is metaphysical, historical, psychobiological, etc.) or toward a signified outside the text whose content could take place, could have taken place outside of language. . . . There is nothing outside the text."[21] But if there is nothing outside these texts, then they are not identity descriptions of the person Jesus was.

An example from a very different field may help drive the point home. In the 1890s, working with the young women among his first patients, Sigmund Freud reached the disturbing conclusion that the source of many of their hysterical conditions could be traced back to traumatic and repressed experiences of sexual abuse by their fathers. None of Freud's conclusions generated more controversy, for the implications about all too many Viennese families were horrifying. It alienated Freud from his colleagues, to say nothing of its effect on the fathers of his patients, who were often paying the bills.

For whatever reasons, Freud gradually changed his mind. At first he entertained the possibility that a few of these young women might be inventing their stories. By the time he wrote the classical statements of psychoanalytic theory, he had convinced himself that the reports were consistently fictitious, accusations of fantasy. But, he further concluded, it did not matter: the stories dwelt within the unconsciousnesses of these young women, and "this psychical reality requires to be taken into account alongside practical reality."[22] "There can be no doubt," Freud wrote in 1916, "of the imaginary nature of the accusation . . . [but] up to the present we have not succeeded in pointing to any difference in the consequences whether phantasy or reality has had the greater share in these events of childhood."[23]

But of course Freud was wrong. For the process of analysis itself, the distinction between reality and fantasy may not have mattered—although even that could be a subject for debate. For one's picture of Vienna, however, and for a good many questions of public policy, it made every difference in the world. Should Freud's readers have worried about the pathology that produces imaginary accusations or about the sexual violence of Viennese fathers? Freud's decision to avoid the question of fact did much damage by turning attention from problems of real male abuse to supposed problems of overactive female imaginations, and it is therefore disturbing to realize that Freud's growing indifference to the relation of the text—in this case the dream text—to any external reality is very likely the source of so much of the postmodern discourse of intertextuality, as a kind of dirty secret of postmodernism.

In the face of the pain of the world's victims, the Christian gospel and common human decency prohibit saying that one narrative simply interprets another in an infinite regress, with nothing that one might be so old-fashioned as to call "truth." Christian theologians cannot offer good news to the world's victims that claims only to be a story about a story about a story. Theology needs to tell some stories about what is true, and in this case about what is true concerning Jesus.

Yet, in important ways we know about Jesus only as he is presented to us in these stories. John Dominic Crossan, as he bravely embarks on the project yet once again, concedes that "historical Jesus research is becoming something of a scholarly bad joke." Within the last twenty-five years, major works by distinguished scholars have portrayed Jesus as a political revolutionary, a magician, a Galilean charismatic, a Galilean rabbi, a proto-Pharisee, an Essene, and an eschatological prophet, followed by Crossan's own account of Jesus as "a Mediterranean Jewish peasant."[24] Some versions may well have more plausibility than others, but when the experts disagree, the ordinary believer, the preacher, or the theologian cannot make faith rest on any one set of conclusions. As Lessing and Kierkegaard already noted, historical research gives us in the best of cases only probabilities, and faith calls us to a different kind of commitment. And historical research about Jesus is hardly the best of cases.

Similar problems arise with Schubert Ogden's proposal that we should take the New Testament as a witness, not to the historical Jesus, but to "the earliest traditions of Christian witness accessible to us today by historical-critical analysis of these writings."[25] Again we would be left with the faithful having nervously to await the latest word from the scholarly historical front, and at best with fragments and glimpses. For Ogden's existentialist interpretation, what the gospel needs to do is to confront us with a moment of decision, and a minimal earliest kerygma will do. But if we need to learn from the gospel who God is, then we need an identity description, and that means requiring more content.

In the confessional tradition of the Presbyterian church, when the Confession of 1967 claims that the Bible is not just "a witness" but "the witness without parallel," or when the Barmen Declaration calls believers to trust and obey not just in Jesus Christ but in "Jesus Christ, as he is attested for us in Holy Scripture,"[26] they are not proposing simply to use the Bible as one source on a par with others in an attempt to retrieve the historical Jesus or the earliest accessible layer of Christian witness but affirming that, in the complex sense earlier described, Christians should believe that the picture the New Testament provides of Jesus' identity gets it right.

Starting with these texts does not mean tying ourselves to textual literalism, because the texts themselves keep pushing us in varied directions: their diversity invites attention to a range of voices, they pose questions about their relation to history, and they challenge us to think about the relation of the stories they tell to our own lives. Starting with the texts might seem the "conservative" strategy, but it turns out to open up a richer, more complex field of interpretation than does limiting ourselves to the historical Jesus or the earliest kerygma.[27]

These narratives provide only a witness. Find the irrefutable letters in which the apostles describe their conspiracy to invent the whole story and, yes, Christians need to concede, that would mean we were wrong. But if historical evidence can refute, it cannot establish. The biblical narratives give us much more than historical evidence about Jesus or the earliest kerygma warrants. If the pattern of a Christian life, following a Jesus whom Christians claim to know, seems possible only by accepting an essential rightness in these narrative descriptions, therefore, the question arises inevitably: Why should one do that?

"The reasons for adopting just these writings as 'authority,'" David Kelsey has observed, "are as complex, unsystematic, and idiosyncratic as are the reasons individual persons have for becoming Christians."[28] Living one's life within a community whose corporate life these texts contribute to shaping, looking at the world in terms of the patterns and structure they describe, finding one's life transformed by the Jesus whose identity they narrate, one accepts the stories they offer. That act of acceptance does not imply believing the truth of their every proposition—as already indicated, the texts themselves resist such a way of interpreting them. It is not incompatible with finding that some of the things they say are very puzzling or utterly infuriating, as one continues to struggle with them.[29] Most basically, it simply means saying that, yes, Jesus is the One they say he is: the human person whose identity they narrate, and the self-revelation of God. To think through Christian claims about the relation of these texts to the Jesus to whom they witness is therefore to find oneself also thinking about their relation to one's own life.[30] If one accepts the account they give, that is not because of some doctrine of the authority of scripture that serves as a foundational starting point for a system of belief but because of the compelling quality that a whole web of belief has come to have for a particular reader. Reading these texts leads one to reflection not only on the narration and the history behind it but also on one's own world. Cornel West puts it well, casting the comment, as one must, in the mode of personal testimony:

> The self-understanding and self-identity that flow from this tradition's insights into the crises and traumas of life are indispensable *for me*. . . . Of course, the fundamental philosophical question remains whether the Christian gospel is ultimately true. And, as a Christian prophetic pragmatist whose focus is on coping with transient and provisional penultimate matters yet whose hope goes beyond them, I reply in the affirmative, bank my all on it, yet am willing to entertain the possibility in low moments that I may be deluded.[31]

Living with any number of doubts and questions, a Christian nevertheless finds these stories compelling in the interrelated accounts they give of Jesus' identity and of the character of our world—interrelated first because this can be the sort of world they claim only if Jesus was the one they assert him to be. I understand the world in the way that I do, I live in the world in the way that I do, as a Christian because of what I believe about Jesus' identity. But the dialectic works both ways: I find the Gospel accounts of Jesus persuasive in part because I understand and live in the world in the way that I do as a Christian. To live a Christian life is to find, however tentatively, what John Rawls would call a kind of reflective equilibrium between life and text.[32]

In thus interconnecting the world that the Gospels narrate with the world of our own lives, Christians are again doing something that the texts themselves seem to invite. To come full circle, reading the ends of the Gospels nicely illustrates just this point. Having earlier subjected those texts to a hermeneutics of suspicion, let me now look at them through the lens of a hermeneutics of faith chastened, I hope, by the lessons of suspicion. My claim will be that the relation of narrative world and readers' world I have been describing is not a hermeneutical approach simply imposed on the Gospels but one that grows naturally out of the forms of the narratives themselves. I begin considering the Gospels' ends with the Fourth Gospel.

John, notoriously, has two endings. John 20 ends with what seems like a full conclusion:

> Now Jesus did many other signs in the presence of his disciples, which are not written in this book. But these are written so that you may come to believe that Jesus is the Messiah, the Son of God, and that through believing you may have life in his name. (John 20:30–31)

But then John 21 starts up again, with the story of Jesus' appearance to the disciples by the Sea of Tiberias, again a complex story about Simon Peter and the disciple Jesus loved, and again a conclusion in which the narrator steps forward to speak directly to the readers.

The second half of John 20, which many scholars judge to be the original concluding narrative, tells the familiar story of doubting Thomas, who happens to be absent on the first occasion when Jesus appears to the disciples and will not believe; Jesus appears again, and Thomas can only exclaim, "My Lord and my God!" Jesus then replies, "Have you believed because you have seen me? Blessed are those who have not seen and yet have come to believe" (John 20:29). And who are they, these people who have believed without seeing? Readers have not yet encountered any such folk in the Gospel story—even the beloved disciple entered the tomb "and he saw and believed" (John 20:8). So the people who have not seen yet have come to believe can only be, actually or potentially,

97

those reading the Gospel. Indeed, at the end of John 20 the narrator pulls out of the narrative frame. These things are written, he says, "so that you may come to believe that Jesus is the Messiah, the Son of God, and that through believing you may have life in his name" (John 20:31). Notice, incidentally, that the "things" are "written" rather than "done"—the verb itself moves the focus from the characters in the story, who could witness Jesus' actions, to readers confronted by the written word.[33]

Then in John 21 something similar happens. The Gospel continues with the story of Jesus' appearance to the disciples by the Sea of Tiberias, but, in a way that has not happened before, the narrator keeps breaking in to make connections with the later life of the Christian community. Jesus speaks to Peter within the story—and his remark, the narrator explains, predicts something about how Peter will meet his death. Jesus answers a question about the beloved disciple enigmatically, and the narrator connects that answer with a rumor later "spread in the community" that that disciple would not die (John 21:23). These notes may or may not represent later editorial interpolations, but the text as we have it is suddenly pulling in and out of the narrative frame. Then it finally pulls out altogether. The next-to-the-last verse reveals that the beloved disciple "is the disciple who is testifying to these things and has written them, and we know that his testimony is true," not only an author announced but a community—that sudden "we"—verifying his testimony. The story includes the telling of the story and the life of its community of readers within itself. Raymond Brown puts it eloquently:

> Throughout the Gospel and more particularly in the Last Discourse, in what the evangelist has been describing on the stage of early 1st-century Palestine, he has had in mind an audience seated in the darkened theater of the future, silently viewing what Jesus was saying and doing. True to the limitations and logic of the stage drama imposed by the Gospel form, the Johannine Jesus could address that audience only indirectly through the disciples who shared the stage and gave voice to sentiments and reactions that were shared by the audience as well. But now, as the curtain is about to fall on the stage drama, the lights in the theater are suddenly turned on. Jesus shifts his attention from the disciples on the stage to the audience that has become visible and makes clear that his ultimate concern is for them—those who have come to believe in him through the word of his disciples. [34]

The endings of the Fourth Gospel, therefore, thrust its readers into a decision, for they bring us into the story and confront us with the Jesus whose identity they narrate. If this Jesus is the person the story claims, then, these two endings say, we ought to shape our lives accordingly. If we live our lives as Christians, then we presuppose that Jesus has this identity.

The same theme appears in the ends of Luke and Matthew as well. Consider, for instance, just how odd is Luke's introduction of the good news of resurrection. On the first day of the week, a group of women go to Jesus' tomb, only to find the stone rolled away and the tomb empty. They are perplexed (Luke 24:4). Then two men in dazzling clothes appear to them, and they are terrified (Luke 24:5). In the end they tell the news to the apostles, to whom the words seemed "an idle tale, and they did not believe them" (Luke 24:11). Peter goes to the tomb himself, as recounted in a verse that may or may not be an editorial addition,[35] and he is amazed, astonished. The whole first section of resurrection accounts has passed by without a single unambiguously positive verb to describe a response. Even later, when Jesus appears to the eleven, the only description of their reaction is that "they were startled and terrified, and thought that they were seeing a ghost" (Luke 24:37).

It is an ironic narrative that presents the victory of the resurrection in such nontriumphant language. As Wayne Booth has explained, one of the functions of irony can be to create a community of readers.[36] Authors invite readers to join them in the company of those who get the joke or see the point, precisely in contrast to the insensitive characters in the story, or hypothetical insensitive readers, who are missing it. So here the author of Luke invites us to join him, the author of a Gospel, in the community of those who have responded in faith to events that draw such ambiguous responses from the characters within the narrative.

Similarly, at the very end of Matthew, as the eleven disciples come to the mountaintop for their final commissioning, "they saw him, they worshiped him; but some doubted" (Matt. 28:17). Is one to infer that some of the disciples doubted? The text mentions no one else's presence. At any rate, here are some folk or other in the story face to face, as it were, with the resurrected Jesus—and doubting. References to doubt appear in a number of later resurrection traditions, but there, in the story of doubting Thomas for instance, they have an apologetic function: Doubts provide the occasion for decisive evidence.[37] Here, however, no such demonstration follows, and the only role of the doubt seems to be to leave the response within the narrated world ambiguous and thrust readers into the story as those called to make a decision. The enigmatic end of Mark performs the same function even more dramatically.[38] The story ends with the women running away in fear and telling no one. The rhetorical strategy is almost exactly the opposite of John's. Where that Gospel consciously stepped out of the frame of the narration to address the readers, Mark leaves its readers in a closed narrated world that seems to have come to a dead end—the only witnesses told no one.[39] Except that here is this Gospel. Someone must have talked. We are addressed from a community of faith, although no such community appears within the story itself. "The key to understanding the ending of Mark," as Robert Fowler puts it, "is not to understand the women or men in the story, but to understand what is happening in the women or men reading the story."[40] The effect of opposite narrative strategies is thus very similar: to ask, What about you, *hypocrite lecteur, mon semblable, mon frère?*

Michel Foucault's *Les mots et les choses* begins with a kind of meditation on Velazquez's painting *Las Meninas*.[41] On this canvas we see a number of figures from the Spanish court of the seventeenth century—the young daughter of the royal family, her ladies-in-waiting, a dwarf, a handsome dog, and, not least, the court artist, Velazquez himself. Nearly all the figures stare intently at the viewer, and the artist thoughtfully holds his brush and palette. The frame of the picture includes, left foreground, the edge of the back of a canvas, so that it is as if Velazquez had paused in the painting of our portrait, while the others from the court stare out at us attentively.

In the back of the room, however, one sees what seems at first to be a picture on the wall, but on closer examination it turns out to be a mirror, and in the mirror appear the king and queen of Spain, Philip IV and his wife Mariana. Of course, a reflective viewer realizes, it is *their* portrait that Velazquez has been painting, *they* at whom everyone is staring. We viewers cannot fit into the space of the world of this picture.

Velazquez has invited us, Foucault suggests, to reflect on the nature of our relationship to a painting. Looking on such a domestic scene, we are apt to locate ourselves in the room, a few feet to the front of the painting's foreground. But of course we cannot be in that sort of spatial relation to these people, for they are seventeenth-century Spaniards, now long dead, and we are in an art gallery, looking at a canvas. Velazquez uses all his artistry to bring us into the painting with vivid realism, and then he reminds us, with figures in a mirror, that there is literally no place for us in this world.

The artistry of the Gospel writers accomplishes something like the opposite effect. A realistic painting using the rules of perspective invites viewers into its space, so that a Velazquez or a Foucault has to shock us out. A narrative provides its readers with distance. We hear a story in the narrator's voice; even reading words on a page, we are somehow located in the narrator's world, not the world of the storied action. "Once upon a time . . . " the best stories begin, and we know that that time is not our time. But just as that mirror in the Spanish court shocks us out of the picture, so the Gospels' ends shock us into the story.

In his classic study of realistic narrative, *Mimesis*, Erich Auerbach contrasted Homer, whose narratives seek "merely to make us forget our own reality for a few hours," with the Bible, which "seeks to overcome our reality. We are to fit our own lives into its world, feel ourselves to be elements in its structure of universal history."[42] As a literary critic and not a theologian, Auerbach remained neutral on the question of the *truth* of the biblical narratives, but as to their *meaning*, he insisted that they make a "tyrannical" claim:

> It excludes all other claims. The world of the Scripture stories is not satisfied with claiming to be a historically true reality—it insists that it is the only real world, is destined for autocracy. All other scenes, issues, and ordinances have no right to appear independently of it, and it is promised that all of them, the history of all mankind, will be given their due place within its frame, will be subordinated to it. The Scripture stories do not, like Homer's, court our favor, they do not flatter us that they may please us and enchant us—they seek to subject us.[43]

As Robert Scholes and Robert Kellogg put it in a standard recent study of narrative,

> Meaning, in a work of narrative art, is a function of the relation between two worlds: the fictional world created by the author and the "real" world, the apprehendable universe. When we say we "understand" a narrative, we mean that we have found a satisfactory relationship or set of relationships between these two worlds.[44]

Christians understand the biblical texts to mean that the world they narrate *is* the real world, that we should place our lives within the framework they present. "It is within this framework," Karl Barth explains, "that the whole history of nature and the universe plays its specific role, and not the reverse, although logically and empirically the course of things ought to have been the reverse."[45] These narratives invite their readers to find themselves living in the world of the narratives. Those who accept that invitation will of course find themselves in a world where these stories have correctly narrated Jesus' identity. And Jesus' identity, as narrated in these texts, is that he is the one who has been resurrected. Each of the Gospels, in a different way, looks back on Jesus' life from the perspective of a community that believes in his resurrection, and they sort out the events of his life from that perspective. The resurrection provides the standpoint that in different ways gives each Gospel its narrative coherence as an identity description; absent the resurrection, they dissolve away from any clear picture of who this person is.[46] If Jesus was not resurrected, then we would be thrown back on the methods of critical historians to figure out as best we could some reality behind these misinterpretations of his life.

Mark, however, does not narrate resurrection appearances at all. His portrait of Jesus (I am, like most contemporary scholars, rejecting the longer Markan ending) concludes with Jesus dying on the cross as the centurion proclaims, "Truly this man was God's Son" (Mark 15:39). The fact of the Gospel, and the picture of Jesus it offers, imply that that was not the end of the story, for it is only a resurrected Jesus of whom this story, as it is told, makes sense. As chapter 1 above argued, however, part of Mark's point was to undercut the ideology of Christians who thought of Jesus as a powerful wonder-worker and themselves as continuing his triumphs. It would distort the point of the story, therefore, to have a resurrected Jesus "revealed" at the end of the story as really a figure of power after all. Jesus is revealed as the Son of God as the vulnerable, crucified one, since, after we see him hanging on the cross, we never see him again.

Any narrative of resurrection appearances, therefore, might seem to undercut Mark's narrative logic, and yet each of the other three Gospels finds a way to present such accounts that preserves Mark's point by consistently identifying the resurrected one as the crucified one. In Luke, the two disciples on the road to Emmaus remember that their hearts were burning just at the moment when this mysterious stranger was interpreting how the scripture shows that the Messiah must suffer. When the gathered disciples find that doubts arise in their hearts, he resolves them by showing the wounds on his hands and feet (Luke 24:40). The same thing happens in both appearances in the Thomas story in John 20. When Thomas finally cries, "My Lord and my God," incidentally, the phrase may well have been redolent with irony, for Domitian, a particularly brutal emperor, had begun to demand its use as one of his official titles, *Dominus et Deus noster*, likely about the time this Gospel was written.[47] "Lord and God" was the terminology of the most cynical worship of raw power. Yet Thomas bursts forth with this exclamation precisely when Jesus points to his wounds, a reminder yet again of the challenge that the Gospels embody to the usual assumptions about power. Matthew's resurrection narratives come closest to a *theologia gloriae*, with the angel who has an appearance like lightning and clothing white as snow. Still the first words of the first announcement of the resurrection are, "Do not be afraid; I know that you are looking for Jesus who was crucified. He is not here; for he has been raised" (Matt. 28:5–6). The Jesus who has been raised, the one who is not here, is the Jesus who was crucified.[48]

The identification of the resurrected one with the crucified one looks back to the story of Jesus' ministry, but the ends of the Gospels also point forward by identifying the resurrected one with the one Christians know in communities of word and sacrament. In the resurrection narratives, the moment of recognition regularly comes when Jesus speaks or shares in a meal. He speaks to Magdalene, and she knows that this is no gardener. He breaks bread with the disciples on the road to Emmaus, and they realize his identity. Such moments of recognition do two things. First, they bring the readers into the story. When the focus is on the resurrection appearance, it excludes its readers, for Jesus does not appear to us. But when the story says that the appearance fails to generate recognition, but the word or the shared meal does so, then Christian readers come into the story, for we too can know the narrated identity of Jesus—indeed, we are reading a Gospel—and we too can share the presence of Christ in the breaking of bread. At the same time, the word is always a word about love willing to suffer rather than power determined to coerce, and the bread is the body that has been broken for us, so that these moments also remind us of the identity of the one who appears with the one who was crucified.

The question of the relation of the narrated world of the Gospels and "our world" is therefore not a question invented by contemporary theologians and biblical scholars but one the Gospels themselves implicitly address. They address it by a variety of strategies that pull out of the narrative frame to challenge their readers, thus contrasting two worlds, and by then connecting those two worlds through the connection between the risen Christ in the narrated world and the word and sacraments in the world of their Christian readers. Thus the theological tradition that calls Christians to trust and obey Jesus Christ as attested in Holy Scripture points to a dialectic between the narrated world, the history behind it, and the world of the reader, a dialectic that the Gospels' ends themselves capture with varied narrative strategies.

We can recognize those narrative strategies, however, only if we respect the narrative logic of the individual Gospels. Conflation of the Gospels, in the manner of Tatian's *Diatesseron*, would muddle the ways in which each Gospel narrative develops such matters in a quite different way. The Jesus we encounter in these stories rejects coercive power, and both the stories and the dominant Christian tradition of interpreting them also reject coercion. The different stories stand in their odd juxtaposition. Reading them pulls us into a complex dialectic between their narrations and the world of our experience. Only if we refuse to let any single narrative overpower the diversity of these texts can we authentically encounter the vulnerable one who turned away from the misuse of power, the one whose identity they narrate, and find ourselves living in a world in which just this victim of crucifixion is the one who has been resurrected.

NOTES

1. Bruce M. Metzger, *The Text of the New Testament* (New York: Oxford University Press, 1964), 89. Theodoret tells the story in his *Treatise on Heresies* 1.20.
2. A very good recent book on new ways of reading Mark begins by contrasting the diversity of contemporary approaches to the Bible with the monolithic traditional reading, oddly using Tatian's project as characteristic of the "tradition," without any reference to how rare his sort of compilation has actually been or how widely his project was condemned (Janice Capel Anderson and Stephen D. Moore, eds., *Mark and Method: New Approaches in Biblical Studies* [Minneapolis: Fortress Press, 1992], 1–2).
3. See Michael Goldberg, "God, Action, and Narrative: *Which* Narrative? *Which* Action? *Which* God?" *Journal of Religion* 68 (1988): 39–56.
4. Paul Ricoeur, "Naming God," *Union Seminary Quarterly Review* 34 (1978–79): 222.
5. See David Tracy, "On Reading the Scriptures Theologically," in *Theology and Dialogue: Essays in Conversation with George Lindbeck,* ed. Bruce D. Marshall (Notre Dame, Ind.: University of Notre Dame Press, 1990), 45.

6. George A. Lindbeck, *The Nature of Doctrine: Religion and Theology in a Postliberal Age* (Philadelphia: Westminster Press, 1984), 121. See also George A. Lindbeck, "The Church's Mission to a Postmodern Culture," in *Postmodern Theology: Christian Faith in a Pluralist World*, ed. Frederic B. Burnham (San Francisco: Harper & Row, 1989), 38–43.

7. Gabriel Fackre, *The Christian Story* (Grand Rapids: Wm. B. Eerdmans Publishing Co., 1978).

8. Stanley Hauerwas, *A Community of Character: Toward a Constructive Christian Social Ethic* (Notre Dame, Ind.: University of Notre Dame Press, 1981), 10, 37, 91. To be fair, Hauerwas also acknowledges, "The social ethical task of the church, therefore, is to be the kind of community that tells and tells rightly the story of Jesus. But it can never forget that Jesus' story is a many-sided tale. We do not have just one story of Jesus, but four. . . . We . . . must learn that understanding Jesus' life is inseparable from learning how to live our own. And that there are various ways to do this is clear by the diversity of the Gospels" (ibid., 52).

9. Susan A. Handelman, *The Slayers of Moses* (Albany, N.Y.: State University of New York Press, 1982), xiv.

10. John R. Donahue argues (in "Jesus as the Parable of God in the Gospel of Mark," *Interpretation* 32 [1978]: 380–81) that "fear" here is not a negative word but means awestruck in the face of the numinous. But Andrew Lincoln makes, to me, a more persuasive case that "fear" has been consistently linked in the Gospel with disobedience and failure to understand and that, in this case, the women in fact disobey the command given them (Andrew Lincoln, "The Promise and the Failure—Mark 16:7,8," *Journal of Biblical Literature* 108 [1989]: 286).

11. For a sensible review of the basic issues, see C. S. Mann, *Mark* (Garden City, N.Y.: Doubleday & Co., 1986), 659–63; and Lincoln, "The Promise and the Failure—Mark 16:7,8," 283–300.

12. Raymond E. Brown, *The Gospel according to John* (Garden City, N.Y.: Doubleday & Co., 1970), 1078.

13. For a thoughtful argument, see R. Alan Culpepper, *Anatomy of the Fourth Gospel: A Study in Literary Design* (Philadelphia: Fortress Press, 1983), 5.

14. "Matthew is the only gospel which has anything that can properly be called an ending" (W. F. Albright and C. S. Mann, *Matthew* [Garden City, N. Y.: Doubleday & Co., 1971], 361).

15. See Brown, *The Gospel according to John*, 1126; and Culpepper, *Anatomy of the Fourth Gospel*, 45.

16. Martin Luther, *Kritische Gesamtausgabe der Werke*, vol. 19 (Weimar, 1883–), 350; quoted in Herbert Marks, "On Prophetic Stammering," in *The Book and the Text: The Bible and Literary Theory*, ed. Regina Schwartz (Oxford: Basil Blackwell Publisher, 1990), 60.

105

17. Frank Kermode, *The Genesis of Secrecy: On the Interpretation of Narrative* (Cambridge, Mass.: Harvard University Press, 1979), 33.
18. Ludwig Wittgenstein, *Culture and Value*, ed. G. H. Von Wright, trans. Peter Winch (Oxford: Basil Blackwell Publisher, 1980), 32e.
19. Rudolf Bultmann, *New Testament and Mythology*, trans. Schubert M. Ogden (Philadelphia: Fortress Press, 1984), 10.
20. Ludwig Wittgenstein, *Lectures and Conversations on Aesthetics, Psychology and Religious Belief* (Berkeley and Los Angeles: University of California Press, 1967), 62.
21. Jacques Derrida, *Of Grammatology*, trans. Gayatri Chakravorty Spivak (Baltimore: Johns Hopkins University Press, 1976), 158. Another scholar writing from a very different point of view makes an analogous point: "The events the Bible describes are what some scholars call 'language events,' brought to us only through words; and it is the words themselves that have the authority, not the events they describe" (Northrup Frye, *The Great Code: The Bible in Literature* [New York: Harcourt Brace Jovanovich, 1981], 60). For Derrida, this would be true of any text, however; Frye seems to be using the point to distinguish the particular kind of text the Bible is.
22. Sigmund Freud, "On the History of the Psycho-analytic Movement" (1914), *The Standard Edition of the Complete Psychological Works of Sigmund Freud*, trans. James Strachey (London: Hogarth Press, 1953–74), 14:17. The whole story is told with panache and occasional paranoia in Jeffrey Moussaieff Masson, *The Assault on Truth: Freud's Suppression of the Seduction Theory* (New York: Farrar, Straus & Giroux, 1984).
23. Sigmund Freud, *Introductory Lectures on Psycho-Analysis*, in Strachey, *Standard Edition*, 16: 369.
24. John Dominic Crossan, *The Historical Jesus* (San Francisco: Harper, 1992), xxvii–xxviii. The book's subtitle is "The Life of a Mediterranean Jewish Peasant," and the front of the dust jacket identifies it as "the first comprehensive determination of who Jesus was, what he did, what he said." One hopes that Crossan is not responsible for that rather astonishing claim.
25. Schubert M. Ogden, *On Theology* (San Francisco: Harper & Row, 1986), 64.
26. *Book of Confessions*, Presbyterian Church (U.S.A.), 9.27; 8.11.
27. The kind of project Elisabeth Schüssler Fiorenza undertakes in *In Memory of Her: A Feminist Theological Reconstruction of Christian Origins* (New York: Crossroad, 1984)—looking behind the New Testament texts to find a more sexually egalitarian community in earliest Christianity—would be *one* of the enterprises one might undertake in reflection on the texts. But one would not rest as much theologically as Schüssler Fiorenza does on particular historical claims about that earliest community—a methodological point

where some other feminists are also nervous about her book even while greatly admiring its remarkable accomplishment.

28. David H. Kelsey, *The Uses of Scripture in Recent Theology* (Philadelphia: Fortress Press, 1975), 164.

29. For an eloquent and more developed statement of the point I am trying to make here, see Phyllis Trible, "The Pilgrim Bible on a Feminist Journey," *Princeton Seminary Bulletin* 11 (1990): 232–39. I will return to these questions at the end of the next chapter.

30. "The readers are brought into the narratives; it becomes a context for reflection and action. . . . What is achieved is not simply read off the text and accepted but is rather created through the engagement of the readers—who have their distinctive backgrounds and locations—with the text. . . . Thus, although the text is normative, in that it is by the text that the appropriateness of Christian belief and conduct is to be judged, its normativeness does not stifle diversity and creativity. Indeed, it positively mandates them" (Charles M. Wood, "Hermeneutics and the Authority of Scripture," in *Scriptural Authority and Narrative Interpretation*, ed. Garrett Green [Philadelphia: Fortress Press, 1987], 13–14).

31. Cornel West, *The American Evasion of Philosophy: A Genealogy of Pragmatism* (Madison, Wis.: University of Wisconsin Press, 1989), 233.

32. John Rawls, *A Theory of Justice* (Cambridge, Mass.: Harvard University Press, 1971), 20, 48–51. In thinking about such matters, I am indebted to the work of William Werpehowski.

33. Gail R. O'Day, *Revelation in the Fourth Gospel* (Philadelphia: Fortress Press, 1986), 94.

34. Brown, *The Gospel according to John*, 1049.

35. The point is debated, although Fitzmyer makes a good case that it "has to be regarded as part of the original text of the Lucan Gospel" (Joseph A. Fitzmyer, *The Gospel according to Luke* [Garden City, N.Y.: Doubleday & Co., 1985], 1542). The NRSV has moved it back up to the main text.

36. "The building of amiable communities is often far more important than the exclusion of naive victims. Often the predominant emotion when reading stable ironies is that of joining, of finding and communing with kindred spirits" (Wayne C. Booth, *A Rhetoric of Irony* [Chicago: University of Chicago Press, 1974], 28).

37. Luke 24; John 20:25; *Pseudo-Mark* 16:11–14; and even more dramatically in the apocryphal *Epistula Apostolorum* 1–10. See Reginald H. Fuller, *The Formation of the Resurrection Narratives* (New York: Macmillan Co., 1971), 81.

38. I am generally in agreement with Andrew Lincoln's interpretation of Mark 16:7–8 as a story of divine promise followed by human failure, "and yet the word of promise prevailing despite human

failure" (Lincoln, "The Promise and the Failure—Mark 16:7, 8,"
292). My (small) disagreement with Lincoln's interpretation comes
when he says that the human failure at Mark 16:8 "is by no means
the end of the Gospel's narrative world" (p. 291). As evidence, he
cites the fact that Mark 13 had already ascribed a postresurrection
role to the disciples and that Mark 16:7 offers a promise that remains in the reader's mind as part of the narrative even after the
following verse and the abrupt conclusion. But I would rather say
that the Gospel thereby thrusts us out of the narrative world into
our world and forces us to reflect on these two worlds' relations.

39. "The story *in* Mark's Gospel seems to preclude the telling *of*
Mark's Gospel" (Robert M. Fowler, "Reading Matthew Reading
Mark," *SBL 1986 Seminar Papers*, ed. Kent Harold Richards [At-
lanta: Scholars Press, 1986], 14).

40. Robert M. Fowler, "Reader-Response Criticism: Figuring Mark's
Reader," in Anderson and Moore, *Mark and Method*, 80.

41. Michel Foucault, *The Order of Things: An Archaeology of the
Human Sciences* (New York: Random House, Vintage Books,
1973), 3–16.

42. Erich Auerbach, *Mimesis: The Representation of Reality in Western
Literature*, trans. Willard R. Trask (Princeton: Princeton University Press, 1968), 15.

43. Ibid., 14–15.

44. Robert Scholes and Robert Kellogg, *The Nature of Narrative*
(New York: Oxford University Press, 1966), 82. "The sense or the
significance of a narrative stems from the intersection of the world
of the text and the world of the reader" (Paul Ricoeur, "Life in
Quest of Narrative," in *On Paul Ricoeur*, ed. David Wood [Lon-
don: Routledge & Kegan Paul, 1991], 26).

45. Karl Barth, *Church Dogmatics*, 2/2, trans. G. W. Bromiley et al.
(Edinburgh: T. & T. Clark, 1957), 136.

46. See Hans W. Frei, *The Identity of Jesus Christ* (Philadelphia:
Fortress Press, 1975), 145.

47. Brown, *The Gospel according to John*, 1047.

48. "The Easter stories . . . tell of a victory. However, it is significant
that the description is not of a God who strides through the gates
of death as though through a triumphal arch. . . . The One who
has been raised from the dead remains the crucified One. And the
marks of his dominion which he will forever bear are the scars on
his body (Eberhard Jüngel, *Death*, trans. Iain and Ute Nicol
[Philadelphia: Westminster Press, 1974], 111–12).

5 The Savior and the Vulnerable

Earlier chapters have emphasized concern for the vulnerable, the outsiders, the marginalized of the world's societies, and have urged mistrust of those who revel in power, especially when that power implicitly or explicitly turns to violence. I have simultaneously been proposing a Christian theology that begins with what we know about God in Jesus Christ, as witnessed by the biblical narratives, a God who turns out to be triune. This is the vulnerable God who can most be with us in our sufferings. Many thoughtful people today, however, find these ideas inconsistent. Christ, the authority of the Bible, and the doctrine of the Trinity, they argue, have too long functioned as slogans of oppression. The themes and the language of patriarchy pervade the Bible and serve to oppress women and homosexuals. The name of Christ, and doctrines such as the Trinity, have been the mottos for rampages against non-Christians. Brutal invaders of much of the world bore flags with a cross or some triune symbol. Biblical stories speak of a God who urges mass murder, a monster of power. These narratives above all offer no help to the world's vulnerable.

An honest response to such concerns should not try to defend the indefensible. Horrible things have been done in the name of Christ. Horrible things have also been done in the name of liberty, and peace, and Mohammed, and the workers of the world, and any number of other causes, but Christendom had a long run, and

109

Christians have had a chance at more than their share of horror. This hard reality, to be sure, leaves open the question of whether or not such evil has distorted the true meaning of the gospel, and in earlier chapters I have been arguing that it has. Jesus was himself a marginalized outsider. The God he revealed is a God of love, not of violence. The Trinity reminds us that mutual love between equals, not a hierarchy of power, lies at the heart of who God is. The Bible is not a single master narrative that represses all other voices but a complex text in which many sometimes conflicting voices can be heard.

Such analyses, however, may still seem to avoid a direct facing of some of the issues that are very much in some people's minds these days. This chapter will take some steps toward remedying that fault. It will address three issues in particular, all of them instances of ways in which Christianity can be used to oppress rather than liberate the vulnerable. To summarize, the theology here proposed refers to a *male* savior, a *suffering* savior, and a *unique* savior. Reflection on any of those three adjectives raises some challenging questions. (1) Should theology call upon women to put their trust for salvation in a male savior? (2) Does a theology that begins with the crucified Jesus glorify suffering and thereby encourage victims to accept their victimization? (3) Is a theology that begins with Jesus Christ inappropriately exclusivistic in a world of religious pluralism and therefore a way of oppressing non-Christians?

Addressing even these three questions within a single chapter may seem to treat them too hastily, but it can offer at least the sketch of responses. The more serious issue may be that these are only some of the topics worthy of attention in this context. The first paragraph of this chapter already alluded to a number of others. The conclusion of this chapter will undertake some more general reflections, but, the truth is, one cannot talk about everything. Perhaps discussing some representative questions can suggest directions for dealing with others.

More problematically still, I am, as the Introduction acknowledged, writing all of this as a white male of some social privilege. That fact poses many pitfalls when one is dealing with issues like these. One can continue old patterns of insensitivity and indifference to voices and issues that too often are repressed in our culture. Alternatively, trying to attend to those voices respectfully, one can listen to them in a completely uncritical fashion that becomes condescending and ironically fails to take them seriously as conversation partners. Yet again, one can get scared off, try to avoid the topics where these issues arise, and thereby again seem not to be attending. No easy path leads through these dangers. The third, however—that of avoiding such controversial issues altogether—seems the worst of all, and therefore I proceed as best I can, trying to listen, disagreeing cautiously when that seems necessary.

The first issue concerns Jesus' maleness. It is only one of the issues that confront many women, and men sensitive to their questions, as they read the Bible. As Sandra Schneiders puts it,

> Whereas the Bible permits a fairly straightforward connection between the oppression of the poor and the stranger in the biblical story and analogous oppression of the poor and racial-ethnic minorities in contemporary society, the biblical text is not only frequently blind to the oppression of women in the Israelite and early Christian communities, but the text itself is pervasively androcentric and patriarchal, frequently sexist, and even misogynist.[1]

Men who suffer from economic and political oppression can find the Bible speaking particularly to them and written by people like them. Women encounter a text written (at least almost entirely) by men and most of the time taking male social superiority for granted.

A careful reading of the texts informed by contemporary concerns yields at least partial resolutions of many of the apparent problems. Elisabeth Schüssler Fiorenza, for instance, argues that Jesus, quite remarkably for his time and place, invited women into a community of the discipleship of equals.[2] "The New Testament does not transmit a single androcentric statement or sexist story of Jesus although he lived and preached in a patriarchal culture."[3] As Patricia Wilson-Kastner puts it, "In the perspective of his time, Jesus' treatment of women was uncondescendingly attentive." He taught women as well as men. He praised Mary of Bethany for abandoning her stereotypically female household tasks to listen to his teaching. In the Gospels, he never says anything demeaning about women or praises them for some supposedly distinctly feminine contribution; he uses female imagery to describe both himself and God.[4] One could address other issues in similar fashion, at least up to a point.

Concede all that. Still, as Mark Kline Taylor writes in *Remembering Esperanza*, "Even if 'the brother' Jesus is interpreted as, say, a feminist, a hero crusading against the patriarchy . . . even then, he is still a male."[5] Traditional Christian theology—and in this respect this book is traditional enough—therefore seems to be asking women yet once more to solve their problems by throwing themselves on the mercy of some man. For some radical post-Christian feminists, the only viable alternative is to abandon Christian faith. Taylor and others urge instead, as a compromise strategy, a shift "*away from* exclusive preoccupation with the man Jesus *toward* the center of the Christ event."[6]

That old Tillichian phrase "the Christ event," however, expresses a notoriously slippery concept. Mark Kline Taylor will serve as an example here because of the particular sensitivity with which he engages in the effort to move away from the male Jesus to a more abstract Christ event. Any such effort finds itself facing a trilemma. The trick would be to find a middle ground between three unsatisfactory positions. First, there is a view that Taylor criticizes Peter Hodgson for holding: "God was 'incarnate,' not in the physical nature of Jesus as such, but in the gestalt that coalesced both in and around his person."[7] But for Hodgson, Taylor says, Jesus still in some sense becomes identical with, or the bearer of, that gestalt, and "especially given the problems entailed in identifying the incarnation so closely to the male figure Jesus, it is important today to emphatically resist that identification."[8] Hodgson, in other words, fails to move far enough to get away from the problem as Taylor has defined it; his Christ is still at base the male Jesus.

A second alternative would be to identify all or part of the ongoing Christian community as "the Christ event." The work of Christ, Taylor says, "cannot be only the activity or practice of Jesus . . . but is rather *these as narrated and practiced by* historical communities of disciples contemporary with and subsequent to Jesus' period . . . [which may] include selective appropriations (involving suspicion as well as trust) of Jesus' activity"[9]—and that Christian community, of course, includes women as well as men. The obvious problem here is that, at least if we accept the conclusions of Schüssler Fiorenza and others, the church has been more problematically patriarchal than Jesus was. To let the Christian church in its history serve as the norm for Christology would only make things worse. One would have to find criteria for identifying some parts of Christianity—and perhaps some phenomena outside the church too—as "the Christ event" in order to do what Taylor wants to do and find a Christ event that escapes patriarchy by moving away from the male Jesus.

That leads, however, to the third vertex of the trilemma. What is the source of those criteria for determining which aspects of Jesus and the Christian tradition should be counted as legitimate parts of the Christ event? In Taylor's words, "while the actions of

Jesus are an important part of Christian criteria they cannot be 'the foundation' for judging Christian actions. Ultimately, we must have recourse to ethical reflection ongoing in the whole communal dialogue, wrestling with the meaning of the whole Christ dynamic disclosed in the Christian movement in light of dialogue about contemporary needs."[10]

But how does one decide about which contemporary needs are most important or about who gets to participate in the dialogue that defines them? Kant thought he could rationally establish a universal set of ethical concerns and then emphasize the themes within Christianity that best addressed those concerns. But the last two hundred years have made most philosophers and theologians (Taylor among them) suspicious of such claims to universal ethical principles. If one simply gathered together the churchgoers in my part of Indiana to set the agenda, however, most of them would turn out to be conservative Republicans, and their lists of concerns would differ widely from Taylor's. If communal dialogue is to define what really counts as part of the Christ event, by what criteria could one tell them they were wrong? The danger is, in short, that a "Christ event" quite so willing to yield its definition to the voices of our contemporaries and so little tied to the gospel that it will give up the centrality of Jesus of Nazareth will lack the bite to challenge contemporary culture forcefully enough. Standing with Jesus, one can say no to the ideologies of power, violence, and material success. If one is willing to give up Jesus, on what will one insist? The question, at any rate, is worrisome enough for us to want to see whether Jesus' maleness is really such an insurmountable problem.

That it has been a problem ought to stand beyond debate. Within the last twenty years, after all, there has been an official Vatican declaration opposing women's ordination on the grounds that "there must be a physical resemblance between the priest and Christ."[11] One cannot honestly say that the fact that Jesus was male has made no difference; the difference is real and often appalling. A response might begin by arguing that the Christian church has been unable to understand Jesus' maleness aright because it has so consistently repressed his Jewishness.[12] This repression does not only consist in the disgraceful history of pseudoscholarly efforts, some but not all simply Nazi, to show that Jesus was not ethnically Jewish. But in most American churches hang pictures of Jesus as some sort of northern European, or certainly not a Middle Eastern Jew. In this we both follow and lead the images of the popular culture, most egregious in the case that virtually every production of *Jesus Christ*

113

Superstar has cast not only a blond- or light-brown-haired Jesus but an African American Judas. Little wonder that episodes take place like that described by Elisabeth Schüssler Fiorenza:

> One of my friends spoke about Jesus, the Jew, to an adult education class in her parish. She encountered vehement objections to such a notion. Finally, after a lengthy discussion a participant expressed the religious sentiment underlying it: "If you are so insistent that Jesus was Jewish, then you are probably right. But the Blessed Mother for sure is not."[13]

The instinct of our culture may well be that sexual difference is more basic than the difference between Jew and Gentile, but that was not so in the world of the New Testament. Krister Stendahl's studies on Paul make a strong case that Paul's theology was much more about particular problems concerning the relations between Jews and Gentiles than about supposedly universal questions concerning justification.[14] Christians have too often misunderstood Paul by pulling him out of that original context. To first-century Jews like Paul, or like Jesus or any of his original followers, the distinction between those who were among the chosen people of God and those who were not may well have seemed the most basic of all divisions within humanity.[15] From that biblical standpoint, to tolerate a northern-European-looking Jesus, deny Jesus' Jewishness, but then recoil in complete horror at a female Christa symbol, is to have one's priorities backward.

Male Christians say, "Oh, Jesus was male—like us." He was not like us, not like the vast majority of us, for we are Gentiles and he was a Jew. In terms of human categories, he comes to us as different, we come to him as different—male and female alike. Only if we really come to terms with that fact of difference will the significance of the claim that "there is no longer Jew or Greek, there is no longer slave or free, there is no longer male and female; for all . . . are one in Christ Jesus" (Gal. 3:28) come home to us. To say that, of course, is to leave many questions—questions about language and about patriarchal patterns, for instance—unanswered. It can at most serve as one beginning for reflections, reflections that will be discussed below in chapter 6, about how Christian churches might define themselves as communities of equals welcoming outsiders. For now, it should at least be clear that for male Christians to divide the world by gender and claim a privileged position on Jesus' side is to miss the point. Humankind divides along any number of lines, and all of us are in some ways like Jesus and in other ways not. Elizabeth Johnson notes that too often the alternatives have been either to emphasize the male/female dichotomy in a way that includes males and excludes females or else to deny that sexuality makes any difference at all. Then she adds:

> A way beyond the impasse of these options is emerging: one human nature celebrated in an interdependence of multiple differences. Not a binary view of two forever predetermined male and female natures, nor abbreviation to a single ideal, but a diversity of ways of being human, . . . of which sexuality is but one.[16]

To acknowledge that diversity is to subvert binary oppositions between insiders and outsiders. All of us fit into, and slip out of, too many categories to permit such easy classifications. If in some cultural settings some are particularly marginalized or oppressed, then the Gospels suggest that it is they, if any are, who are in the most important ways like Jesus.

To speak of the identification of those who suffer with Jesus, however, is to raise another question that has also been of particular concern to feminists. In a way, it is the obverse of the first, for the question is now not the valorization of the powerful, male Jesus but of the weak, suffering Jesus on the cross. Joanne Carlson Brown and Rebecca Parker state the issue:

> Christianity has been a primary—in many women's lives *the* primary—force in shaping our acceptance of abuse. The central image of Christ on the cross as the savior of the world communicates the message that suffering is redemptive. If the best person who ever lived gave his life for others, then, to be of value we should likewise sacrifice ourselves. Any sense that we have a right to care for our own needs is in conflict with being a faithful follower of Jesus.[17]

If Christians are called to identification with the suffering Jesus on the cross, does that generate an ideology that urges them, if they are among the world's oppressed, to accept their suffering in humble obedience?[18] In one sense, this is hardly a new question. African Americans have long worried that Christianity functioned to keep slaves docile with the promise of reward when the sweet chariot came to carry them home. And, after all, what does it mean to speak of religion as the opiate of the people? But the example of abuse within the family serves particularly well just now, in part because we are beginning to learn something about just how pervasive the abuse of women and children is.[19] None of us should assume that our own social circles and congregations are exempt. In liberal mainline congregations, however, the weekly announcements may include a call for volunteers at the women's crisis shelter. We may forget how many congregations there are in which the advice to abused women and children still involves urging the endurance of suffering and preservation of the family at all costs as Christian virtues. Barth once remarked of self-love, "God will never think of blowing on this fire, which is bright enough already."[20] In terms of social psychology, he was simply wrong, and that is a lesson the church has begun to learn largely through listening to women's voices. At least if self-love means a sense of self-worth, a determination to stand up for one's own rights, then some folk, and in our culture they are most apt to be women, do need more self-love. The Presbyterian Church (U.S.A.)'s 1991 A Brief Statement of Faith makes just this point when it says that the Holy Spirit sets us free first "to accept ourselves" and *then* "to love God and neighbor" (line 55). Christians have to find an acceptance of themselves that makes them less vulnerable to manipulation and abuse so that they can find the integrity to love God and neighbor most fully.

If we want to urge victims of abuse to get out of the abusive situation, right now, and urge people who are being cheated or mistreated or oppressed to fight back, but also want to say that the Jesus whose life led to the cross reveals God to us, however, then is our Christology in danger of undercutting our social ethic? What follows can only begin to answer that question, but four points contribute to that beginning.

First, as already noted above in chapter 1, it is God's vulnerability, God's willingness to *risk* pain and suffering in being open in love, that is good. Suffering in itself is not good. In the best of situations, one would open oneself to suffering by risking love but would never suffer. Love would be met by love, and joy would respond to joy. But the story of God's love for humankind is not such a happy story because of the fact of our sin. "God so loved the world that he gave his only Son . . . not . . . to condemn the world, but in order that the world might be saved through him" (John 3:16–17). "Yet the world did not know him. He came to what was his own, and his own people did not accept him" (John 1:10–11). Because of sin, God's willingness to risk suffering led in fact to suffering, and such is love that God does not regret the risk. Christians even celebrate the wonder of redemptive suffering, but, still, the suffering as suffering is not a good.

116

Calvin captures this point when he says that Christ abolished sin and banished the separation between God and us "by the whole course of his obedience."[21] That is, in obedience the Christ who reveals God came to be with us and thereby set forth on a journey into the far country that led finally to the cross. It is that journey, and the willingness to undertake it, for which we give thanks and praise. Christian faith gives thanks that Christ was willing to follow this road even when it led to a cross, but not thanks for the cross itself.

Suffering, then, is not itself a good but one of the risks of the kind of vulnerable love that is good. Moreover—a second point— even Christ's suffering on the cross is the suffering of someone out to win in the struggle with evil, not the suffering of a passive victim only enduring suffering for the sake of the purported virtue of passive endurance.

To put the matter more concretely, contrast Martin Luther King, Jr., urging protesters to put their bodies on the line in the struggle against injustice, to risk beatings and even death in a campaign of nonviolent resistance, with a pastor telling an abused woman to go home and let the beating continue, because Jesus treasures her suffering. The analogy to Jesus' way to the cross lies in the first case, in an active resistance that demands change even as it eschews violence.[22]

The language of traditional Christology, after all, includes what Gustaf Aulén called the classical model of soteriology. In his words, "The Word of God who is God Himself, has entered in under the conditions of sin and death, to take up the conflict with the powers of evil and carry it through to the decisive victory."[23] Christ defeats the forces of evil, although, Irenaeus says, not by violence but "by persuasion."[24] God's justice and God's refusal of violence determine the means of achieving victory, but the conflict is engaged, and the victory is won. Some of the imagery of this soteriological model is no doubt problematically mythological, but it at least makes the point that orthodox Christology does not offer a model of lying down and letting evil roll over you.

In such a model of nonviolent resistance to the forces of violence, christological doctrine follows the pattern of the Gospel narratives. Jesus challenged the powerful, challenged a religious establishment become hypocritical and a political empire firmly oppressive. Those who do things like that, then or now, risk getting beat up or killed. Reinhold Niebuhr once said that "the perfect disinterestedness of the divine love can have a counterpart in history only in a life which ends tragically," since "the power of sin makes a simple triumph of love impossible."[25] That seems unqualifiedly dogmatic; one might allow for the occasional temporary anticipation of the eschatological triumph of love. But in the medium run, Niebuhr was probably right. Those who challenge violence and injustice without resort to violence themselves will have, often enough, a tough time of it. To follow Jesus is to believe that it is worth it—that injustice needs to be challenged but that the cycle of violence needs to be broken.[26] But nonviolent resistance, as Gandhi and King both often pointed out, is still resistance; it is not "passive," it does the very opposite of accepting the violence and injustice against which it protests.[27] Third, in his thoughtful analysis of *agapē*, Gene Outka makes the useful point that the Golden Rule says, "Do unto others as you would have them do unto you," not, "Do unto others as *they* would have you do unto them."[28] As I think about how I hope that others would treat me, I hope that they would love me in spite of my faults and help me out when I need it. I also hope they would tell me when I am becoming an unreasonable tyrant. I do not hope that they would pander to my every whim until I become a monster of selfishness. If I should come to be in some state where I tried to assault or abuse them, I hope they would stop me. Quite apart from questions of *their* integrity, I hope that is what they would do for *me*. Although it may insist that resistance should not turn to violence, Christian love never simply gives in to abuse.

Fourth, it is worth remembering that Christ's self-abnegation was the reaching down of a superior to a position of equality, not the groveling of an inferior. Think of the words of Gregory of Nazianzus:

> Let us become like Christ, since Christ became like us. Let us become God's for His sake, since He for ours became human. He assumed the worse that He might give us the better; He became poor that we through His poverty might be rich; He took upon Him the form of a servant that we might receive back our liberty; He came down that we might be exalted.[29]

Christ humbles himself to reach down to those who are humble, but his goal is that the humble might be exalted. To follow the pattern of Christ is therefore to develop an ideology of equality, not one of the downtrodden letting themselves be beaten ever farther into the ground.

René Girard's remarkable studies of scapegoats bring many of these themes together. One is overwhelmed at the thought of summarizing, let alone evaluating, Girard's work. Anyone who can entitle a book "Things Hidden since the Foundation of the World" without a whiff of irony is not addressing small questions in a small way.[30] It is easy enough, however, to state one of his central themes. At the foundation of culture and religion lies a scapegoating of the outsider, the other, the one who does not belong, a phenomenon so pervasive that we consistently fail to recognize it.[31] Few stories, for instance, have been so thoroughly analyzed as that of Oedipus, from Aristotle to Freud and beyond. Yet in regard to this lame and apparently orphaned foreigner become king with a terrible secret, the one thing in the story virtually every interpreter seems to accept is that Oedipus really caused the plague. "Certainly, Sophocles suspects something," Girard writes, "but he never goes as far in revealing the structural principle of the scapegoat as the Gospels or even the Prophets. Greek culture forbids it. The myth does not burst apart in his hands and show its inner workings."[32] The question that cannot be asked is: Why does everyone assume that a deformed outsider is responsible for the problem that afflicts the city?

The Bible, Girard says, does burst open the myth to reveal the secret that scapegoats are innocent. For literally as long as there has been history, mobs have been uniting into communities by finding a common victim. The propaganda machines that defended America with anti-Communist witch-hunts have now, lacking enough Communists, had to turn to homosexuals. What is different about the biblical narratives, and, above all, the story of Jesus, is that they expose the workings of the device and therefore, if we can have eyes to see, disarm it. From Abel to Job to Jesus, the biblical stories proclaim that victims are innocent. If Peter tries to join the social circle around the fire of culture by denying Jesus, by making Jesus the radical rejected outsider just as his own Galilean accent threatens to cast Peter himself for the role, then there is a cock crow to remind him and us that justice and God stand with the condemned outsider Jesus.

Stated as simply as possible: A great many cultures tell stories of oddly different folk who are the source of trouble. The Bible insists that the trouble comes not from these innocent victims but from the way everyone else gangs up on them. Therefore anyone who reads these texts above all as an exercise in blaming victims is misreading them drastically. The story of Jesus tells us that love in its vulnerability risks suffering, that in a world of violence those who tackle injustice will sometimes suffer, and that, for those who

119

have power, to renounce violence is the only way to move toward a world of equality. It is therefore a story that teaches its readers how to work to struggle against suffering, not how to glorify it.

Within the last generation, victims of family abuse in our society, most of them women, have begun to be able to tell their stories. Those who live in communities where such tales are told and heard—and liberal Protestant churches and seminaries are apt to be such places—have come to be justifiably suspicious of anything that sounds like a call to suffering. Yet most of us in "mainline" churches in the United States, men and women alike, remain, as the world goes, in so many ways among the privileged. The voices of victims ought to continue to make easy rationalizations about the value of suffering ring hollow. But if they start to encourage the thought that Christian faith need never involve anything by way of sacrifice, then their message will have been misheard. Nothing should be farther from Christian faith than the easy acceptance of the continuing suffering of victims, but Christian faith does often imply sacrifice, and it may well call individuals to stand up against injustice and violence at real personal risk. Concern for the victimized above all should not turn Christianity into an ideology of comfortableness.[33]

To identify the gospel with the world's victims may, however, seem ironic in a different way. Throughout much of its history, Christianity has been associated with the culture of Europe, and Europeans (and more recently North Americans) have often encountered much of the rest of the world as colonizers, conquerors, or the wealthy who control and consume much of the world's resources—although it is worth emphasizing that by every statistical measure Christianity is today predominantly a third-world religion. Christians thus have often encountered non-Christians in circumstances where those non-Christians were in some sense their victims, and that history colors thoughts about the relations between Christians and non-Christians today. Having considered the way a male savior might marginalize women and a suffering savior might lead to a paradoxical lack of concern for those who suffer, it seems appropriate to turn to the question of Christians' relations with those of other faiths. Do claims of Christ's uniqueness as savior, with the implication that other religious traditions have somehow gotten things wrong, intrinsically continue a history of Christian oppression?

Here I have to confess to a kind of tone deafness to issues that bother some other folk very much indeed. In writing about the Spanish invasion of the Americas, Tzvetan Todorov compares Pedro de Alvarado, who murdered native Americans, with Bartolomé de Las Casas who, as a Christian, loved them, opposed violence, and sought to convert them. Todorov finds little enough difference: "Is there not already a violence in the conviction that one possesses the truth oneself, whereas this is not the case for others . . . ?"[34] Such attitudes appear often among those who discuss interreligious dialogue. "It is," Wilfred Cantwell Smith argues, "morally not possible actually to go out into the world and say to devout, intelligent fellow human beings . . . 'We believe that we know God, and we are right; you believe that you know God, and you are totally wrong.'"[35] John Hick or Paul Knitter or many others would say much the same,[36] and, indeed, discussions of such matters at the American Academy of Religion often take such a principle so much for granted that questioning it would seem to leave the bounds of civilized society altogether. One would want to be cautious about saying that anyone was "*totally* wrong," but, when in conversation with someone about religion, why feel such horror in disagreeing?

Most people have intelligent, well-meaning friends we believe to be fundamentally mistaken about politics, educational policy, or the designated hitter rule in baseball. We often do not hesitate to tell them that we think they are wrong. To be sure, etiquette requires that one do this politely. If the conversation partner does not join the discussion as an equal (if I as a college faculty member, for instance, am arguing with a student or an untenured colleague), then it is particularly important to make sure that disagreement does not make it impossible for the conversation to continue honestly and openly. Sometimes, if one cannot think how to make a point without risking intimidation, it is probably best to let it pass. Nevertheless, on a variety of topics most people find themselves from time to time telling someone that they believe them to be wrong about something.[37] Why should religion be any different? To deny honest religious difference, Paul Griffiths says, "produces a discourse that is pallid, platitudinous, and degutted. Its products are intellectual pacifiers for the immature: pleasant to suck on but not very nourishing."[38]

To be sure, conversations between Christians and adherents of other faiths have, historically, often taken place with a colonial army—or a mob ready to launch a pogrom—at least potentially behind the Christians. Serious interreligious dialogue needs to begin with Christian acknowledgment of that evil history, and

121

understanding if potential conversation partners prove reluctant or suspicious. But what Christians need to do is to make it clear that the days of intimidation are over—and make sure they really are over—and then get on with talking about honest disagreement. In a provocative article, Kenneth Surin has argued that the refusal to point out honest disagreement can be the most oppressive stance of all. Sometimes it becomes a strategy for saying, "You really agree with me, you just fail to realize it," which refuses even to acknowledge the other person's position. On other occasions, it treats the fact of disagreement, and therefore of difference, as a matter for such embarrassment that it cannot be discussed in public.[39] Why should we not rather say, with Audre Lorde, "Difference must be not merely tolerated but seen as a fund of necessary polarities between which our creativity can spark like a dialectic"?[40] Why be so embarrassed about disagreement unless one covertly assumes that there is something basically wrong with being different?

Surin further makes a persuasive case that this antipathy to religious disagreement itself grows out of a set of Enlightenment assumptions that are very much the product of Western culture, so that imposing them on interreligious dialogue is just one more case of trying to impose the values of the modern West on the rest of the world, just the sort of thing Todorov and so many others want to protest. Muslims in much of the Middle East, or Hasidic Jews in Brooklyn, or Reformed Christians in Grand Rapids for that matter, likely do not at all think that all religions are somehow saying the same thing. Who has the right to denounce them as irrational if they fail to accept the assumptions of a subset of Western academics? As Langdon Gilkey has written, an approach like that of Smith, Hick, and Knitter

> represents—try as it may to avoid it—a particular way of being religious. . . . Thus it has to *misinterpret* every other tradition in order to incorporate them into its own scheme of understanding. In the end, therefore, it represents in a new form the same religious colonialism that Christianity used to practice so effectively: the interpretation of an alien viewpoint in terms of one's own religious center and so an incorporation of that viewpoint into our own system of understanding.[41]

Is it not more genuinely pluralistic, more honest, more respectful of others, to admit that sometimes people really disagree, to assume that one's conversation partners understand what they mean, even when they mean to disagree? The conversation should be a conversation among equals, with no one presiding from the head of the table—not the Christian, but also not the expert, Western academically trained philosopher of religious dialogue.[42] In such a conversation, Christians, like anyone else, could say, "Here is what we believe, sometimes the rest of you will not agree, but this is what we believe to be true."

Having set forth this unfashionable thesis, let me qualify or clarify it in four ways.

First, to say that other folks are wrong about religion is not necessarily, as Smith and Hick and Knitter often assume, to say that they are damned.[43] To claim that those intelligent, devout folk are fundamentally wrong, the argument goes, implies that they will burn in hell forever. And there are, certainly, reasons, Christian reasons among them, for being reluctant to say that. What is not clear is that it follows from judging them wrong. Two of the theologians in our century most unbending about the errors of other faiths, Karl Barth and Hans Urs von Balthasar, also entertained at least a strong hope for universal salvation.[44] Barth believed that we could at least hope that all will be saved, since we cannot imagine that anyone could hold out against the reality of what one already is in Christ. What crucially distinguishes Christians is that we already know the good news.

George Lindbeck wants to make it clearer that salvation depends on an individual response to the word of the gospel in faith; in that sense he is more cautious on this issue than Barth or von Balthasar. But he suggests that that response might happen at, or just beyond, the moment of death:

> All previous decisions whether of faith or unfaith are preliminary. The final die is cast beyond space and time, beyond empirical observation, beyond all idle speculation about "good" and "bad" deaths, when a person loses his rootage in this world and passes into the inexpressible transcendence surpassing all words, images and thoughts. We must trust and hope, though not know, that in this dreadful yet wondrous end and climax of life no one will be lost.[45]

Those who in this life failed to believe the truth could nevertheless be saved, even if salvation depends on true belief. Catholics might propose an analogous solution by way of the doctrine of purgatory.[46]

Whether or not one accepts any of these particular proposals, they at least make it clear that the conviction that important beliefs of a particular religious tradition are false need not in any way imply that its adherents are damned. It is a cheap shot, and quite unfair, to connect the two issues.

Second, the qualification already mentioned in reference to Wilfred Cantwell Smith's claim that no religion can be dismissed as "totally wrong" deserves further comment. God is a mystery beyond human comprehension. No one, no group of humans or human institution, can claim to understand all there is to understand of God. We may not even understand the language we use when we speak of God.[47] In such matters, all claims to truth must be partial at best. Moreover, given the lessons that the church fathers learned from Greek philosophy or that Aquinas learned from Maimonides and the Arab commentators, given lessons that Christian theologians have begun to learn from Buddhists about ways of understanding Paul's talk of self-emptying,[48] Christians can and should acknowledge that adherents of other religions sometimes have grasped important truths from which they can learn. So it goes in many conversations about a variety of topics. Even while arguing for the essential truth of one's own position, one can acknowledge that the truth one holds is only partial, that others have hold of real truths too, and that one can learn from them in ways that will lead to correcting one's own position.

Third, Christians might even hold that some non-Christians best serve the providence of God by continuing to live in their particular non-Christian faiths. J. A. DiNoia has written eloquently about a "providential diversity of religions" which might involve unforeseen roles for other religions in the divine plan for the human race.[49] Given the richness that Buber found in Judaism or that Gandhi found in Hinduism, how much they contributed to their own traditions, and for that matter how much Christians have learned precisely from what they developed by probing the heights and depths of a standpoint outside our own, it seems an oddly limited vision of God's providence whose comment would be, "If only they had become Christians." In such cases we can already see God's providence at work in non-Christians' explorations of the depths of their own traditions. Those explorations may provide further insights and values beyond anyone's current capacity to imagine. For Christians to say that non-Christian systems of belief are in some respects false need not imply that it would be more in accord with God's plan for things if all non-Christians converted to Christianity.

Fourth and finally, Judaism seems to be a special case, and Jews who complained about Vatican II's classifying them under the rubric of non-Christian religions were thoroughly justified.[50] The God we know in Jesus Christ is a God who made promises to Abraham and to the descendants of Abraham and Sarah forever, and this is not the sort of God who breaks promises.[51] The recent statement of the Presbyterian Church (U.S.A.) on this matter takes an important step in the right direction: "The church has not 'replaced' the Jewish people. Quite the contrary! The church, being made primarily of those who were once aliens and strangers to the covenants of promise, has been engrafted into the people of God."[52] Christians are the branch grafted onto the tree of the descendants of Abraham, and we have heard and believed the good news of God's self-revelation in Jesus Christ. But that self-revelation as known in scripture confirms God's history with and commitment to the people Israel.

Take Judaism as a special case, then, and recognize that adherents of other religions may well be saved, may well have hold of partial truths on matters where our own truths are partial as well, and may well be serving God's providential purposes in pursuing the depths of their own faiths. One could still believe that on fundamental matters they are wrong, and Christians who believe Christ to be in some sense uniquely God's self-revelation do presumably believe just that. Such a belief provides a more promising beginning for honest conversation than either the claim that we do not really disagree or the claim that none of our disagreements are really important.

This chapter began with some worries. The crucified Jesus surely seems to be the revelation of a God self-identified with the vulnerable and the outsiders of the world. Yet there are reasons to wonder whether the triune God revealed in Jesus Christ as known through the biblical narratives turns out to be at least in some respects on the side of the oppressors after all. The three issues discussed—the fact of Jesus' maleness, the possibility that Christian attitudes toward Jesus' suffering encourage oppressed people simply to accept their suffering, and the relation of Christians to adherents of other religions—serve only as examples; similar issues are of equal importance. Perhaps the responses to these cases can at least provide examples of the kinds of strategies one might use in thinking about others. What has been said in this chapter, moreover, ought to be set in the context of the preceding chapter's discussion of the diversity and ambiguities of biblical narratives. The Bible does not offer *the* Christian story or *the* Christian code of ethics. It presents a range of different stories and different commentaries on those stories, with complex relations to the history behind them and the readers in front of them.

Out of this mix, Christians can come to have a sense of the God who moves at the center of the stories and to learn something about the identity of that God, some of which, perhaps, we do not know how to express except by retelling the stories—every conceptual summary of the narrative seems to lose something. Given the mix of these texts, however, it is not always clear how to fit all the pieces together. Some seem clearly central to the identity of this God as it emerges, while others seem more peripheral. Something like this happens often enough as one comes to know a human person from a variety of data. Think of the task of a biographer, although that only formalizes what we do with acquaintances all the time. An anecdote may contradict a remembrance but is supported by some other testimony, and slowly a picture emerges. As the Westminster Confession of Faith states with remarkable understatement, "All things in Scripture are not alike plain in themselves."[53] Still, the Confession declares, all things necessary for our salvation, faith and life, are either to be found in scripture or derivable from it,[54] and the infallible rule of interpretation of scripture is scripture itself.[55] That is to say, there is not some prior, universally derivable rational set of rules as to which parts of scripture we can believe, or as to what God has to be like, known in advance.

Parts of the Bible, moreover, appear surely to have mostly to do with human responses to this God—to flow out of what Calvin called accommodation, the fact that revelation to human beings is always of necessity to *particular* human beings and therefore, if it is to be *to* them, will be expressed in categories and thereby embody assumptions such that they can understand it.[56] Sometimes one can see that principle at work in the Bible. "I can see," we say, "that that is how you would have to say it to those people back then if you wanted them to understand it—just as, no doubt, you would have to find ways of communicating with us if you wanted us to understand." The way one communicates a message to a particular audience is not necessarily part of the message; it is not necessarily something that would have to be transferred when one is addressing a different audience.

In some cases, then, the overall account of God that the Bible yields encourages us to move some admittedly still puzzling passages to the periphery of things. In other cases, the principle of accommodation helps us understand a passage in a different light, as something like a strategy for communication with the text's

126

original audience. But sometimes, to be honest, we Christians encounter things in the Bible that leave us just struggling, not knowing what to say.

What deserves emphasis is that it is all right to struggle—indeed, the Bible itself calls its readers to do so. Job's comforters find
everything easy to understand; Job moans and cries and protests.
But the friends, the Lord says, "have not spoken of me what is
right, as my servant Job has," and they have to ask Job to pray God
not to deal with them according to their "folly" (Job 42:7–8). This
is, after all, a Lord who seems to welcome it when Abraham, hearing that God would save Sodom if it contained fifty righteous men,
says, "What about forty-five?" (Gen. 18:28, paraphrased). In these
matters, incidentally, Judaism has much to teach Christians, for the
rabbis have long understood that interpretation involves an ongoing argument with the text.

In reading the Bible, we Christians find ourselves presented
with a vision of the world, a world that is the world of a particular
sort of God, a world in the context of which our own lives could
make a certain kind of sense, and may find ourselves captured by
that vision. Given the diversity within scripture, given the parts of
scripture we resist or just find puzzling, how can the vision hold together? Why do we still believe that it makes sense of our lives?
Such questions admit of no quick answers. The answer lies in the
doing, in a life of reading, prayer, and action, in which the internal
coherence of the text and the shape it gives one's life keep out-
weighing the internal inconsistencies and the passages that worry or
even appall. Or, for some Christians at some point, they do not.

As mentioned in the Introduction, contemporary philosophers of science such as Thomas Kuhn and Imre Lakatos have argued that even for scientific theories there is no way of setting
down in advance the set of rules to determine when one should
abandon a theory. A scientific theory of sufficient scope opens up a
set of interesting research projects to be pursued, and that research
produces a combination of positive and anomalous results. At some
point, the interesting results may no longer seem to justify the embarrassment of the anomalies, but such decisions always involve a
subjective component. Often neither giving up in the face of the
problems nor continuing in hopes of resolving them can be judged
irrational.[57] The sort of theology here described has neither a doctrine of the authority of scripture nor a set of philosophical prolegomena that would function as some sort of foundation to the
whole. It has a set of doctrines and practices, among which there

are some beliefs about the function of scripture in the life of the Christian community. To live as in the world of the God whose identity these texts narrate is not to stop struggling but to ask hard questions in the way the text itself urges even as one finds oneself formed by the text and thereby transformed away from the patterns of the larger society, toward the surprising, vulnerable God whom the texts identify and the kind of life one might live in discipleship to such a God.

The temptation in reading these texts is always simply to discard what makes us uncomfortable, but of course cultural norms shape what we find awkward and uncomfortable, and in every society those with power will in the long run contribute most to shaping cultural norms. Those of us who live in academic settings can sometimes think that our own countercultural norms can carry the day and therefore appeal with confidence in our theological work to accepted values of solidarity with the oppressed. Our students may have a more cynical view of how academic institutions and the power relationships within them really work, and they are also destined soon to leave the academy for a wider world. They know, as those working in many local congregations or struggling for social change know, that we do not live in a society eager to attend to the voices of the oppressed and the marginalized. If we have let the values and assumptions of our society guide us, even in matters of faith, then where will we stand when the powerful impose their agendas? Perhaps we should stand, from the start, with the crucified Jesus and the vulnerable God he makes known to us.

NOTES

1. Sandra M. Schneiders, *The Revelatory Text: Interpreting the New Testament as Sacred Scripture* (San Francisco: Harper, 1991), 181–82.
2. Elisabeth Schüssler Fiorenza, *In Memory of Her: A Feminist Theological Reconstruction of Christian Origins* (New York: Crossroad, 1983), 140.
3. Elisabeth Schüssler Fiorenza, "Interpreting Patriarchal Traditions," in *The Liberating Word*, ed. Letty M. Russell (Philadelphia: Westminster Press, 1976), 52.
4. Patricia Wilson-Kastner, *Faith, Feminism, and the Christ* (Philadelphia: Fortress Press, 1983), 72. See also Winsome Munro, "Women Disciples in Mark," *Catholic Biblical Quarterly* 44 (1982): 232–37; and Anne Carr, *Transforming Grace* (San Francisco: Harper & Row, 1990), 15, 180.

5. Mark Kline Taylor, *Remembering Esperanza: A Cultural Political Theology for North American Praxis* (Maryknoll, N.Y.: Orbis Books, 1992), 157.

6. Ibid., 171.

7. Peter C. Hodgson, *God in History: Shapes of Freedom* (Nashville: Abingdon Press, 1989), 209; quoted in Taylor, *Remembering Esperanza*, 171.

8. Taylor, *Remembering Esperanza*, 171.

9. Ibid., 173.

10. Ibid., 277.

11. "Declaration of the Question of Admission of Women to the Ministerial Priesthood," October 15, 1976; quoted in Rosemary Radford Ruether, *Sexism and God-Talk: Toward a Feminist Theology* (Boston: Beacon Press, 1983), 126. It was a statement whose content actually led Karl Rahner to condemn it as "heretical." Rosemary Radford Ruether discusses the point in *To Change the World: Christology and Cultural Criticism* (New York: Crossroad, 1981), 47.

12. "The Word did not simply become any 'flesh,' any man humbled and suffering. It became Jewish flesh. The Church's whole doctrine of the incarnation and the atonement becomes abstract and valueless and meaningless to the extent that this comes to be regarded as something accidental and incidental" (Karl Barth, *Church Dogmatics*, 4/1, trans. G. W. Bromiley [Edinburgh: T. & T. Clark, 1956], 166).

13. Schüssler Fiorenza, *In Memory of Her*, 105–6.

14. "The main lines of Pauline interpretation . . . have for many centuries been out of touch with one of the most basic of the questions and concerns that shaped Paul's thinking in the first place: the relation between Jews and Gentiles. . . . We think that Paul spoke about justification by faith, using the Jewish-Gentile situation as an instance, as an example. But Paul was chiefly concerned about the relation between Jews and Gentiles—and in the development of *this* concern he used as one of his arguments the idea of justification by faith" (Krister Stendahl, *Paul among Jews and Gentiles* [Philadelphia: Fortress Press, 1976], 1, 3). Stendahl is making a stronger claim than I need to defend for the sake of my point.

15. Think for instance of Jesus' reason for not preaching to Gentiles in the story of the Syrophoenician woman in Mark 7:24–30 and parallels: "It is not fair to take the children's food and throw it to the dogs." None of the misogyny or androcentrism of the Gospels ever reaches that level.

16. Elizabeth A. Johnson, *She Who Is: The Mystery of God in Feminist Theological Discourse* (New York: Crossroad, 1992), 155. Bernard Häring alternatively proposes that, since men have mostly dominated women throughout history, "it might be appropriate" for Christ

to be a male, "to break the fetters of sexism by his absolute humility" (Bernard Häring, *Free and Faithful in Christ* [New York: Crossroad, 1984], 139). It is an intriguing idea, but it makes Jesus' maleness unnervingly important to his salvific work. See Rosemary Radford Ruether's more careful account of the "kenosis of patriarchy" in *Sexism and God-Talk*, 137.

17. Joanne Carlson Brown and Rebecca Parker, "For God So Loved the World?" in *Christianity, Patriarchy and Abuse*, ed. Joanne Carlson Brown and Carole R. Bohn (New York: Pilgrim Press, 1989), 2. The classic discussion of these issues is Valerie Saiving, "The Human Situation: A Feminine View," in *Womanspirit Rising: A Feminist Reader in Religion*, ed. Carol P. Christ and Judith Plaskow (New York: Harper & Row, 1979), 25–42. "The ideal of the helpless divine victim serves only to strengthen women's dependency and potential for victimization, and to subvert initiatives for freedom, when what is needed is growth in relational autonomy and self-affirmation. The image of a powerless, suffering God is dangerous to women's genuine humanity, and must be resisted" (Johnson, *She Who Is*, 254).

18. Even so sensitive a theologian as John Cobb at one point identifies the Logos as masculine with order, novelty, agency, and transformation, and the Spirit as feminine with receptivity, empathy, suffering, and preservation (John B. Cobb, Jr., *Christ in a Pluralistic Age* [Philadelphia: Westminster Press, 1975], 264). As Elizabeth Johnson points out, this "boxes actual women into a stereotypical ideal" (Johnson, *She Who Is*, 51).

19. See Mary D. Pellauer, Barbara Chester, and Jane Boyajian, *Sexual Assault and Abuse: A Handbook for Religious Professionals* (San Francisco: Harper & Row, 1987).

20. Karl Barth, *Church Dogmatics*, 1/2, trans. G. W. Bromiley and T. F. Torrance (Edinburgh: T. & T. Clark, 1956), 388.

21. John Calvin, *Institutes of the Christian Religion* 2.16.5, ed. John T. McNeill, trans. Ford Lewis Battles (Philadelphia: Westminster Press, 1960), 507.

22. Schillebeeckx says that the Christian tradition went wrong when it separated Jesus' suffering and death from the particular circumstances that caused it and therefore began to value suffering in the abstract. See Edward Schillebeeckx, *Christ: The Experience of Jesus as Lord*, trans. John Bowden (New York: Crossroad, 1990), 699.

23. Gustaf Aulén, *Christus Victor*, trans. A. G. Hebert (New York: Macmillan Co., 1969), 32. Aulén is here describing Irenaeus's position, but he takes it for his own.

24. Irenaeus, *Against Heresies* 5.1.1, trans. Edward Rochie Hardy, in *Early Christian Fathers*, ed. Cyril C. Richardson (New York: Macmillan, 1970), 385.

25. Reinhold Niebuhr, *The Nature and Destiny of Man*, vol. 2 (New York: Charles Scribner's Sons, 1949), 72, 290.

26. "To believe that the suffering Messiah will return at the end of history as a triumphant judge and redeemer is to express the faith that existence cannot ultimately defy its own norm" (ibid., 290).

27. "I make a definite distinction," bell hooks writes, "between that marginality which is imposed by oppressive structures and that marginality one chooses as a site of resistance—as location of radical openness and possibility" (bell hooks, *Yearning: Race, Gender, and Cultural Politics* [Boston: South End Press, 1990], 153). For analogous points, see Søren Kierkegaard, *Concluding Unscientific Postscript*, trans. David F. Swenson and Walter Lowrie (Princeton: Princeton University Press, 1941), 387–88; and Dorothee Soelle, *Suffering*, trans. Everett R. Kalin (Philadelphia: Fortress Press, 1975), 103.

28. Gene Outka, *Agape: An Ethical Analysis* (New Haven: Yale University Press, 1972), 275.

29. Gregory of Nazianzus, *Orations* 1.5, trans. Charles Gordon Browne and James Edward Swallow, *The Nicene and Post-Nicene Fathers*, 2d ser., vol. 7 (New York: Christian Literature Co., 1893), 203.

30. René Girard, *Things Hidden since the Foundation of the World*, trans. Stephen Bann and Michael Metteer (Stanford, Calif.: Stanford University Press, 1987).

31. "Beyond a certain threshold of belief, the effect of the scapegoat is to reverse the relationships between persecutors and their victims, thereby producing the sacred, the founding ancestors and the divinities" (René Girard, *The Scapegoat*, trans. Yvonne Freccero [Baltimore: Johns Hopkins University Press, 1986], 44).

32. Ibid., 122.

33. As thoughtful a theologian as Anne Carr writes that models of the imitation of Christ developed by male theologians that "counteract *their* experience of sin as prideful self-assertion; the healing of grace is then understood as sacrificial love . . . are of no help to women" (Carr, *Transforming Grace*, 174). But women are also of some particular class, race, nationality, and so on—and they are simply human beings. The rhetoric that says they need not concern themselves at all ("of no help") about sins of pride or the need for sacrificial love seems to me excessive.

34. Tzvetan Todorov, *The Conquest of America*, trans. Richard Howard (New York: Harper & Row, Harper Torchbooks, 1987), 169. To be fair, the passage continues, "and that one must further impose that truth on those others." But given that Todorov has made Las Casas's renunciation of violence clear, "impose," I should think, can only mean, "try to persuade."

35. Wilfred Cantwell Smith, *Religious Diversity* (New York: Crossroad, 1982), 13.

36. See, among many works, John Hick, *An Interpretation of Religion* (New Haven: Yale University Press, 1988); and Paul F. Knitter, *No Other Name? A Critical Survey of Christian Attitudes Toward the World Religions* (Maryknoll, N. Y.: Orbis Books, 1985).

37. "Political liberalism," John Rawls writes, "does not argue that we should be hesitant and uncertain, much less skeptical, about our own beliefs. Rather, we are to recognize the practical impossibility of reaching reasonable and workable political agreement in judgment on the truth of comprehensive doctrines" (John Rawls, *Political Liberalism* [New York: Columbia University Press, 1993], 63). I will have more to say about Rawls below in chapter 7, but note here that even his liberal commitment to pluralism does not require, or even encourage, doubt about the truth of one's own position.

38. Paul J. Griffiths, *An Apology for Apologetics* (Maryknoll, N.Y.: Orbis Books, 1991), xii.

39. Surin quotes Theodor Adorno on how such attitudes treat "actual or imagined differences as stigma indicating that not enough has yet been done" (Kenneth Surin, "Towards a 'Materialist' Critique of 'Religious Pluralism,'" *The Thomist* 53 [1989]: 664–73; the quotation is from Theodor W. Adorno, *Minima Moralia: Reflections from Damaged Life*, trans. E. F. N. Jephcott [London: Verso, 1974], 102).

40. Audre Lorde, *Sister Outsider: Essays and Speeches* (Freedom, Calif.: Crossing Press, 1984), 111–12.

41. Langdon Gilkey, "A Retrospective Glance at My Work," *The Whirlwind in Culture: Frontiers in Theology*, ed. Donald W. Musser and Joseph L. Price (Bloomington, Ill.: Meyer Stone Books, 1988), 35.

42. See William C. Placher, *Unapologetic Theology: A Christian Voice in a Pluralistic Conversation* (Louisville, Ky.: Westminster/John Knox Press, 1989), chap. 9. Like Gilkey, J. A. DiNoia points out that pluralists like Hick, who "argue that the various foci of worship and question in the major, soteriologically oriented religious communities represent a focus that transcends them all" are ultimately making "an independent religious proposal" of their own. All the more reason not to grant them any special status (J. A. DiNoia, *The Diversity of Religions* [Washington, D.C.: Catholic University of America Press, 1992], 140).

43. See, e.g., Smith, *Religious Diversity*, 13.

44. Karl Barth, *Church Dogmatics*, 2/2, trans. G. W. Bromiley et al. (Edinburgh: T. & T. Clark, 1957), 417-18, 476; and Hans Urs von Balthasar, *Dare We Hope "That All Men Be Saved"?* trans.

David Kipp and Lothar Krauth (San Francisco: Ignatius Press, 1988). For a discussion of the complexity of von Balthasar's position on this matter, see Gerard O'Hanlon, *The Immutability of God in the Theology of Hans Urs von Balthasar* (Cambridge: Cambridge University Press, 1987), 74.

45. George A. Lindbeck, "*Fides ex auditu* and the Salvation of Non-Christians," in *The Gospel and the Ambiguity of the Church*, ed. Vilmos Vajta (Philadelphia: Fortress Press, 1974), 115.

46. For some interesting reflections, see DiNoia, *The Diversity of Religions*, 104–6.

47. Note Lindbeck's appeal to Aquinas's distinction between the *modus significandi* and the *significatum* (George A. Lindbeck, *The Nature of Doctrine: Religion and Theology in a Postliberal Age* [Philadelphia: Westminster Press, 1984], 65–66).

48. See, e.g., John B. Cobb, Jr., and Christopher Ives, eds., *The Emptying God: A Buddhist-Jewish-Christian Conversation* (Maryknoll, N. Y.: Orbis Books, 1990).

49. J. A. DiNoia, "The Universality of Salvation and the Diversity of Religious Aims," *Worldmission* 32 (1981–82): 12; and idem, *The Diversity of Religions*, 90. See also Lindbeck, *The Nature of Doctrine*, 54.

50. One can also understand that, given the horrible history of Christian anti-Semitism, *some* Jews welcome an attitude that treats them as just one more world religion.

51. DiNoia, *The Diversity of Religions*, 91.

52. "A Theological Understanding of the Relationship between Christians and Jews," study paper commended to the church for study by the 199th General Assembly (1987) of the Presbyterian Church (U.S.A.), 9.

53. *Book of Confessions*, Presbyterian Church (U.S.A.), 6.007.

54. Ibid., 6.006.

55. Ibid., 6.009.

56. See Calvin, *Institutes* 1.14.3, pp. 162–63; 1.17.13, p. 227; 2.11.13, pp. 462–63. See also *Commentary on Genesis* (3:8), trans. John King, *Calvin's Commentaries*, vol. 1 (Grand Rapids: Baker Book House, 1989), 161; and *Commentary on First Corinthians* (2:7), trans. John Pringle (Grand Rapids: Baker Book House, 1989), 103–4. Of Calvin, Jackson Forstman says that accommodation "is perhaps his most widely used exegetical tool" (H. Jackson Forstman, *Word and Spirit* [Stanford, Calif.: Stanford University Press, 1962], 13).

57. See Placher, *Unapologetic Theology*, chap. 3. See also, e.g., Paul Feyerabend, *Farewell to Reason* (London: Verso, 1987), 169–79.

Part 3

Discipleship

6 Eating Gracefully

The Church of a
Vulnerable God

If we Christians understand ourselves to be living in a world defined by the biblical narratives that identify this vulnerable God, then that makes a difference not only in how we think about God but also in how we think we ought to live our own lives. This chapter and the next turn to the question of what it means to live in discipleship to such a God. It is perhaps surprising that the answer to that question begins not with ethical precepts but with an old-fashioned Reformation doctrine of the church: Christians should live as members of a community in which the Word of God is preached and heard and the sacraments are properly administered.[1] Indeed, much of this chapter will consist of rather straightforward exposition of Calvin, whose definition of a church was just paraphrased, focusing on church as community, on preaching as the telling of the stories that define this community, and on sacraments as creators and signs of its communal virtues.

Those who talk about community in Christian theology today find themselves in dialogue with Stanley Hauerwas. The popularity of his many works indicates the deep chord he has struck, particularly among Christian pastors. At several points in this chapter Hauerwas will come in for criticism—for not giving enough attention to the sacramental character of Christian communities and for lacking a strong enough theology of grace—so it is worth emphasizing at

137

the start how much what follows owes to his work. In particular, Hauerwas has reminded contemporary Christian theologians of the importance of church as community for Christian faith. Nearly a hundred years ago, the great Adolf von Harnack, addressing his audience on the essence of Christianity, declared, "The kingdom of God comes by coming to the individual, by entering into his soul and laying hold of it. . . . It is not a question of . . . thrones and principalities, but of God and the soul, the soul and its God"[2] The interviews that Robert Bellah and his coworkers conducted for *Habits of the Heart* indicate how pervasive individualism has become in religion and every other aspect of American culture.[3] Sheila Larson, the young nurse who describes her religious belief as "Sheilaism," is only the extreme case of a common pattern.[4]

The biblical narratives, however, do not generally tell stories about individual souls alone with their God. Consider, for instance, the story of Paul's conversion in Acts 9. The story often gets told only partway through: Saul of Tarsus, off to Damascus, "breathing threats and murder against the disciples of the Lord," encounters a mysterious light from heaven and the voice of Jesus and is converted.[5] But as Acts tells it, that moment on the Damascus road left Saul blind and neither eating nor drinking for three days: so far it sounds more like a nervous breakdown than a successful religious conversion. The story concludes only when Ananias, in obedience to a vision from the Lord, seeks out Saul, speaks to him, and restores his sight, whereupon Saul is baptized, eats, spends some time with the Christian community in Damascus, and begins to proclaim the gospel. When God "willed to call Paul to the knowledge of himself and to engraft him into the church," Calvin noted, "he does not address him with his own voice, but sends him to a man from whom he is to receive both the doctrine of salvation and the sanctification of baptism."[6] In other words, Saul becomes a Christian only by entrance into a Christian community.

To be sure, some historical question marks surround this story, which the Bible never gives in Paul's own words. But the narrative as we have it does seem to present a pattern to be seen repeatedly in scripture and in the lives of Christians. This particular story has a special dramatic force, since Saul had been throwing Christians into prison and stood witness to the stoning of Stephen; he presumably still had the warrants he was issued against the Damascus church in his back pocket. The story reaches its conclusion only because Christians, first Ananias and then the whole Damascus community, were willing, in love and obedience, to risk vulnerability in a very concrete way, to return forgiveness for violence, and to make an outsider welcome in their midst.

All Christians are called to live in that kind of community, to help create it. In Dietrich Bonhoeffer's words, "It is the mystery of the community that Christ is in her and, only through her, reaches to men. Christ exists among us as community, as Church in the hiddenness of history. The Church is the hidden Christ among us."[7] That claim refers to the church universal, to be sure, but also to the particular congregation. When in the creed Christians say, *credo ecclesiam*, they mean, Karl Barth says, that in "each particular congregation of Christ, . . . here, at this place, in this assembly, the work of the Holy Spirit takes place."[8] Such an ideal may seem a long way from Calvin's apparently pedestrian marks of a church of God, where the Word of God is preached and heard and the sacraments properly administered, or a long way from most contemporary congregations. The thesis of this chapter, however, is that a community that hears, really hears, the Word preached and shares, really shares, in the sacraments will be just this kind of community, modeling the God it knows and worships, the vulnerable God known in biblical narratives.

To begin where Calvin did, with the preaching and hearing of the Word of God: "The social ethical task of the church," Hauerwas writes, "is to be the kind of community that tells and tells rightly the story of Jesus."[9] We Christians enact that telling in our liturgy and our lives, but it also needs to happen in sermons, for only in regularly reading scripture and reflecting on it in the gathered community can there develop a common language and a framework of shared stories and understandings of those stories within which we can live our lives together as Christians.[10] One needs no particularly theologial warrants to make such a claim; a good social anthropologist could affirm it, and, for that matter, common sense discloses that communities, from families to nations to the campers of Camp Cucamonga, become communities in part by sharing stories. Sermons provide the space for inviting the community to reflect together in the context of the language of the scriptural texts, thereby at once learning to use that language and learning to think about the world in its terms.

From this it follows that, in the phrase of Hughes Old, "a sermon is not just a lecture on some religious subject, it is rather an explanation of a passage of Scripture."[11] My late friend and colleague Eric Dean did a good bit of supply preaching in Indiana and told the story of one congregation where he filled in for the regular pastor. A number of people afterward remarked, "You know, what we particularly liked about that sermon was that you tied what you said to the passage that had been read from the Bible earlier in the service." Given their usual experience, this was apparently a new idea to them.

The language and stories that Christians as Christians share come first of all from the Bible. In Christian worship, therefore, the sermon, whatever else it does, ought to present and interpret scripture to the assembled people. Vivid stories, humor, intellectual brilliance, challenging social commentary may all be helpful and appropriate, but if one is not at some level retelling the stories, then it is not Christian preaching. "What surprises the modern reader of Calvin's sermons," to quote Hughes Old again,

> is the simplicity of his sermons. We find no engaging introductions, no illustrative stories nor anecdotes, no quotations from great authors, no stirring conclusions. . . . The forcefulness of his sermons is to be found in the clarity of his analysis of the text. Calvin seems to have no fear that the Scriptures will be boring or irrelevant unless the preacher spices them up.[12]

The need for explicitly scriptural preaching in our time derives in part from realities noted in earlier chapters: in contemporary American society the dominant images of divinity and success and community are in some respects radically un-Christian. It cannot be taken for granted that Christians generally remember or ever understood the sort of God in whom we believe and the sort of people we are therefore called to be. James Cone somewhere explains that African American sermons have characteristically been so long because the whole rest of the week the dominant white society was telling black people they were of no worth, and so it took a while to talk them back into knowing who they really were. All Christians need some reminding of who we are, and worship ought to provide it.

If preaching is not just good jokes and intellectual brilliance but serious reflection on biblical texts, then it becomes God's Word addressed to God's people. "The preaching of the Word of God," the Second Helvetic Confession asserts, "is the Word of God."[13] The great Reformed theologian of worship Jean Jacques von Allmen faithfully represents the Reformed tradition in presenting this as a kind of secondary incarnation: "Preaching . . . expresses one of the deepest mysteries of the love of God: If God gives Himself to us, it is to enter into the depth of our being and invite us to disclose Him to the world, clothed with our flesh."[14] At one level, any preacher ought to find terrifying the call to speak God's Word. As Annie Dillard writes,

> The churches are children playing on the floor with their chemistry sets, mixing up a batch of TNT to kill a Sunday morning. . . . We should all be wearing crash helmets. Ushers should issue life preservers and signal flares; they should lash us to our pews.[15]

It ought to be a terrifying business to find yourself speaking the Word of God to the people of God. "Biblical preaching" should never be the slogan for noncontroversial, nostalgic piety, for the Bible tells about a covenant that shaped every aspect of people's lives, prophets who challenged the powers-that-be, and a Christ murdered by the establishment of his time. These narratives of a vulnerable God are not safe stories. Indeed, the call to preach the Word of God may sometimes be a call to cause pain, to make yourself unpopular, to lose your job. The gospel of the crucified Jesus is not a safe retreat from the storms of contemporary social issues but sometimes the most direct and radical address to them that one can imagine.

On the other hand, the Second Helvetic Confession goes on to say, using the male pronouns that that age took for granted as applied to preachers, that "the Word itself which is preached is to be regarded, not the minister that preaches; for even if he be evil and a sinner, nevertheless the Word of God remains still true and good."[16] Calvin even suspects it may not be a bad thing to have a less than perfect preacher:

> This is the best and most useful exercise in humility, when he [God] accustoms us to obey his Word, even though it be preached through men like us and sometimes even by those of lower worth than we. . . . When a puny man risen from the dust speaks in God's name, at this point we best evidence our piety and obedience toward God if we show ourselves teachable toward his minister, although he excels us in nothing.[17]

To face the task of preaching God's Word, Calvin wanted to say, is first to realize that it is difficult, then to realize that it is impossible, and then to realize that it must therefore depend on grace. Like every other form of Christian life, preaching is a calling into which one puts the best possible efforts in gratitude to God but in which one learns about God's grace when the best-planned efforts fail and mistakes succeed beyond any expectations. Trying to shock or offend the congregation is as bad as trying not to shock or offend them, and trying to capture them with the peculiar genius of a gifted preacher misses the point altogether. When directors try to liven up a production with all sorts of gimmicks, it shows that they do not really trust the quality of the play. Sometimes, in the theater, such directors may be right, but preachers should learn to trust their material.

It is also worth noting that Calvin defines a church as a place where the Word of God "is purely preached *and heard.*"[18] The good news is that even that puny preacher of little worth can be heard as speaking God's word; the bad news is that, no matter how good the preacher, a congregation where everyone else is daydreaming or asleep is at that moment, in Calvin's terms, not a church. Congregations need reminding from time to time that the preaching of the Word of God is not a spectator sport.

The preaching of the Word, the telling of the stories of God's work with Israel and of the crucified Jesus, plays its part in making a Christian community by issuing reminders of the sort of God Christians worship. In Calvin's terms, it recalls the "promise." The sacraments then "confirm" and "seal" that promise; they are "covenants," "tokens," or "visible words," that "ratify among us those things given us by divine bounty."[19]

It is one of the great failures of contemporary Reformed worship that the sacraments have come to have such a peripheral role and usually get done in such uninspired fashion. Karl Barth focused the question well:

> Would the sermon not be delivered and listened to quite differently, . . . if everything outwardly and visibly began with baptism and moved towards the Lord's Supper? Why do the numerous movements and attempts to bring the liturgy of the Reformed church up to date . . . prove without exception so unfruitful? Is it not just because they do not fix their attention on this fundamental defect, the incompleteness of our usual service, i.e. its lack of sacraments?[20]

Unless Presbyterians start having more children, baptisms at every service seem an impractical ideal, and, although Calvin wanted a weekly Eucharist, with many American Presbyterian congregations moving to monthly celebration only reluctantly, doing it every week may for the time being remain unrealistic. Still, did not Barth have an important point to make? Christians need to find ways of remembering that the service of Word and sacraments is the norm, that anything else is, for one reason or another, an abbreviation. For all of Stanley Hauerwas's emphasis on worship,[21] incidentally, in many of his works he seems to talk about Christian congregations as ethical communities that hear and remember the biblical stories in preaching and teaching but not much about them as sacramental communities.[22]

What kind of community should Christians form? The first answer is that they are a people who tell particular stories, but for the Reformed tradition the second and third have to do with sacraments. First, they are people who have been baptized. "Baptism is the sign of the initiation by which we are received into the society of the church, in order that, engrafted in Christ, we may be reckoned among God's children."[23] In the midst of his trials and spiritual struggles, Luther used to repeat to himself, again and again like a talisman, "I have been baptized,"[24] and Calvin recommended the same practice:

> All pious folk throughout life, whenever they are troubled
> by a consciousness of their faults, may venture to remind
> themselves of their baptism, that from it they may be con-
> firmed in assurance of that sole and perpetual cleansing
> which we have in Christ's blood.[25]

The way one becomes a member helps define the nature of a community. One gets into Congress by election, and that creates at least the temptation for political posturing, the pressure of constant fund raising, and so on. One joins a symphony orchestra through audition, and that creates a particular mixture of pride, discipline, and insecurity among the successful. One enters a country club after the approval of the membership committee, with resulting possibilities of exclusion, snobbery, and bigotry. But one enters the Christian church by being baptized, and any infant can do it.

Much of the Christian tradition has held that in an emergency anyone, even a non-Christian, can baptize. No doubt this has sometimes led to, or grown out of, superstitious interpretations in which the external sign of water took on complete and magical significance. Still, it seems rather wonderful that, even in medieval periods when the church seems, to a modern Protestant eye, to have been most problematically hierarchical, there remained this almost casual sense that, when push comes to shove, anyone can baptize.

In so many communities the ritual of initiation is rigorous and daunting, and those who have survived wear its scars as a matter of

143

pride, as much, incidentally, in academic communities as in tribes of hunter-gatherers. Robert Bly and some of his admirers think that males in our culture need more of such rituals, the moral equivalent of killing our first bear. But how can anyone brag about having gone through baptism? To be sure, some come to Christian faith as adults, through difficult paths, and parts of the patristic era, when most Christians postponed baptism, often required the most rigorous of preparatory disciplines.[26] Yet even then it took only a bit of water in infancy to make one just as fully a Christian. All in all, one can hardly imagine a better symbol for a community of equals and a community of grace.[27]

Down through the years, Presbyterians have from time to time suspected Methodists of a perfectionism and Arminianism that lose strong enough doctrines of sin and grace, so perhaps it only revives old battles to raise another question about Hauerwas at this point. He does seem to say, however, that the moral quality of the Christian community counts as evidence for the truth of the stories it tells, and even that our belief in the truth of the story depends on the moral virtues of the community that tells it.[28] Now sometimes Christian congregations do anticipate the virtues of the heavenly city. But oftentimes, deeply flawed as we are, they do not and even then they are still God's church, the community of the baptized. A community free to tell the truth is, among other things, free to tell the truth about its own sins, and free to do so precisely because it knows itself to belong to God even in the midst of its sin, in a way that baptism so marvelously symbolizes. That is one of the reasons it is so important that a Christian church be a sacramental community as well as a storytelling one. We Christians know who we are because of the stories we tell, but part of what we know is that we are sinners who could not stand, individually or together, were we not sustained at every turn by God's grace.

The community that tells the stories, the community of the baptized, is also the community that gathers around a table and shares a meal. One way to reflect on the nature of that meal is to turn once again to the Gospel narratives. In those stories, Jesus eats or defends or distributes a good many meals, and they often occasion controversy. Commentators often read the texts backward, taking these other meals as types or anticipations of the Last Supper and therefore as implicitly eucharistic meals. And fair enough. The Gospels were written and first read in communities that already celebrated the Lord's Supper, which would naturally have provided an interpretive context for these parts of the narrative. Drawing on reader-response theory, however, Robert Fowler has suggested that there is, after all, also something natural about reading the story forward, interpreting the Eucharist in the light of these earlier stories about eating in the Gospels. [29]

Although this is hardly an exhaustive categorization, the stories include at least meals that Jesus eats with a variety of people, defenses of his disciples when they eat in some violation of ritual law, and miraculous feedings.

Except for the Last Supper, the most formal occasion in the Gospels on which Jesus ever sits down to dinner takes place at the house of Levi, where Jesus eats with tax collectors and sinners (Mark 2:13–17 and parallels). The scribes of the Pharisees react with horror, and Jesus replies, "Those who are well have no need of a physician, but those who are sick; I have come to call not the righteous but sinners" (Mark 2:17). Luke tells a similar story about dinner at the house of the chief tax collector, Zaccheus (Luke 19:1–10). A meal shared with Jesus, it seems, is a place where just about anyone might be found—except those too proud or fussy to join the company. Some may exclude themselves, but Jesus excludes no one.

In Jesus' controversies about his disciples' eating, he likewise consistently challenges rules and restrictions. If his disciples pluck heads of grain on the Sabbath—well, "the sabbath was made for humankind, and not humankind for the sabbath" (Mark 2:27). If his disciples eat without washing their hands first—well, it is what comes out of a person that can defile, not what goes in (Mark 7:15). If his disciples do not fast, as do the disciples of John—well, the bridegroom is here, this is a party, no time for fasting (Mark 2:19). Jesus has in all this a certain insouciance, the self-confident indifference to legalistic rules that aristocracy and urban underclass alike can manifest to the judgment of the bourgeousie, the attitude that Augustine captured when he summarized Christian ethics in the phrase, "Love and do what you will."[30] Love, as Whitehead said, is "a little oblivious as to morals."[31]

This Jesus who eats with sinners and seems so indifferent to the rules of proper eating feeds multitudes. In Mark's version of the feeding of the five thousand—the only miracle, incidentally, to appear in all four Gospels—Jesus has compassion on the crowd who seem like sheep without a shepherd. The disciples urge him to stop teaching these people and send them off to buy something to eat, and Jesus replies—the retort sounds harsh—"You give them something to eat." Jesus had sent his disciples off a-preaching, with explicit instructions to take no bread and no money, but they prove to have two hundred denarii, which is most of a year's wages, and five loaves of bread—and no interest at all in spending them on this crowd of strangers.[32] And Jesus blessed and broke the bread and all ate and were filled. Whatever we make of what really happened that afternoon—and I for one just do not know—the story as a part of the larger gospel story certainly tells us something about Christian community.

Mark tells the story just after his account of a very different feast, the banquet where the daughter of Herodias dances before Herod and receives the head of John the Baptist as her reward.[33] It is an obscene story, beginning with a scandalous marriage, a family conflict, and royal power exercised by unwarranted arrest to satisfy a family grudge. Herod's niece or daughter—the text is unclear—dances in public, "for his courtiers and officers and for the leaders of Galilee," and Herod is so excited that he offers her half his kingdom. It is hard for us to read the story without echoes of Richard Strauss or Oscar Wilde intruding, but the text itself does seem to have, in the public dancing of a royal daughter, in the king's excessive promise, undertones of a very odd sensuality.[34] "What should I ask for?" the child asks her mother. "The head of John the baptizer." Only a metaphor for his murder, perhaps. It is the child herself who adds the literalistic detail of wanting it on a dish. The scene ends with the bare report: "Then the girl gave it to her mother." After a single sentence in which John's disciples bury his body, the text shifts to the story of the feeding of the five thousand.

Fowler, thinking about how the narrative strikes a reader, invites us to contrast "the banquet of Herod" with "the banquet of Jesus."[35] On the one hand, a family torn apart by hatred and at least a hint of incestuous love; on the other, a crowd of strangers united in listening to Jesus' teaching and sharing the meal he provides. In one case a banquet where taxation that has bled the countryside must have provided every kind of delicacy but the only item actually mentioned on a dish is disgustingly inedible. In the other case, a situation of poverty without enough food to stave off hunger, but in the end basketfuls of food. Eros at its most grasping and self-indulgent. Agape at its most generous.

The Gospel narratives, then, reach the Last Supper with a set of images about meals and eating implanted in the minds of their readers. We know that Jesus sat at table with all sorts of sinners and outsiders, that he was a bit indifferent to rules about the proper occasions and formulae for eating, and that somehow he could feed

146

multitudes of strangers, so that no one who had come to listen to his words went hungry. Such images do not provide a bad context for thinking about the Eucharist.

Calvin resisted clear explanations of the Lord's Supper. It is not, he said, "as if the body of Christ, by a local presence, were put there to be touched by the hands, to be chewed by the teeth, and to be swallowed by the mouth."[36] At the same time, "greatly mistaken are those who conceive no presence of flesh in the Supper unless it lies in the bread."[37] "Now, if anyone should ask me how this takes place, I shall not be ashamed to confess that it is a secret too lofty for either my mind to comprehend or my words to declare."[38] What matters to Calvin at minimum, over against Zwingli at his worst,[39] is that Christ's presence in the sacrament is real and something that God does, not merely something we create by remembering something God once did. "I indeed admit that the breaking of bread is a symbol; it is not the thing itself. But, having admitted this, . . . unless a man means to call God a deceiver, he would never dare assert that an empty symbol is set forth by him. . . . And the godly ought by all means to keep this rule: whenever they see symbols appointed by the Lord, to think and be persuaded that the truth of the thing signified is surely present there."[40]

If Christ is present in the sacrament, then the table around which the people gather is Christ's table, and, in the face of the attitudes the Gospels portray of Jesus, it is not for us to set overfussy limits about who may come or how to proceed.[41] For someone generally so concerned that things be done decently and in order, indeed, Calvin could be oddly relaxed about the form of the Lord's Supper. The practice of the ancient church was for all to take the elements in their hands, he noted, but such things do not really matter much. Using unleavened bread rather than an ordinary loaf seemed to have no purpose "unless to draw the eyes of the common people to wonderment by a new spectacle." If one could only "get rid of this great pile of ceremonies," we could do the thing every week.[42] Calvin's anti-Catholic polemics, uncomfortable as they sometimes make readers in our more ecumenical age, generally make the point that, although we ought to feel awe at Christ's presence, this meal should be joyous and welcoming. The Lord, he wrote, has "given us a Table at which to feast, not an altar upon which to offer a victim; he has not consecrated priests to offer sacrifice, but ministers to distribute the sacred banquet."[43] "The Supper was to have been distributed in the public assembly of the church to teach us of the communion by which we all cleave together in

Christ Jesus. The sacrifice of the mass dissolves and tears apart this community."[44]

It is a paradox of the Lord's Supper that this commemoration of Christ's passion should also be a joyous feast. To celebrate the Lord's Supper, then, is to enact and manifest a theme emphasized above in chapter 1. Mark's Gospel does not give its readers an unambiguously happy ending with all Christ's suffering cast aside like a mask. Yet it does proclaim itself to be good news. So the Lord's Supper provides the occasion to remember the night Jesus was betrayed, and how he said, "This is my body . . . ." "This is my blood . . . ." Yet the occasion is a celebration: the feast is spread before us, and Jesus is our host. "What stands out," Edward Schillebeeckx has remarked, in the Gospel accounts of Jesus' role as host, "is the sheer abundance of Jesus' gifts. . . . Although he had not a stone on which to lay his head, he and his disciples, even the listening bystanders, never went short of anything."[45] The very pattern of the Lord's Supper, like the pattern of Jesus' story, thus makes a significant point about the Christian life. As Christians we are called to take risks, to make ourselves vulnerable in love, to share with strangers, to dare to challenge unjust power and take the consequences. And we are promised joy and celebration, not as a reward bestowed extrinsically after having paid the price of enough suffering, but rather in that a life of vulnerable love is itself a life of joy. "Over against the dissatisfied 'Acquisitive Man,'" Gregory Dix wrote, "Christianity sets the type of 'Eucharistic Man'—man giving thanks with the product of his labours upon the gifts of God, and daily rejoicing with his fellows in the worshipping society which is grounded in eternity."[46] In a broken world, one cannot quite draw such claims as an empirical conclusion; we know only by faith and not by sight. Still, to contrast the quiet (or sometimes not so quiet) desperation of those who live lives dedicated to the fulfillment of id and ego with the lives of those dedicated to love and service is to notice how the latter so often seem to have found a strange kind of joy.

Few human gestures are as basic as the offering of food and drink. In our culture, where every visitor has passed three fast food franchises and a convenience store on the way to any destination, it is easy to forget how fundamental in most of history has been the host's first responsibility to offer something to eat. Those who counsel runaways or the homeless do still remember: so often, the first question ought to be, Are you hungry, have you eaten?

At this meal, all are invited, never matter class or race or gender, and all come as equals, for Jesus is the host. Let a Moor or a barbarian come among us, Calvin said in a sermon on Galatians, whoever, and inasmuch as they are human they come as our brother or sister and our neighbor.[47] He was nervous about those who insisted that only the "pure," "purged of all sin," could come to the Lord's Table: "Such a dogma would debar" all those "who ever were or are on earth from the use of this Sacrament."[48]

In many congregations today, however, the Lord's Supper has become a joyless and unwelcoming affair. Part of the problem is that so many churches are too big for the size of the regular congregation, so that worshipers sit widely spread out, alone or in small clumps, and cannot feel that they are sharing the Supper. This is a feast. It should begin with bread that looks like bread, broken off in honest, healthy chunks, with the congregation forward to gather round the table—and with a table they can gather round rather than a pseudo-altar. The people should pass the elements to each other. Someone ordained to the ministry of Word and sacrament consecrates the elements, but she or he is neither host nor priest, for this is a gathered community sharing a meal. Symbolically, for everyone to be separated, lay people seated, pastor standing and presiding, could hardly be more wrong.[49]

A church where the gospel is preached and heard and the sacraments properly administered, then, ought to be a community that tries to live by the stories of the crucified Jesus, a community of the baptized free to be honest about its faults, and a community gathered around the Lord's Table in equality, celebration, and openness. To say that is to recall one of the most powerful slogans of the modern world, the French Revolution's cry for liberty, equality, and fraternity (translating the last into the gender-neutral ideal of community). Has an analysis of the church where the Word is preached and the sacraments properly administered simply generated a description of a community that instantiates these ideals of modernity?

Not quite, because Christians mean something different by these ideals. Too often in the modern world, liberty has meant the right to satisfy all of one's desires, equality only the assurance that one's rights are secure, and community only the exclusion of outsiders. The community of the baptized will have a different understanding of liberty; the community gathered around the Lord's Table will mean something different by equality; the community that tells the stories of the crucified Jesus will understand community itself in a different way. The rest of this chapter will explore some of those differences.

For liberal, capitalist society, Milton Friedman says, liberty or freedom "is our ultimate goal in judging social arrangements. In a society freedom has nothing to say about what an individual does with his freedom."[50] I am most free when I can do whatever I want. Sail to Tahiti, feed the hungry, make a fortune in the stock market, drink myself to oblivion—after all, it is my life. Society can justly require only that I not interfere with the freedom of others. But communal ideals that require self-sacrifice or a sense of vocation that somehow limits my choices—these seem unwarranted interference with freedom. I am left to do whatever I want, in a context where my very freedom guarantees that there be no right answer as to what I should want. And then I find it odd that it should be so hard to find meaning or purpose to life.[51]

Christian liberty is different: it is freedom *for* a life of service, and it is such because it is freedom *from* sin and the law—the freedom, first of all, of the baptized to be truthful about themselves. In an essay published in *The Christian Century*, Eberhard Jüngel wrote eloquently about how in his youth in East Germany he discovered "the church as the one place within a Stalinist society where one could speak the truth without being penalized."[52] And that discovery was radically liberating.

In the no doubt much freer society of the United States too, citizens live much of their lives in communities of pretense. If I have a problem with alcohol, I have to hide it. If I am a teacher or a student, I have to pretend that I have read more books than I have read and that I understood the argument that others are discussing with such confidence. If I am white or male, I have to pretend that I have no feelings of racism or sexism. If I am African American or a woman or gay, I have to pretend that being in the mostly white, male, straight environment of my office does not intimidate me. All of this I have to do because otherwise this community might not accept me.

The church ought to be different, ought to be a community of the baptized who recognize that all are sinners, but that all have been accepted by God, and can therefore start to tell the truth to each other. As Calvin puts it,

> Among the Corinthians no slight number had gone astray; in fact, almost the whole body was infected. There was not one kind of sin only, but very many; and they were no light errors but frightful misdeeds; there was corruption not only of morals but of doctrine. What does the holy apostle . . . do about this? Does he seek to separate himself from such? Does he cast them out of Christ's Kingdom? Does

he fell them with the ultimate thunderbolt of anathema? He not only does nothing of the sort; he even recognizes and proclaims them to be the church of Christ and the communion of the saints.[53]

Churches are, to be sure, often not in fact very free places. Christians retreat from too much risk, thinking that too much honesty might scare people off. After all, the argument goes, most people do not want to admit that they are sinners, do not want to admit just how much all depend on grace. And so Christian churches play it safe, keeping the pretenses of respectability in place and trying not to notice all the people flooding the church basement for meetings of twelve-step groups as the size of the regular congregation declines. People will find a place where they are free to tell the truth. A community where all know themselves to be sinners who yet live in a grace of which their baptisms are the sign ought to be that kind of place.

If the church of the baptized should be a community of a new kind of liberty, so the church that gathers around the Lord's Table ought to form a community of a new kind of equality. In the words of the World Council of Churches document *Baptism, Eucharist and Ministry,*

> As Jesus went out to publicans and sinners and had table-fellowship with them during his earthly ministry, so Christians are called in the eucharist to be in solidarity with the outcast and to become signs of the love of Christ who lived and sacrificed himself for all and now gives himself in the eucharist.[54]

Given the inequalities that afflict our society, nearly any kind of commitment to equality would be an improvement. Yet even our ideals of equality too often focus on rights and calculation. In a most careful and balanced contemporary account of justice, John Rawls writes that that principle requires that

> all social primary goods—liberty and opportunity, income and wealth, and the bases of self-respect—are to be distributed equally unless an unequal distribution of any or all of these goods is to the advantage of the least favored.[55]

Such a definition is not a bad principle of economic distribution, but as a general rule for determining justice and put into practice, it raises alarming images of trying to calculate each person's allotment of "the bases of self-respect." The very calculation of appropriate distributions, particularly according to a rather complicated principle, seems inimical to some characteristics of a good society.

As suggested above in chapter 3, the doctrine of the Trinity offers a different model for thinking about equality.[56] Within a triunity of equals, there is room for all sorts of relative subordination. If people have really acknowledged one another as equals in a community of love, then we do not have to measure rights down to the last inch, in part just because the members of such a community will be giving each other more than their technical entitlements, and everyone can let different gifts flourish.[57] "When people are friends," Aristotle wrote in the *Nicomachean Ethics*, "they have no need of justice."[58]

Most Christian congregations rarely approach such an ideal of equality. Lines of social class do not disappear at the church door; every congregation has its influential members, its "important people," and therefore, tragically, Christians do not gather as equals even around the Lord's Table. Moreover, at the door of the church a new line between "clergy" and "lay people" appears. That lay theologian John Calvin worried about such distinctions and regretted that "clerics" had become a term applied only to some members of the church, since First Peter so clearly "calls the whole church 'the clergy,' that is, the inheritance of the Lord."[59] "The Lord . . . alone," he wrote, "should rule and reign in the church."[60]

Those ordained to the ministry of Word and sacrament—I write as one who is not—are not always very good at equality. In many congregations, there may be people who are better organizers than the pastor, more empathetic listeners, maybe people who know more about theology. Some of those with such special gifts will not count among the prestigious as the world counts prestige. It will be hard, sometimes, for "the minister" to encourage and value their ministries, for the paradigm of the professional ministry is one of expertise in such matters. But those ordained to particular ministries in the end do not have a profession but a calling—within a Christian community of equals gathered around the Lord's Table.

In a variety of ways the lives of Protestant denominations in particular have in recent years become a matter of the fine calculation of rights, seeking at best the kind of justice that a large political society can hope to achieve. Such calculations produce frustration, and amid the careful figuring of representation of various groups on every committee it is tempting for conservative forces to blame those who are introducing such "political" considerations into the life of just the communities that ought to be modeling a different ideal. It is worth remembering that people do not fight for their rights when they have been living in communities of loving equality. They fight for their rights when they have not even been getting their rights. As Paul Tillich once observed,

> Nothing is more false than to say to somebody: since I love you and you love me, I don't need to get justice from you or you from me, for love eliminates the need for justice. Such language is used by people who want to avoid the obligations which are connected with justice. It is said by tyrannical rulers to their subjects and by tyrannical parents to their children.[61]

Christian communities have often tolerated the worst injustices and inequalities, and the process of rectification and the creation of trust will necessarily involve elements of the calculation of rights. But Christian communities also have to begin to model a higher ideal, which begins with equality around the Lord's Table. One of the greatest challenges contemporary American denominations face is that of seeking political justice within their corporate lives while remembering that they are communities for which justice in such a political sense is not the highest ideal of equality.

The community of the baptized should be a free community; the community around the table should be a community of equals; the community that tells the stories of the vulnerable God revealed in Jesus should be an inclusive community—that is, a community that does not define itself by the outsiders it rejects.

Most communities, of course, define themselves by exclusion. We are ourselves, so a persistent theme of human history goes, because *we* are not *they*. The school finds its moments of greatest unity on the night of the game with the archrival. Phi Beta Kappa is worth the membership fee only because not everyone gets elected. Even the most open of nations does not forever welcome the tired, the poor, the huddled masses yearning to breathe free.[62]

A church united around the story of Jesus is thus a very different sort of community. The New Testament word for "hospitality," *philoxenia*, means "love of strangers"; it is the opposite of *xenophobia*, the fear of those whom one does not know. New Testament texts find a variety of ways to challenge the model of a community of insiders who exclude. First Peter and James, for instance, addressing communities of struggling, displaced foreigners, identify them as a model of Christian community. Ephesians bursts open all boundaries with a vision of Christ for the whole world.[63] Both make the same point: a Christian church cannot define itself as a

153

NARRATIVES OF A VULNERABLE GOD

community of privilege. "There is not," Justin Martyr wrote, "one single race of [people]—whether barbarians, or Greeks, or persons called by any other name, nomads, or vagabonds, or herdsmen dwelling in tents—among whom prayers and thanksgivings are not offered to the Father and Creator of the universe in the name of the Crucified Jesus."[64] Today there truly is no race, no nation, where there are not fellow Christians, no sort of person who might not gather around the Lord's Table. In urban America where homeless people may be sleeping in the church doorway, the issue of inclusivity may literally concern vagrants; in the southwest it may involve Central American refugees; and in a small-town church, a son with AIDS come home to die. The principle remains the same: a community that faithfully attends to the narratives of the crucified Jesus cannot be a community that excludes. Christians are a people who have seen that scapegoats are innocent. When we try to get into the in-crowd by joining in their ridicule or persecution of those they exclude, we find, as Peter did in that courtyard so long ago, that Jesus stands among those we have just excluded, and we have separated ourselves from him.

Alice Walker's marvelous short story "The Welcome Table" tells of an old African American woman, tired and thirsty, entering the vestibule of a white church.

> Some of them there at the church saw the age, the dotage, the missing buttons down the front of her mildewed black dress. Others saw cooks, chauffeurs, maids. . . . Many of them saw jungle orgies in an evil place, while others were reminded of riotous anarchists looting and raping in the streets.

And so the hierarchy of the church mobilizes in defense of the racism of the congregation:

> The reverend of the church stopped her pleasantly as she stepped into the vestibule. . . . "Auntie, you know this is not your church?" As if one could choose the wrong one.[65]

Out on the hot highway, dying as her heart gives out, she sees Jesus walking down the road and tells him, indignantly, "how they had tossed her out of his church."[66] So should Christians always be indignant when what ought to be Jesus' church becomes a community of exclusion, celebrating, in Robert Bellah's phrase, "the narcissism of similarity."[67]

Few issues illustrate so clearly the relation of liturgy and Christian life as this question of inclusiveness. John Zizioulas recalls the strict ancient canonical rule that one could celebrate only one Eucharist in the same place on the same day.[68] No special services for students or particular social classes or anyone else. The Christian community consists of all the Christian people in that place on that day—and they gather around a table together. When one thinks of the tragedies that followed when the Dutch Reformed Church in South Africa, in 1857, in deference to "the weaknesses of some," allowed the Lord's Supper to be celebrated in separate services for different races—it was the beginning of apartheid—one sees how our worship shapes our identity as a community, for better or worse.[69]

Just as the community of the baptized is one where one can be free to speak the truth and the community around the Lord's Table is one in which we share an equality so firm that different gifts can flourish within it, so a community that tells and truly hears the stories of the crucified Jesus will of necessity remain open to the outsiders and strangers of the world.[70] A place where the Word of God is preached and heard and the sacraments properly administered makes for a pretty good church.

NOTES

1. "Wherever we see the Word of God purely preached and heard, and the sacraments administered according to Christ's institution, there, it is not to be doubted, a church of God exists" (John Calvin, *Institutes of the Christian Religion* 4.1.9, ed. John T. McNeill, trans. Ford Lewis Battles [Philadelphia: Westminster Press, 1960], 1023).
2. Adolf von Harnack, *What Is Christianity?* trans. Thomas Bailey Saunders (New York: Harper & Brothers, Harper Torchbooks, 1957), 56.
3. "Individualism lies at the very core of American culture" (Robert N. Bellah et al., *Habits of the Heart: Individualism and Commitment in American Life* [New York: Harper & Row paperback, 1985], 142.
4. Ibid., 221, 235.
5. For a recent example of telling only part of the story, see Peter Berger, *A Far Glory: The Quest for Faith in an Age of Credulity* (New York: Free Press, 1992), 88–89, where Paul serves with Abraham as an example of biblical "proto-individualism," in support of Berger's odd (especially for a sociologist) argument for the essential solitariness of religious belief.
6. Calvin, *Institutes* 4.3.3, p. 1056.
7. Dietrich Bonhoeffer, *No Rusty Swords*, trans. Edwin H. Robertson and John Bowden (New York: Harper & Row, 1965), 68.

8. Karl Barth, *Dogmatics in Outline*, trans. G. T. Thomson (New York: Harper & Brothers, Harper Torchbooks, 1959), 142–43.

9. Stanley Hauerwas, *A Community of Character: Toward a Constructive Christian Social Ethic* (Notre Dame, Ind.: University of Notre Dame Press, 1981), 52.

10. Stanley Hauerwas, *Against the Nations: War and Survival in a Liberal Society* (Minneapolis: Winston Press, 1985), 5; and George A. Lindbeck, *The Nature of Doctrine: Religion and Theology in a Postliberal Age* (Philadelphia: Westminster Press, 1984), 128–29.

11. Hughes Oliphant Old, *Worship* (Atlanta: John Knox Press, 1985), 60.

12. Ibid., 75–76.

13. *Book of Confessions*, Presbyterian Church (U.S.A.), 5.004.

14. Jean Jacques von Allmen, *Worship: Its Theology and Practice* (London: Lutterworth Press, 1965), 143.

15. Annie Dillard, *Teaching a Stone to Talk* (New York: Harper & Row, 1982), 40.

16. *Book of Confessions*, Presbyterian Church (U.S.A.), 5.004.

17. Calvin, *Institutes* 4.3.1, p. 1054.

18. Michael Root pointed out to me that Luther and Melanchthon would not usually have added this phrase, not because they thought faithful hearing unimportant but out of the conviction that the Word rightly preached is never altogether without effect.

19. Calvin, *Institutes* 4.14.3, 6, 17, pp. 1278, 1280–81, 1293. The description of sacraments as "visible words" seems to come from Augustine, *Homilies on the Gospel of John* 80.3, trans. John Gibb and James Innes, *The Nicene and Post-Nicene Fathers*, 1st ser., vol. 7 (New York: Christian Literature Co., 1888), 344–45.

20. Karl Barth, *The Knowledge of God and the Service of God*, trans. J. L. M. Haire and Ian Henderson (London: Hodder & Stoughton, 1938), 211–12.

21. "Worship, at least for Christians, is the activity to which all our skills are ordered. . . . As Christians, our worship is our morality, for it is in worship we find ourselves engrafted into the story of God" (Stanley Hauerwas, *After Christendom* [Nashville: Abingdon Press, 1991], 108).

22. This is a comment about Hauerwas's published work. The church as sacramental community is very important, I am told, in his thinking and in his teaching. Dare one say that this is a topic about which he has not published enough?

23. Calvin, *Institutes* 4.15.1, p. 1303.

24. Roland H. Bainton, *Here I Stand* (Nashville: Abingdon-Cokesbury Press, 1950), 367.

25. Calvin, *Institutes*, 4.15.4, pp. 1306–07.

26. Indeed, Hughes Old concludes, "Baptism had become a sign of salvation by works rather than salvation by grace" (Old, *Worship*, 14).

27. "The readiness of the churches in some places and times to allow differences of sex, race, or social status to divide the body of Christ has further called into question genuine baptismal unity of the Christian community (Gal. 3:27–28) and has seriously compromised its witness" (*Baptism, Eucharist and Ministry* [Geneva: World Council of Churches, 1982], 3).

28. See, e.g., Hauerwas, *A Community of Character*, 2.

29. Robert M. Fowler, *Loaves and Fishes: The Function of the Feeding Stories in the Gospel of Mark* (Chico, Calif.: Scholars Press, 1981), 134. "The meals which Jesus is recorded as sharing during his earthly ministry proclaim and enact the nearness of the Kingdom, of which the feeding of the multitudes is a sign. In his last meal, the fellowship of the Kingdom was connected with the imminence of Jesus' suffering. After his resurrection, the Lord made his presence known to his disciples in the breaking of the bread. Thus the eucharist continues these meals of Jesus during his earthly life and after his resurrection" (*Baptism, Eucharist and Ministry*, 10).

30. Augustine, *Homilies on 1 John* 7.8, trans. Mary T. Clark, in *St. Augustine: Selected Writings*, ed. John Farina et al. (Ramsey, N.J.: Paulist Press, 1984), 305.

31. Alfred North Whitehead, *Process and Reality*, corrected edition (New York: Free Press, 1978), 343.

32. Fowler, *Loaves and Fishes*, 81, 118.

33. The NRSV has Herodias as the name of the dancing daughter. The name Salome comes from Josephus, *Antiquities*, in *The Life and Works of Flavius Josephus*, trans. William Whiston (Philadelphia: Universal Book and Bible House, 1936), 541.

34. I am intrigued but not persuaded by Janice Capel Anderson's claim that such interpretations reflect a male bias that sees women as the source of temptation and a European bias that sees things Oriental as exotic and immoral (Janice Capel Anderson, "Feminist Criticism: The Dancing Daughter," in *Mark and Method: New Approaches in Biblical Studies*, ed. Janice Capel Anderson and Stephen D. Moore [Minneapolis: Fortress Press, 1992], 122). As I read the story, the daughter is something more like a victim of child abuse than a woman challenging male stereotypes, and it surely requires no cultural prejudices to think of the Herodians as a corrupt dynasty.

35. Fowler, *Loaves and Fishes*, 86.

36. Calvin, *Institutes* 4.17.12, p. 1372.

37. Ibid., 4.17.31, p. 1403.

38. Ibid., 4.17.32, p. 1403.

39. Zwingli mixes the language of "memorial" and "sacramental presence" and never very clearly defines the latter, but Brian Gerrish does seem right to think that Zwingli's whole way of talking about the sacraments invites thinking of them as finally *human* actions,

with a logic that raises questions about his justification of infant baptism (Brian A. Gerrish, "The Lord's Supper in the Reformed Confessions," in *Major Themes in the Reformed Tradition*, ed. Donald K. McKim [Grand Rapids: Wm. B. Eerdmans Publishing Co., 1992], 253). For Calvin, "a sacrament is first and foremost an act of God or Christ rather than of the candidate, the communicant, or the church. Zwingli had the priorities wrong. Indeed, he not only put first what can only be secondary but made it the whole sacrament; he imagined that a sacrament is only an act by which we attest our faith and not rather, as it truly is, a sign by which God strengthens our faith" (Brian A. Gerrish, *Grace and Gratitude: The Eucharistic Theology of John Calvin* [Minneapolis: Fortress Press, 1993], 8).

40. Calvin, *Institutes* 4.17.10., p. 1371. See *Baptism, Eucharist and Ministry*, 12–13, for an ecumenical statement thoroughly compatible with these conclusions.

41. See Sallie McFague, *Models of God: Theology for an Ecological, Nuclear Age* (Philadelphia: Fortress Press, 1987), 52–53.

42. Calvin, *Institutes* 4.17.43, p. 1421. Calvin would have sympathized with Robert Jenson's views: "Whether the cup is kept from most of the congregation by the clergy's metaphysical scrupulosity or by the laity's own hygienic scrupulosity, the result is the same. Substitution of small quantities of wine distributed in little glasses helps not at all; it is precisely sharing a cup that is the mandated action. . . . Anticipating the promises of the Supper, if Christ gives himself over to us in the bread and cup, then crumbs and spills are part of the humiliation he assumes, and if he makes us brothers and sisters in the cup, then sharing one another's human messiness belongs to the humiliation *we* thereby assume" (Robert W. Jenson, "The Sacraments," in *Christian Dogmatics*, ed. Carl E. Braaten and Robert W. Jenson, vol. 2 [Philadelphia: Fortress Press, 1984], 343–44).

43. Calvin, *Institutes* 4.18.12, p. 1440. "Another regulation . . . has either stolen or snatched half the Supper from the greater part of God's people. The symbol of the blood, which, denied to lay and profane persons (these are titles they apply to God's inheritance [I Peter 5:3]), was given as a special property to a few shaven and anointed men" (ibid. 4.17.47, p. 1425).

44. Ibid. 4.18.7, pp. 1435–36.

45. Edward Schillebeeckx, *Jesus: An Experiment in Christology*, trans. Hubert Hoskins (New York: Crossroad, 1981), 213.

46. Gregory Dix, *The Shape of the Liturgy* (Westminster: Dacre Press, 1945), xviii–xix.

47. John Calvin, Sermon on Galatians 6:9–11, quoted in Nicholas Wolterstorff, "Worship and Justice," in McKim, *Major Themes in the Reformed Tradition*, 315.

48. Calvin, *Institutes* 4.17.41, p. 1418. "The inclusion of sinners in the community of salvation, achieved in table-fellowship, is the most meaningful expression of the message of the redeeming love of God" (Joachim Jeremias, *New Testament Theology*, vol. 1 [London: SCM Press, 1971], 117).

49. "The Reformers . . . tried to make the celebration look like a real meal. They replaced altars with tables and they used bread which looked like real bread. In many places they actually sat at the table" (Old, *Worship*, 173).

50. Milton Friedman, *Capitalism and Freedom* (Chicago: University of Chicago Press, 1962), 12.

51. "Western societies have continued the search for spiritual consolation in the only manner consistent with the freedom of the seeking subject: by making every person the judge of his own spiritual satisfaction. . . . What would astonish a primitive tribesman about the state of our spirits is that we believe we can establish the meaningfulness of our private existence in the absence of any collective cosmology or teleology" (Michael Ignatieff, *The Needs of Strangers* [Harmondsworth, Middlesex: Penguin Books, 1984], 78).

"A liberal nation," Michael Walzer writes, "can have no collective purpose. . . . Liberalism, even at its most permissive, is a hard politics because it offers so few emotional rewards; the liberal state is not a home for its citizens; it lacks warmth and intimacy" (Michael Walzer, *Radical Principles* [New York: Basic Books, 1980], 69, 68).

52. Eberhard Jüngel, "Toward the Heart of the Matter," in *How My Mind Has Changed*, ed. James M. Wall and David Heim (Grand Rapids: Wm. B. Eerdmans Publishing Co., 1991), 146.

53. Calvin, *Institutes* 4.1.14, p. 1028.

54. *Baptism, Eucharist and Ministry*, 15.

55. John Rawls, *A Theory of Justice* (Cambridge, Mass.: Harvard University Press, 1971), 303.

56. "The manifest inadequacy of the theology of the church derives from the fact that it has never seriously and consistently been rooted in a conception of the being of God as triune" (Colin E. Gunton, "The Church on Earth: The Roots of Community," in *On Being the Church*, ed. Colin E. Gunton and Daniel W. Hardy [Edinburgh: T. & T. Clark, 1990], 48).

57. For the Reformation, "every legitimate calling has exactly the same worth in the sight of God" (Max Weber, *The Protestant Ethic and the Spirit of Capitalism*, trans. Talcott Parsons [New York: Charles Scribner's Sons, 1958], 81).

58. Aristotle, *Nicomachean Ethics* 8.1, trans. Martin Ostwald (Indianapolis: Bobbs-Merrill Co., 1962), 215; I have slightly altered the translation.

59. Calvin, *Institutes* 4.4.9, pp. 1076–77, reference to 1 Peter 5:3.

Moltmann calls the various gifts of leadership for the church "assignments," as a way of avoiding the hierarchical implications of more traditional terms (Jürgen Moltmann, *The Church in the Power of the Spirit*, trans. Margaret Kohl (San Francisco: Harper & Row, 1977), 296–300. It is significant that the New Testament has no word for "office," and the closest equivalent in use is *diakonia*, which means "service" (Anne E. Carr, *Transforming Grace: Christian Tradition and Women's Experience* [San Francisco: Harper & Row, 1988], 26).

60. Calvin, *Institutes* 4.3.1, p. 1053.

61. Paul Tillich, *Love, Power and Justice* (London: Oxford University Press, 1954), 82.

62. The very "idea of distributive justice," Michael Walzer writes, "presupposes a bounded world within which distributions take place: a group of people committed to dividing, exchanging, and sharing social goods, first of all among themselves" (Michael Walzer, *Spheres of Justice: A Defense of Pluralism and Equality* [New York: Basic Books, 1983], 31).

63. Letty M. Russell, *Church in the Round: Feminist Interpretation of the Church* (Louisville, Ky.: Westminster/John Knox Press, 1993), 168.

64. Justin Martyr, *Dialogue with Trypho* 117, in *Saint Justin Martyr*, trans. Thomas B. Falls (New York: Christian Heritage, 1948), 329.

65. Alice Walker, "The Welcome Table," in *In Love and Trouble* (New York: Harcourt, Brace & World, 1967), 82–83.

66. Ibid., 86.

67. Bellah, *Habits of the Heart*, 72.

68. John D. Zizioulas, *Being as Communion: Studies in Personhood and the Church* (Crestwood, N.Y.: St. Vladimir's Seminary Press, 1985), 60.

69. Robert E. Webber and Rodney Clapp, *People of the Truth* (San Francisco: Harper & Row, 1988), 103.

70. "I describe the church as a community of Christ, bought with a price, where everyone is welcome. It is a *community of Christ* because Christ's presence, through the power of the Spirit, constitutes people as a community gathered in Christ's name (Matt. 18:20; 1 Cor. 12:4–6). This community is *bought with a price* because the struggle of Jesus to overcome the structures of sin and death constitutes both the source of new life in the community and its own mandate to continue the same struggle for life on behalf of others (1 Cor. 6:20; Phil. 2:1–11). It is a community *where everyone is welcome* because it gathers around the table of God's hospitality. Its welcome table is a sign of the coming feast of God's mended creation, with the guest list derived from the announcements of the Jubilee year in ancient Israel (Luke 14:12–14)" (Russell, *Church in the Round*, 14).

7 Risking Vulnerability

Christian Faith in Academy and Society

David Tracy has written about the "three publics" of Christian theology. Theologians, he says, address the church, the society, and the academy, and they need to reflect on what they say and how they say it in terms of all three of those audiences.[1] The preceding chapter argued that the church represents the primary community of Christians, and it follows that it constitutes the primary audience or public for Christian theologians. In times of persecution, theologians may be cut off from the wider conversations in academy and society; in other times, they may just find themselves ignored and ridiculed. They can still do their community-shaping, possibly countercultural work in the church. But a theologian who gets no hearing in the church has in some sense failed as a theologian. The cause of the problem may lie in the church rather than with the theologian, but the failure remains a failure. One may serve the church in part by connecting one's Christian conclusions to wider social concerns or making a Christian case in the intellectual world of the academy, but one undertakes such tasks too in large part precisely to serve the church.

If the primary "public" of Christian theology is thus the church, theologians nevertheless address these other audiences as well. In a pluralistic culture, the writing of books or articles or the delivery of public speeches involves at minimum being regularly "overheard" by non-Christians. Many Christian theologians also

161

live their lives as members of academic communities, and in this past generation in the United States theology has increasingly been written by people teaching in a variety of colleges and universities, not just or even principally denominational seminaries. As Christian theologians we will thus regularly find ourselves giving an account of what we are doing to non-Christian colleagues and fellow citizens.

In this too, Christians generally share the situation of theologians. All of us live within wider societies to which we bear some civic responsibilities. All of us find ourselves talking about Christianity in conversations with non-Christians. If, just as the primary audience of a theologian ought to be the church, so the primary community of any Christian ought to be the church, so other Christians, like theologians, find themselves involved in these other communities too.

What should theologians do in the academic settings in which they find themselves? How should Christians live in their societies? These are not easy questions. Chapter 5 made the case that we Christians ought to assert the truth of what we believe, and what we believe makes a difference not only for the private corners of our lives but sometimes for matters of social policy. The Bible's claim to truth, Erich Auerbach wrote, "is tyrannical—it excludes all other claims."[2] In a pluralistic society, that kind of tyranny can seem deeply threatening to our non-Christian neighbors.

But these "tyrannical" narratives are the narratives of a vulnerable God. If their form imposes a structure on all of reality, their content centers on a story about the rejection of force, the willingness to suffer in love. Those who find themselves caught up in *these* stories, therefore, cannot try to accumulate enough power to impose their vision of the world on those around them without contradicting themselves, for the strategies of power are at odds with the vision these stories embody. To think about one's wider intellectual and social roles in the context of these narratives is neither to retreat from wider responsibilities nor to attempt the forceful imposition of one's views but to adopt strategies of vulnerable love. If the questions are not easy, neither are these answers, and their difficulty reaches beyond that of intellectual puzzles to challenge the pattern of one's life.

These issues are not new. One hundred fifty years ago Søren Kierkegaard faced analogous questions in his native Denmark. How do you preach Christianity, he asked himself, to a country full of people who scarcely understand it at all but who think they are already Christians? In a non-Christian land, one could say, "Here is something new—let me tell you about Jesus Christ." Nearly all Danes, however, would have responded, "Yes, yes, we know all about it. You see, our whole country is Christian." And yet, they hardly grasped the Christianity of the New Testament at all:

> The truth is that Christianity really involves suffering (it invites those who suffer—and in becoming a true Christian you come to suffer). But in "Christendom" it is actually the favored ones who have taken possession of Christianity, the rich and powerful who in addition to all their enjoyment of life also want all their power and might and wealth interpreted as proof of God's grace.[3]

So Kierkegaard had to develop a radical strategy of indirection to try to introduce Christianity into Christendom.

The situation in the contemporary United States is, in one respect, even more complex. Kierkegaard's Denmark was an officially Christian state with a vast majority of inhabitants who were officially Christian. If he found a dramatic way to call people to true Christian faith, they were hardly in a position to protest; it was the goal they had claimed for themselves all along. We live, however, officially and actually, in a religiously diverse nation. Although most of our citizens are nominally Christians, Kierkegaard would probably judge that very few of them are real Christians, and many of the policies and aspirations of our society hardly seem to be those to which the gospel calls us. Yet non-Christian neighbors still think of "Christians" as a dominant and possibly dangerous force. One way to reassure them would be to say that Christianity concerns only the private lives and particular communities of Christian people, that it has no implications for national policy or public affairs.[4] But such a reassurance would betray the meaning of the gospel, which does embody a vision for nearly every aspect of the lives of its adherents and for any number of issues that, in our society, have come to be matters of public policy. Even if Christians make no effort to convert our non-Christian neighbors, therefore, given the large number of at least nominal Christians in our society, efforts to get them to take their Christian faith more seriously might well make some sizable social and cultural differences. Non-Christians, understandably enough, might find that prospect threatening.

After all, in certain obvious ways, the United States today remains a Christian culture. Most Americans remain members of one or another Christian church. Christmas, however secularized, remains the dominant national holiday. The chaplain of the United States Senate and the chaplains of many of the great universities are

Christian pastors. Atheists running for political office tend to keep their views quiet. Ask a Jew living in many a small American town, or a Hindu trying to find appropriate food in an American restaurant, or a Muslim exchange student whose final exams fall during Ramadan, the month of fasting, and they will tell you in this culture they are outsiders and Christians are insiders. A theology that talks about Jesus' vulnerability on the cross faces the reality that the cross on the spire of the big church downtown or on the university chapel often feels to members of non-Christian minorities like a symbol of power, even of potential intimidation.

On the other hand, it is not just a clever turn of phrase to speak of our time and place as post-Christian. In *Resident Aliens*, Stanley Hauerwas and William H. Willimon tell the story of the rabbi in Greenville, South Carolina, a friend, who used to challenge the values of the society around him by telling his children, "That's fine for everyone else, but it's not fine for you. You are special. You are different. You are a Jew. You have a different story. A different set of values." What is striking, Hauerwas and Willimon argue, is how many Christian parents today, even in the midst of a Bible Belt town like Greenville, would want to say the same thing to their kids: "Such behavior is fine for everyone else, but not fine for you. You are special. You are different. You have a different story. You have a different set of values. You are a Christian."[5] When one walks the streets of our cities and sees the homeless hungry in juxtaposition to great wealth, when one considers the foreign and military policies of our nation, when one reflects on the values with which television advertising floods our consciousness, the images of success and love that it fosters, by New Testament standards, this hardly looks like a Christian society.[6]

Yet just because of the residually dominant place of Christianity in American society, some strategies for social change seem thoroughly inappropriate. One can call for a Republican nation, or a socialist nation, or say that the values of existentialist humanism or Zen Buddhism ought to come to dominate our culture. But to call for a "Christian nation," or for the dominance of "Christian values," is to sound as if one is planning to organize a pogrom—to sound that way to any sensitive person who knows some history, to sound that way to oneself.

Should Christians therefore remain silent? Silent in the midst of a culture where materialism and militarism are so powerful, where too many new values turn out to be the merest cloak for selfishness? If Christian values get betrayed and ignored on every side, is silence the only acceptable response, given that any forceful speech may sound to non-Christians potentially oppressive in a culture still nominally Christian?

One answer is that problems arise only when a Christian voice tries to dominate. Christians should be content to be one voice among others in a pluralistic conversation. But confronted with pressing social problems, someone who feels that the gospel has something to say to contemporary society finds it hard to rest satisfied with the view that one can advocate Christianity as long as one is careful not to be too successful. In the course of the conversation, one would like to persuade others, to carry the day enough to be able to get on with the business of social change.

It is often easy for those of us who live in the academic world to discuss such issues of public policy with the relative security of kibitzers on the sidelines. Yet we face analogous problems. How should a Christian teach Christian theology in a pluralistic academy?

The difficulties reach beyond general questions of advocacy in the classroom. One hopes that everyone on a college faculty realizes the evils of manipulating students and the need to give alternative points of view a hearing. Still, if faculty members teaching libertarian economics or feminist literary interpretation or Zen Buddhism give other points of view an honest shot, but teach with an enthusiasm that wins significant numbers of students over to their own point of view, the institutional ethos congratulates them on their success. Suppose, however, one teaches a course on Calvin, fair as one can, pointing out the problems, encouraging disagreement, but still inviting students to see Calvin's vision, based as it is in biblical narratives, in all of its power. Suppose several Catholic or Muslim or agnostic students turn up at the Presbyterian church the next Sunday wanting to join. In most academic institutions, that means trouble for their teacher—trouble with parents, with colleagues, with one's own conscience.

William Scott Green, editor of the *Journal of the American Academy of Religion*, states the problem:

> Faculty in other fields often are glib, ignorant, or hung up about religion and tend to trivialize its study or confuse teaching it with proselytizing about it. . . . Despite its formal presence in curricula and catalogues, religion frequently lacks the neutrality and plausibility of other mainstream and established fields of learning. For very many students and faculty members, religion remains—intellectually and emotionally—a problematic, awkward, sensitive, and volatile

topic that seems extraneous to the central educational
agenda of secular colleges and universities.[7]

And Christian theology remains the most problematic, awkward,
sensitive, and volatile subject of all. Those who teach it are often
themselves Christians, which raises questions about what some of
their colleagues will call their "objectivity," and the nature of the
subject—in contrast, say, to the sociology of religion—invites exer-
cises in empathetic imagination that can look, to the suspicious, like
calls for sympathy, or even for belief. Moreover, in the contemporary American academy, Christianity itself sometimes seems, in
principle, suspect. In much of academia, pluralism and respect for
different cultural backgrounds and points of view seem central values, and yet pluralism turns out to have its limits. Ridiculing students of evangelical Christian piety can often be not only tolerated
but even encouraged, as if it were part of the mission of an intellectual institution.

Misunderstanding plays a role in all of this. Many academics
turn from church or synagogue sometime in early adolescence, and
their image of religion remains what they learned in fourth-grade
Sunday school. It is as if one assumed that the curriculum of a college mathematics department culminated in long division, or that
biological research consisted exclusively in gathering leaves from
different species of trees and pressing them flat under three volumes of the *World Book Encyclopedia*. If those no longer involved
with churches want to update their views of religion, moreover,
they sometimes turn their television dials to the cable evangelists
and find most of their prejudices confirmed.

But the issue does not always rest on misunderstanding.
When some in the academic world mistrust theologians, they justifiably recognize an enemy. For one thing, American higher education is dedicated to producing people who will go on to successful
careers in late capitalist society. The Christian gospel, with its narratives of a vulnerable God, does not fit comfortably into such an
agenda. Writing of the English public school he loathed, George
Orwell remarked that part of the problem was that, at Crossgates,
"You were bidden to be at once a Christian and a social success,
which is impossible."[8]

Imagine, after all, the admissions literature: "We groom you
to success in your careers. Our graduates on average make x thousand a year. We will prepare you for graduate and professional work
at the best universities or for cocktail party conversation at the best
country clubs. And also, we will get you thinking about the service

of the crucified son of a carpenter who calls his disciples to give up all they have and to pick up their crosses and follow." On second thought, perhaps best to leave out that last sentence.

If theologians rest content with cynicism about the values of the industrial and commercial system whose largesse probably pays much of their salaries, they will likely hear few objections from most of their academic colleagues. But theology also challenges many of the values of the academy itself. In many ways, after all, contemporary colleges and universities still rest on beliefs about objective truth and disinterested inquiry. Students and faculty members alike are expected to toss aside our heritage and our history as the price of being accepted in the circle of rational discourse. After all, Descartes began the whole project of modern inquiry by trying to suspend belief on all that he had been taught or grown up believing, so that he could start afresh and, thereby, establish a secure foundation for knowledge.[9] It is easy to dismiss his project as naive, but contemporary thought often still owes him more than it would like to admit.

For example, in what may be the most influential book written by a living American philosopher, John Rawls invites his readers to think about the meaning of justice. How do you decide what is just, what is fair? The way to do it, according to Rawls, is to imagine yourself in a hypothetical original position behind what he calls the "veil of ignorance." In that odd position, you cannot know your own religious beliefs, value preferences, or race or gender or social class. Therefore, Rawls says, you can be objective; you can be fair.[10]

As a number of critics have asked, the question is whether, so defined and limited, you can be a human person capable of rational decisions at all. At minimum, Rawls has to claim that religious beliefs and the other traditions within which one normally operates are extraneous, irrelevant to one's essential self, the "I" that makes moral decisions. Suppose someone says, "Given my religious faith, I think that all human activity ought to aim at the one goal of serving the glory of God. So I just can't make moral decisions in abstraction from my religious beliefs." Such a view, Rawls says in a remarkable passage, cannot be disproved, but "it still strikes us as irrational, or more likely as mad."[11] The pronoun "us," with no clear antecedent, invites readers into the circle of intellectually sophisticated insiders who see through this religious madness. It is an invitation that, like most invitations to join the insiders of social and intellectual elites, Christians ought to decline.

167

Rawls assumes that "we" share a set of values and assumptions that derive largely from the Enlightenment and still pervade most colleges and universities.[12] "The fundamental prejudice of the enlightenment," Hans-Georg Gadamer has written, "is the prejudice against prejudice, which deprives tradition of its power."[13] Put aside all those things your grandparents taught you. Put aside what you have simply fallen into the habit of believing. Dare to think for yourself.[14] It is an intellectual vision with its own kind of heroism, and all of us who teach in colleges and universities have proclaimed it at one time or another.

The triumph of such values, however, creates problems for the theologian. I, for instance, am a Christian theologian, doing my theological writing in the context of a particular tradition, that of Reformed Christianity. To do theology in that way presses home the fact of particularity. When you speak, when you think, you always stand somewhere, and the place where you stand helps shape what you see. Theologians know that down to their bones.

It might be protested that the contemporary academic world hardly needs to hear the news of the end of the Enlightenment and the triumph of perspectivalism from theologians. Literary critics, artists, and social theorists these days line up, eager to tell us that something called "postmodernism" is carrying the day, that Nietzche was right and that there is no objective truth. Allan Bloom even made himself rich and famous with a book decrying the triumph of relativism in the contemporary American academy.[15]

Yet, eavesdropping on colleagues when they are not reflecting on methodology but doing their ordinary business as scholars and teachers, one is struck at how often they seem to act as if they were presenting a body of truth, established at the bar of reason. Even a particular form of cultural relativism, oddly enough, seems to be considered proven once and for all, objectively, no doubt through careful statistical research in one of the social sciences. Nietzsche hauntingly pictured a world in which God was dead, but life went on exactly as before because no one had noticed. So the contemporary academy sometimes seems to be a world in which objective truth is dead, but life goes on exactly as before. "Your paper, young student," says the teacher's comment on the last page, "did not fully grasp the consequences of a world in which all truth is relative—C+."

Even in the humanities, more buffeted by the winds of particularity and postmodernism, theology remains a special case. Part of the difference goes back to the problematic issues of power with which this chapter began. In many ways, the theologian stands, at best, at the margins of the contemporary academy, and yet there is a sense in which the Christian theologian in particular is perceived to represent a threat due to an appeal to a surviving external power base. Perhaps it is the residual church affiliation of a college or the survival of an institutional baccalaureate service, but Christian theologians are often perceived as still holding institutional power. Even if they lack even residual power in the university itself, they still have a special social status. Deconstructionist literary critics can distance themselves from academic norms of rationality, but they have no alternative home outside the academy, no club downtown, next to the Burger King, where they can go once a week for bingo and discussions of Derrida and Stanley Fish. They may scatter irony around academia like buckshot from time to time, but we all know that, in the end, they have nowhere else to go. It may all seem a bit silly as seen from over in the school of engineering, but no one thinks it dangerous.

It is the burden and the glory of theologians to strike people as dangerous, in part because theologians do have another base of power. There are churches downtown meeting once a week, and the work of theology belongs there at least as much as to the academy. That feels, to some academic colleagues, threatening. Theologians are not the only folk in such a position. African American scholars and feminists and Marxists who identify their primary loyalty as resting with a community other than the academy make the academy very nervous, just as members of any religious community make the academy very nervous when they say that their primary loyalty, even their primary intellectual loyalty, is to church or synagogue or mosque or temple. The academy is supposed to be a place for rational inquiry, and those who think and live within a particular community that shapes their vision of the world and who do not apologize about the fact raise suspicions about their rationality. Because some form of cultural Christianity still has this odd residual establishment status, Christian theologians seem particularly threatening.[16]

Theologians, like most people, are generally a sociable lot who dislike feeling themselves at odds with friends or out of place in the institutions where they have made their careers. So we theologians tend to look for strategies that show we do fit in after all.[17] One might label the two most common strategies *generic theology* and *tribal theology*.[18]

Generic theology says that what is distinctively Christian—or

169

Buddhist or Jewish—is peripheral to theology's real concerns. Theology, after all, really describes some characteristics of universal human experience or conveys the eternal human quest for the divine. It therefore lies quite comfortably in the bosom of the humanities, for it is simply the study of one aspect of human experience among others. In many departments of "religious studies," such assumptions are built into the introductory course, defined as studying a single phenomenon called "religion," which appears around the world in various manifestations. Such a perspective, George Lindbeck writes, understands "all religions as possible sources of symbols to be used eclectically in articulating, clarifying, and organizing the experiences of the inner self. Religions are seen as multiple suppliers of different forms of a single commodity needed for transcendent self-expression and self-realization."[19]

This is a generous, tolerant point of view, but, as the latter pages of chapter 5 indicated, it does not represent what most religions have traditionally said about themselves. As the thirteenth-century Zen Buddhist, Dogen, put it, "Those who are lax in their thinking are saying that the essence of Taoism, Confucianism and Buddhism is identical, that the difference is only that of entrance into the way. . . . If people say such things, Buddhism is already gone from them."[20] Buddhism, Taoism, and Confucianism, Dogen insisted, are not different ways of saying the same thing; they are saying different things. So it is generally with the world's religions on matters as basic as how many gods there are, whether this world is a good creation or an illusion, how God has been revealed to us, and so on.

If religious faiths so obviously disagree with one another, theologians seeking not to offend their colleagues are tempted to turn to the form of radical relativism that might be called tribalism.[21] Yes, they concede, what we believe is different from what those other folk believe, but it is just what we believe, in our tribe, our particular custom, no judgment of right or wrong implied on anyone else.

Again, a generous point of view, but, again, not what the religions themselves really seem to be saying. In the *Bhagavad Gita*, the Lord Krishna proclaims:

> Of the whole world I am
> The origin and the dissolution too.
> Than Me no other higher thing
> Whatsoever exists. . . .

I am the dolphin of water-monsters,
    Of rivers I am the Ganges,
Of creations the beginning and the end. . . .
I am death that carries off all,
    And the origin of things that are to be.[22]

And in the Hebrew scriptures, the Lord God tells the prophet
Amos of bringing not only the Israelites out of Egypt but the
Philistines from Caphtor and the Arameans from Kir (Amos 9:7;
5:8). Yahweh is the Lord of all history. Indeed:

The one who made the Pleiades and Orion,
    and turns deep darkness into the morning,
    and darkens the day into night,
who calls for the waters of the sea,
    and pours them out on the surface of the earth,
the Lord is his name. (Amos 5:8)

These are not claims about what one tribe believes or how the tribe
happens to do things; they are claims about the universal order of
all creation.

Theology tends to adjust to an academic environment by
adopting an odd mixture of genericism and tribalism. This is just a
symbol of universal experience, they say, and as for the symbol,
well, it's the one we happen to use, but, shucks, pick whatever
makes you feel comfortable.

But that is not what the *Gita* claims, or Amos, or Augustine,
or the Koran. It is not what one says at a deathbed; it is not what
inspired John Calvin or Martin Luther King, Jr., or even now helps
so many struggling Christians keep up their courage. Religious
folk, by and large, believe in their particular religious point of view,
and they believe it is true. Yet it goes against so much of what the
modern academy stands for to claim truth for the conclusions of a
particular religious tradition. At the founding of the first great
modern scientific university, the University of Berlin, in 1809, the
philosopher Fichte proposed getting rid of the theology faculty altogether:

If theology insists on a God who wills anything without
cause, the content of whose will no human being can grasp
through his own capacities but only through direct, divine
communication by way of special emissaries; if it insists that
such a communication has taken place and the result set
forth in certain sacred books . . . , then a school of the use
of reason can have nothing to do with it.[23]

171

Fichte's heirs remain with us; their name is legion, and at one level it is hard to disagree with them. The Christian gospel may be true, but even Christians, when honest, do not claim that it is reasonable. And perhaps a college or a university ought to be a school of reason.

If we turn again to the question of Christian contributions to American debates on public policy, analogous questions arise. Just as, perhaps, a university ought to be a school of the use of reason, so, perhaps, American society ought to be a secular state. Just as the Christian theologian, therefore, has an ambiguous place in the academy, so the Christian, therefore, has an ambiguous place in American political life.

It is comforting for those on the left of the political spectrum to think that such problems afflict only Jerry Falwell or antiabortion activists. They, after all, seem to be the ones trying to impose a "Christian" agenda onto American political life. If the problem arises only in relation to the "Christian right," however, that is a devastating comment on many of the rest of us. It may be that liberal, progressive Christians have mirrored values and assumptions already widespread elsewhere in our culture so well that nobody thinks of them as the advocates of a distinctively "Christian" agenda. If there were a larger, serious "Christian left" in this country, it would have serious and distinctively Christian things to say about peace, justice, and much more. Such Christians' views would, no doubt, overlap with those of many non-Christians on a wide range of particular issues, but those who let the narratives of Jesus shape their life and thought would not fit completely into any political categories. Some of their beliefs, and many of their reasons for their beliefs, would be different, perhaps even surprising. To the extent, however, that Christians' views do become distinctive, non-Christian neighbors would raise legitimate questions about their rights as advocates of a religious point of view within American political life.

On these issues, too, one could find "genericists," whose policy positions involve nothing distinctively Christian, and "tribalists," who call for Christian values within the Christian community in a way that could have no application to the wider, pluralistic society. The flaws of unsubtle positions are easy to see, but even thoughtful, nuanced views still raise many of the same questions. Two authors mentioned in the preceding chapter, Robert Bellah and Stanley Hauerwas, have developed two of the most thoughtful recent accounts of how Christians might contribute to public debates in contemporary American society, yet the work of neither solves the question of how Christians can advocate a distinctive point of view without justifiably arousing the worries of our non-Christian fellow citizens.

In *Habits of the Heart*, Bellah and his coauthors express deep concern about nothing less than the future of the United States. "The time may be approaching when we will either reform our republic or fall into the hands of despotism, as many republics have done before us."[24] Central to the danger that confronts us is a "reigning ideology of individualism" that "has become almost hegemonic in our universities and much of the middle class." That individualism teaches that we make moral choices on the basis of personal preferences, that we belong to communities only to the extent that, and only as long as, they serve our personal needs. "The right act is simply the one that yields the agent the most exciting challenge or the most good feeling. . . . The self and its feelings become our only moral guide." A culture dominated by such an individualism, the authors argue, will lack the shared sense of values, purposes, and loyalties necessary to the sustaining of a healthy republic.

Things used to be better, they think. The founders of our republic shared such common purposes and loyalties, and "civic republicanism and biblical traditions" long sustained them. "For a long time, our society was held together, even in periods of rapid change, by a largely liberal Protestant cultural center that sought to reconcile the claims of community and individuality. Rejecting both chaotic openness and authoritarian closure, representatives of this cultural center defended tradition—some version of the civic republican and biblical traditions—but not traditionalism."[25] It is to these traditions that the book seeks to recall us: "Sharing practices of commitment rooted in religious life and civic organization helps us identify with others different from ourselves, yet joined with us not only in interdependence and a common destiny, but by common ends as well. Because we share a common tradition, certain habits of the heart, we can work together to construct a common future."[26]

It is a vision many thoughtful Christians will find attractive. In a culture that often seems to have lost a sense of commonality sufficient to get us to sacrifice for the common good, where "no new taxes" sometimes seems to summarize the national purpose, here is a call to higher aims, and one that sees Christian churches as important to the task at hand.[27] Yet the book raises disturbing questions.

173

Bellah and his coauthors paint a very positive picture of the American heritage. Yet many of the founding fathers they so admire were slave owners who shared a problematically patriarchal view of the world. It has often been only fighting wars or expanding westward at the expense of the indigenous population that gave our citizens that clear sense of national purpose that the authors of *Habits of the Heart* would like to recover.[28] One can overstate such critiques; the American tradition really does contain much to admire. But adherents of "biblical traditions" cannot in conscience simply join in a critique of contemporary individualism. They have to ask hard questions about the traditions and values that existed before that individualism "subverted" them. A truly biblical critique might be far more radical than a call for a return to the good old days.

The problem does not concern only particular issues but the very role one assigns to religion. *Habits of the Heart* properly diagnoses the dangers of a therapeutic culture where religion is valued only as useful to the pleasures of the individual. But it seems to replace that with a still utilitarian view of religion in service of the national good. We need to foster biblical traditions, the authors seem to argue, because, along with civic republicanism, they can help make America a healthier civic culture.[29] But biblical religion, taken seriously, may lead not only to a more radical critique of American culture but also to a nonutilitarian perspective in which Christians follow our calling as Christians simply because that is what our faith calls us to do.[30] Sometimes that might serve the health of the American body politic, sometimes not, and, when not, then Christians may have to say to hell with fostering the American body politic. We are not Christians in service of something else. A story in which Christianity represents one theme in the overall story of America is not an authentically Christian story, for an authentically Christian story has to begin with the biblical narratives. Bellah and his coauthors know that, but their book too often seems to lose sight of it.

Stanley Hauerwas, on the other hand, never loses sight either of the integrity of the church's mission as a church or of the role that Christian narratives play in the formation of the Christian community. In an extensive series of books and articles, Hauerwas has made the case that the primary purpose of the church is not to try to shape the society around it but simply to *be the church*: "The first task of the church is to exhibit in our common life the kind of community possible when trust, and not fear, rules our lives."[31]

This has led some to accuse him of withdrawing from concerns for the wider society, but such charges seem unfair. For Hauerwas, the witness the church can provide of a different sort of life, grounded on different presuppositions, is precisely the most useful contribution it can make to the wider society, because it is the one contribution it uniquely can make.[32] But the reason to be a Christian is not because the Christian community is socially useful: "The church is too often justified by believers, and tolerated by nonbelievers, as a potential agent for justice or some other good effect. In contrast, I contend that the only reason for being Christian . . . is because Christian convictions are true."[33]

Because we Christians believe certain things to be true, we conclude that one ought to live in a certain way, a way that might make no sense to those who do not share our beliefs. For the sake of peace or of justice, those with confidence that God is ultimately in control of history might be willing to take short-term risks that even those of goodwill who do not share such faith and who therefore must depend on the utilitarian calculus of this world would not take. Christians might be willing to eschew violence, even at the price of self-sacrifice, in a way that could be justified only given certain theological assumptions.

In pursuing such a self-consciously Christian ethic, Hauerwas is not, as his critics sometimes charge, advocating withdrawal from concern with public issues. He is simply saying that Christian churches that care for members who have AIDS or that welcome the homeless into their homes or refuse to admit to the Lord's Table "those who make a living from building weapons"[34] and thereby witness to their neighbors the possibility of a different kind of community might make a more significant contribution to our general public discourse than those who pass resolutions urging Congress to take action on one or another matter. As a church, they can take actions that follow from their theological convictions. Such actions might then cause non-Christian neighbors to stop and think about their deepest assumptions and thus have a significant social impact.

All that makes good sense, but Christians in the United States today play roles other than as church members. The members of Methodist or Presbyterian congregations may be state legislators or county judges or editors of local newspapers or school superintendents. They have to decide how to perform those other roles, and one might think their Christian faith would help them. But here Hauerwas gives little guidance. He is himself, for instance, a pacifist, and his reasons for pacifism grow out of his understanding of the distinctively Christian stories. If Congress is considering the appropriate response to "ethnic cleansing" in Bosnia, should Christians in Congress oppose any use of violence? Should they vote for sending in troops but themselves refuse to participate? Should they oppose the use of force only if they can make arguments against it that do not appeal to Christian presuppositions? To what presuppositions should they appeal if they try to make such arguments? Analogous questions arise about any number of social issues.

If Christians take on public roles in a pluralistic society, they will find themselves affecting the lives of, and representing, their non-Christian neighbors. If Christians' ethical decisions emerge from the context of distinctively Christian stories, then those non-Christian neighbors might well resent the Christians' public roles. What then are Christians to do? Avoid all public office? Resign whenever a major issue arises on which they have a distinctively Christian perspective? Advocate one set of policies among fellow Christians but vote for another? Hauerwas will say that what they do as church members is more important to their Christian witness than what they do in these other roles, and fair enough, but in the meantime they have to do *something* in those other capacities, and what should it be?

So the original problem returns, the problem of how to work toward the recovery of authentic Christianity in the midst of a religiously pluralistic society. Bellah's combination of "biblical traditions" and civic republicanism might be inoffensive to non-Christians, but it fails to provide a radical and distinctively Christian critique, not merely of contemporary individualism, but of more traditional American values. In Kierkegaard's terms, it risks inviting a return to "Christendom." Hauerwas provides the radical critique but leaves it unclear how Christians should function in their roles as citizens. If all those nominal Christians were recalled to authentic Christian witness, their faith would have some impact on every aspect of their lives. Since most of our citizens are still at least nominally Christian, if so revivified, they might well start to do things that would leave non-Christian Americans feeling understandably threatened.

Both Bellah and Hauerwas have the virtue of facing the problem. Most denominations have fallen into the habit of passing resolutions urging governmental action on a range of questions, while continuing to assume that the imposition of Christian values on the wider culture is a problem only for the right wing. The so-called mainline denominations get away with it because they have so lost distinctive Christian witness that their resolutions do not seem to represent a particularly Christian point of view—and, perhaps, because they tend to have so little impact.

Christians who teach in colleges and universities, and perhaps particularly those who teach Christian theology, have also fallen into avoiding some difficult issues. Legitimate concerns about the appropriate limits of a teacher's advocacy in the classroom provide a way of avoiding questions about a Christian's role as representative of a particular point of view within the community of scholars. The fact that there are illegitimate ways of trying to impose a point of view serves as the excuse for not thinking too much about whether there are legitimate ways to stand for something.

Christians stand for something in part through the distinctive stories they tell, but those stories are the stories of a vulnerable God, stories about love that avoids violence, even at risk of suffering. The content of those stories, therefore, has implications for the roles that Christians will take in academic settings or the wider social contexts where they work and live. No one provides a better model for what this might mean than Kierkegaard, who dealt so daringly with the problems of preaching Christianity in a culture that thinks of itself as already Christian. Kierkegaard made himself into an outsider, because it was the only way he knew how to preach the gospel. "To become a Christian in the New Testament sense," he wrote, "is such a radical change that, humanly speaking, one must say that it is the heaviest trial to a family that one of its members becomes a Christian. For in such a Christian the God-relationship becomes so predominant that he is not 'lost' in the ordinary sense of the word; no, in a far deeper sense than dying he is lost to everything that is called family."[35]

The strategies of Kierkegaard's authorship have become familiar: indirection, pseudonymity, irony. He keeps starting with the assumptions of his audience and then exploding them from within. He preaches the simplicity of the gospel, and, simultaneously, he sets to work with baroque complexity to undercut alternative visions of the world, until there might just be a moment when, by grace, the word of the gospel could be heard.

But for Kierkegaard—and here comes the hard part—the strategies shaped not just his authorship but his life. He posed as a frivolous young man, he avoided ordination and marriage, he made himself a figure to be ridiculed. He took on the local scandal sheet, the nineteenth-century Danish equivalent of the *National Enquirer*, setting himself up for its campaign to humiliate him. He ended his life impoverished, isolated, ignored.

The only way to communicate Christian faith with passion in a culture like ours without asserting cultural dominance in a way that is offensive to our neighbors and at odds with the central themes of the Christian stories is to keep rejecting the advantages that Christianity's residual cultural status could provide. We as Christians have to keep making ourselves into outsiders who can speak with a prophetic voice. I suspect that this is one reason theologians of liberation have been the most powerful recent public witnesses of Christian faith, and that Martin Luther King, Jr., was the last voice to speak effectively to American public culture in a distinctively Christian voice. For social reasons, figures such as King or theologians of liberation speak from the outside. It is from the margins, from the underside, that one can speak a prophetic Christian word that does not threaten one's non-Christian fellow citizens.

Some of us Christians will find ourselves called to function as Christian outsiders in non-Christian academic settings, consistently reminding our colleagues that we do not quite fit in and, then, living with the consequences, keeping our status and relations a bit uncomfortable. Others will struggle to preserve church-related colleges as countercultural enclaves in tension with some of the dominant themes of American academic life, not as bastions of residual establishment respectability, but, on the contrary, as places devoted to certain kinds of risk, to occasional rebellions—polite but firm— against the dominant values of American society and the academic world that mirrors it in so many ways.

For some, such a practice of vulnerability will mean participation in the political process, but always with a bit of irony, always as uncomfortable allies who ask awkward questions just at the moment of victory. For others, it will mean standing radically outside the ordinary political system, as fundamental critics of the way the United States does its public business, whether the critique is explicit or takes the implicit form of constituting communities founded on different values and different presuppositions. Either way, Christians will likely not make either themselves or their neighbors consistently comfortable.

Rhetorical excess in such matters can quickly become ridiculous. Most Christians in the United States live, by the standards of most of the world, comfortable, privileged lives, and the occasional awkward moment should not be the excuse for claiming martyrdom. But Kierkegaard again provides an interesting example for reflection. He lived in a prosperous country, a male, the child of wealth and privilege, but the isolation and ridicule into which he felt his particular Christian calling drew him involved a high price. Christians in small towns in the United States may find their pleasant lives disrupted by threats or gunshots through the front window if they stand up for an unpopular cause. For those in the academic world, the confession of a devout Christian faith is often not the safest route to tenure. Any Christian may find an unexpected turn in life calling for sacrifices, making demands, transforming one's life in some way that, if it ultimately brings joy, brings it only under the guise of great difficulties.[36] It is a mistake to exaggerate, but it is equally a mistake to ignore the radical demands to which ordinary Christians may suddenly find that their faith subjects them.

Christians are often tempted to accept our welcome as, first of all, colleagues in the academy or citizens of the nation. As Christians, we need to recognize the goods that academy and nation serve and participate in that service as we are called. But we need to remember that these are not our first callings. We live in solidarity with our fellow Christians and with the oppressed of the earth because, first of all, we are who we are, people reconciled to God, people with hope, only in solidarity with the crucified Jesus we have come to know in the biblical stories and the community that tells them.

Martin Buber recounts that someone once asked a rabbi how you should tell a story, and he replied, of course, with a story:

> My grandfather was lame. Once they asked him to tell a story about his teacher. And he related how the holy Baal Shem used to hop and dance while he prayed. My grandfather rose as he spoke, and he was so swept away by his story that he himself began to hop and dance to show how the master had done. From that hour on he was cured of his lameness. That's the way to tell a story![37]

So as we gather as the community of the baptized around Christ's table, and as we stand in unexpected ways among the marginal in society and academy, Christians need to learn to tell faithfully the stories of the one who was wounded for our sakes, that, like the rabbi's grandfather, in the telling of the stories we might be made whole.

179

NOTES

1. David Tracy, *The Analogical Imagination* (New York: Crossroad, 1986), 3–31.
2. Erich Auerbach, *Mimesis: The Representation of Reality in Western Literature,* trans. Willard R. Trask (Princeton: Princeton University Press, 1968), 14.
3. Søren Kierkegaard, *Journals and Papers,* ed. and trans. Howard V. Hong and Edna H. Hong (Bloomington, Ind.: Indiana University Press, 1975), vol. 4, no. 4682.
4. "Narcissus may be allowed his curious pastimes," David Tracy writes in criticism of such a view. "The polis, however, is both unaffected and unimpressed" (Tracy, *The Analogical Imagination,* 9).
5. Stanley Hauerwas and William H. Willimon, *Resident Aliens* (Nashville: Abingdon Press, 1989), 18.
6. Since television helps shape so much of our lives, maybe this isn't a trivial example: In network television, whether sitcoms or dramatic series, church sometimes plays an important role in the life of African Americans, and there is the occasional Catholic priest, from Father Mulcahy to Father Dowling, but there are no identifiably Protestant white characters.
7. William Scott Green, "Something Strange, Yet Nothing New," *Soundings* 71 (Summer/Fall 1988): 272.
8. George Orwell, "Such, Such Were the Joys . . . ," in *The Orwell Reader* (New York: Harcourt, Brace & Co., 1956), 443.
9. René Descartes, *Discourse on Method and the Meditations,* trans. F. E. Sutcliffe (Harmondsworth, Middlesex: Penguin Books, 1968), 95.
10. John Rawls, *A Theory of Justice* (Cambridge, Mass.: Harvard University Press, 1971), 137, 139.
11. Ibid., 554.
12. In his more recent work, Rawls has qualified or clarified his position in at least two ways. First, he now emphasizes that the need to put aside our religious beliefs (or many of our general philosophical beliefs) when setting the rules for social justice does not arise from some eternal truth about human nature but from the particular history that has developed in the West since the wars of religion in the sixteenth and seventeenth centuries. It happens that we cannot persuade everyone in our societies of the truth of any one religious or philosophical point of view, and therefore the alternatives are either to fall into bloody internal conflict or else to find a way to live together in peace while in fundamental disagreement (John Rawls, *Political Liberalism* [New York: Columbia University Press, 1993], xxiv). Second, Rawls now makes it clear that the kind of liberalism he is defending is not "liberalism" as a

complete conceptual framework for understanding the world—we cannot, he acknowledges, expect to persuade everyone of *that* any more than of any other religious or philosophical view—but simply the principles of how we agree to disagree (ibid., 54). Rawls is characteristically honest about the difficulties that emerge when he tries to be only the neutral arbiter between positions. For instance, if some people really believe they should coerce their fellow citizens into sharing their views, or the old order Amish want to keep their children from finding out the range of possibilities open outside their community, political liberals will oppose them (ibid., 196–97). He even argues for a pro-choice position on abortion as part of political liberalism (ibid., 243), and one wonders what has happened to his claims of neutrality. Still, it is hard not to sympathize with his basic thesis: one would rather live in the United States than in Ulster or "greater Serbia," in part because we have learned to live more peacefully with our differences. A Christian theologian might disagree mostly on questions of priority. Rawls's kind of liberalism, since it is not a total worldview, allows that devout Christians might live justly with devout Muslims, the thoroughly secular, and anyone else, so long as none of us tries to coerce any of the others into sharing our beliefs. Yet the political rules of liberalism still have a kind of priority: if our religious beliefs challenge *them*, then the religion has to be overruled. Christians would oppose coercion as contrary to both the nature of belief and the character of the vulnerable God in whom they believe, so in practice they would come to roughly the same place. But I would be reluctant to concede anyone's right to set rules about my belief, even in the name of all the goods of political justice. This theme will come up again later in the chapter in connection with Robert Bellah. I sometimes detect in Rawls a tendency I will point to in Bellah: an optimism about America that seems not to sense how *desperately* we need the kind of vision that might lead us away from violence and toward concern for the oppressed. Such vision, it may be, comes more from particular ways of looking at the world than from principles for adjudicating between them. Perhaps it comes down to a division of labor: if some have the vocation of helping us to live together when we disagree about our passionately held beliefs, others have the calling of helping us find things in which to believe passionately.

13. Hans-Georg Gadamer, *Truth and Method*, trans. Garrett Barden and John Cumming, 2d ed. (New York: Seabury Press, 1975), 139–240.
14. See Immanuel Kant, "What Is Enlightenment?" in *On History*, ed. Lewis White Beck, trans. Lewis White Beck et al. (Indianapolis: Library of Liberal Arts, 1963), 3.

15. Allan Bloom, *The Closing of the American Mind* (New York: Simon & Schuster, 1987).
16. This is not intended as a claim in some contest about who makes the liberal academy feel most threatened. Just at the moment anti-Islamic hysteria seems widespread, and the position of a devout Muslim in an American university has unfortunately often become an uncomfortable one.
17. Jonathan Z. Smith was speaking in Santa Barbara at a conference whose prospectus declared, "It was clearly recognized at Santa Barbara that the task was to develop the academic study of religion in a manner appropriate to the letters and science mission of a modern, secular state university." He observed, "Note which party conforms 'in a manner appropriate' to whom. The political distinction was, at heart, a counsel to passivity and integration, not to interesting thought" (Jonathan Z. Smith, "'Religion' and 'Religious Studies' No Difference at All," *Soundings* 71 [Summer/Fall 1988]: 232).
18. I suppose these conform roughly to the extremes in Hans Frei's typology of theologies. See Hans W. Frei, *Types of Christian Theology* (New Haven: Yale University Press, 1992).
19. George A. Lindbeck, *The Nature of Doctrine: Religion and Theology in a Postliberal Age* (Philadelphia: Westminster Press, 1984), 22.
20. From the "Shobogenzo" of Dogen, in Phra Khantipalo, *Tolerance: A Study from Buddhist Sources* (London: Rider & Co., 1964), 154.
21. I have borrowed the term from James Gustafson's critique of Stanley Hauerwas. See James M. Gustafson, "The Sectarian Temptation," *Proceedings of the Catholic Theological Society* 40 (1985): 83–94. For reasons indicated below, I think Gustafson is unfair to Hauerwas, but the term provides a useful label, even if Hauerwas does not fit the category.
22. *The Bhagavad Gita* 7.6–7, 10.31–32, trans. Franklin Edgerton (New York: Harper & Row, Harper Torchbooks, 1964), 38, 53.
23. Johann Gottlieb Fichte, "Dedusierter Plan einer in Berline zuerrichtenden höheren Lehranstalt," paraphrased in Frei, *Types of Christian Theology*, 105.
24. Robert N. Bellah et al., *Habits of the Heart: Individualism and Commitment in American Life* (Berkeley and Los Angeles: University of California Press, 1985), 294.
25. Ibid., 155.
26. Ibid., 252.
27. See, e.g., ibid., 247.
28. In the volume of essays on *Habits of the Heart*, Charles H. Reynolds and Ralph V. Norman, eds., *Community in America* (Berkeley and Los Angeles: University of California Press, 1988), see particularly Jean Bethke Elshtain, "Citizenship and Armed

Civic Virtue," 47–55, and Vincent Harding, "Toward a Darkly Radiant Vision of America's Truth," 67–83.

29. George Washington, who, "whatever his private beliefs, was a pillar of the Episcopal church . . . a frequent attender . . . [who] long served as a vestryman, though he was never observed to receive communion" (Bellah, *Habits of the Heart*, 222), comes off as a hero of the story. He was involved in the aspects of religion that serve the civic good.

30. See George Hunsinger, "Where the Battle Rages: Confessing Christ in America Today," *Dialog* 26 (1987): 264–74.

31. Stanley Hauerwas, *A Community of Character: Toward a Constructive Christian Social Ethic* (Notre Dame, Ind.: University of Notre Dame Press, 1981), 85.

32. "I have no interest in legitimating and/or recommending a withdrawal of Christians or the church from social or political affairs. I simply want them to be there as Christians and as church" (Stanley Hauerwas, *Against the Nations: War and Survival in a Liberal Society* [Minneapolis: Winston Press, 1985], 1).

33. Hauerwas, *A Community of Character*, 1. "Our ethical positions arise out of our theological claims" (Hauerwas and Willimon, *Resident Aliens*, 75).

34. Hauerwas and Willimon, *Resident Aliens*, 160.

35. Søren Kierkegaard, *Attack upon "Christendom,"* trans. Walter Lowrie (Princeton: Princeton University Press, 1968), 221.

36. See Anne Tyler, *Saint Maybe* (New York: Alfred A. Knopf, 1991), for such a story, told in a remarkable novel.

37. Martin Buber, *Tales of the Hasidim: The Early Masters*, trans. Olga Marx (New York: Schocken Books, 1949), v–vi.

Index

INDEX

Schillebeeckx, Edward, 130 n.22,
148
Schleiermacher, Friedrich, 28
Schneiders, Sandra, 111
Scholes, Robert, 101
Schoonenberg, Piet, 77 n.15
Scots Confession, 27
Second Helvetic Confession,
140–41
Smith, Jonathan Z., 24 n.38,
182 n.17
Smith, Morton, 24 n.32,
Smith, Wilfred Cantwell, 121, 124
Soelle, Dorothee, 131 n.27
Sophocles, 119
Stendahl, Krister, 114
Stump, Eleonore, 46 n.10, 47 n.18
Surin, Kenneth, 122
Swinburne, Richard, 28, 45 n.2,
46 n.10, 47 nn.11,18

Talbert, Charles H., 52 n.75
Tannehill, Robert C., 24 n.37
Tatian, 87, 104
Taylor, Mark Kline, 111–13
Tennis, Diane, 78 n.28
Theodoret of Cyrrhus, 87
Tillich, Paul, 153
Todorov, Tzvetan, 121
Tolbert, Mary Ann, 11
Toledo, Council of, 58

Tracy, David, xvii, 104 n.5, 161,
180 n.4
Tracy, Thomas, 25 n.57
Trible, Phyllis, 60, 107 n.29
Tyler, Anne, 183 n.36

Velazquez, Diego, 100–101

Walker, Alice, 154
Walzer, Michael, 159 n.51,
160 n.62
Weber, Max, 159 n.57
Weeden, Theodore, 11
Werpehowski, William, 107 n.32
West, Cornel, 96
Westminster Confession, 6, 126
Whitehead, Alfred North, 6, 18, 145
Wilken, Robert W., 55
Williams, Jay G., 78–79 n.40
Williams, Rowan, 79 n.41
Willimon, William H., 164
Wilson-Kastner, Patricia, 73, 111
Wittgenstein, Ludwig, 91, 92
Wolfson, Harry A., 82 n.69
Wolterstorff, Nicholas, 21
Wood, Charles M., 22 n.17,
107 n.30

Zizioulas, John D., 54, 81 n.60,
82 n.68, 154–55
Zwingli, Huldreich, 147, 157 n.39

Printed in the United States
1530800005B/196-240

9 780664 255343